BRITISH FOREIGN POLICY IN THE AGE OF WALPOLE

MODERN REVIVALS IN HISTORY

Series Editor: Michael Collinge

Michael Prestwich
War, Politics and Finance under
Edward I
(0 7512 0000 X)

William Lamont
Puritanism and the English Revolution
Vol I: Marginal Prynne, 1600–1669
(0 7512 0001 8)
Vol II: Godly Rule: Politics and
Religion, 1603–1660
(0 7512 0002 6)
Vol III: Richard Baxter and the
Millennium
(0 7512 0003 4)
Set   (0 7512 0004 2)

Jeremy Black
The English Press in the Eighteenth
Century
(0 7512 0007 7)

Patrick Joyce
Work, Society and Politics: the culture
of the factory in later Victorian England
(0 7512 0008 5)

Keith Middlemas
Diplomacy of Illusion: The British
Government and Germany, 1937–1939
(0 7512 0009 3) .

Peter Dickson
The Financial Revolution in England: a
study of the development of public
credit, 1688–1756
(0 7512 0010 7)

Charles Brand
Byzantium confronts the West,
1180–1204
(0 7512 0053 0)

John Kenyon
Robert Spencer Earl of Sunderland
1641–1702
(0 7512 0055 7)

Peter Thomas
The House of Commons in the
Eighteenth Century
(0 7512 0054 9)

Avner Offer
Property and Politics 1870–1914:
Landownership, Law, Ideology and
Urban Development in England
(0 7512 0066 2)

Robert McKenzie
British Political Parties: The
Distribution of Power within the
Conservative and Labour Parties
(0 7512 0067 0)

Michael Hunter
Science and Society in Restoration
England
(0 7512 0075 1)

Jonathan Steinberg
Yesterday's Deterrent: Tirpitz and the
Birth of the German Battle Fleet
(0 7512 0076 X)

Roger Anstey
The Atlantic Slave Trade and British
Abolition, 1760–1810
(0 7512 0112 X)

F B Smith
The Making of the Second Reform Bill
(0 7512 0113 8)

David Fitzpatrick
Politics and Irish Life 1913–1921
(0 7512 0133 2)

J R Western
The English Militia in the Eighteenth
Century: The Story of a Political Issue
1660–1802
(0 7512 0140 5)

Norman McCord
The Anti-Corn Law League 1838–1846
(0 7512 0147 2)

Philip Hughes
The Reformation in England (3 vols)
Set: (0 7512 0154 5)

J M Winter
Socialism and the Challenge of War:
Ideas and Politics in Britain 1912–18
(0 7512 0155 3)

Andrew Rosen
Rise Up, Women!: The Militant
Campaign of the Women's Social and
Poltical Union 1903–1914
(0 7512 0173 1)

Patricia Jalland
The Liberals and Ireland
(0 7512 0182 0)

F B Smith
The People's Health 1830–1910
(0 7512 0185 5)

John Campbell
Lloyd George: The Goat in the
Wilderness 1922–1931
(0 7512 0138 3)

Jeremy Black
British Foreign Policy in the Age of
Walpole
(0 7512 0193 6)

BRITISH FOREIGN POLICY IN THE AGE OF WALPOLE

Jeremy Black

Reader in History
University of Durham

Gregg Revivals

First published in Great Britain in 1985 by
John Donald Publishers Ltd

Reprinted in 1993 by
Gregg Revivals
Gower House
Croft Road
Aldershot
Hampshire GU11 3HR
England

Gregg Revivals
Distributed in the United States by
Ashgate Publishing Company
Old Post Road
Brookfield
Vermont 05036
USA

British Library Cataloguing in Publication Data

Black, Jeremy
  British Foreign Policy in the Age of
  Walpole. - New ed
  I. Title
  327.41

  ISBN 0-7512-0193-6

Printed by The Ipswich Book Co.

Preface

In the age when Lord Grenville is better known as a title of a song by Al
Stewart than as an eighteenth-century Foreign Secretary, it is necessary to
defend briefly the decision to write a book on foreign policy in the Age of
Walpole. For many years diplomatic history has been condemned (largely
though not entirely unfairly) in the historical profession as desiccated. The
great works of the past lie largely unread, the important theses of the
present cannot find publishers. This has been particularly serious in the
case of eighteenth-century British history. Foreign policy has been ignored
by most historians, and the valuable work of diplomatic historians has not
been integrated into the mainstream of scholarship. One sees all too many
studies of ministries and parliamentary sessions that ignore one of the
leading topics of political activity and debate in this period, foreign policy.
The dry husk of political manoeuvre is often of no historical value unless
joined to a study of the substance of policy and policy disagreement.

This work is an attempt to indicate the most important questions
surrounding the debate over, formulation and, to a lesser extent, execution
of foreign policy in the Age of Walpole. It should be read as a whole, but
scholars interested in one particular topic, such as Jacobitism or Trade,
might prefer to read only individual chapters. For that reason there is a
limited amount of repetition, and of reconsideration of certain topics,
particularly the most interesting, that of British neutrality in the War of the
Polish Succession, from different standpoints. Due to a tight word limit,
material discussed already in my articles has not been re-examined, unless
crucial to the argument. It is to be hoped that this work will be read not only
by those interested in foreign policy, but also by those concerned with other
aspects of eighteenth-century history, such as Parliament or the press, who
might be interested to ascertain their importance in the field of foreign
policy.

Jeremy Black

To
Patrick Deane and John Gatehouse

Acknowledgements

In the course of many years' research I have received assistance from a large number of individuals and institutions, for which I am very grateful. Without it I would have been unable to produce this book. It is an honour to be able to head my list of acknowledgements with the name of Her Majesty Queen Elizabeth II by whose gracious permission I was allowed to use the Stuart papers. Prince Kinsky, the Duke of Richmond, the Earl of Egremont, Earl Harrowby, Earl Waldegrave, Lady Agnew and Lady Lucas allowed me to consult their manuscripts. The generosity of the British Academy, the British Council, the German Academic Exchange Scheme, the Gladys Krieble Delmas Foundation, Merton College, the Staff Travel Fund of Durham University and the Zaharoff Foundation has been most helpful. Assistance, hospitality and advice on drafts of this book have been given with great generosity by a host of friends and scholars. I would particularly like to thank David Aldridge, Leopold Auer, Peter Barber, Peter Bassett, Richard Berman, John Blair, Tim Blanning, Tony Brown, Hilmar Bruckner, Marco Carassi, Roy Clayton, Eveline Cruickshanks, Jonathan Dent, Peter Dickson, Grayson Ditchfield, Hugh Dunthorne, Graham Gibbs, Robert Gildea, Lionel Glassey, James and Janet De Groat, Anthony Gross, Michael Harris, Peter Hartmann, Peter Hore, Michael Hughes, Harold James, George Jones, James Kellock, Paul Langford, James Lawrie, Jeremy Mayhew, Derek McKay, Gerhard Menk, Bruno Neveu, Jon Parry, Armin Reese, Bart Smith, Peter Spear, Charles Stephens, Mark Stocker, Peter Tibber, Reg Ward, Philip Winston, Paul Zealander, my parents and Sarah.

Note on Dates and Spelling

The New Year is always taken as starting on 1 January. In the early eighteenth century Britain conformed to the Julian Calendar. Dates recorded in this calendar are referred to as old style. Most of the continent conformed to the Gregorian calendar and recorded its dates in new style. In this book dates are given in old style unless indicated (ns). Where possible, well-established anglicised forms have been used for both place and personal names. The length of proper noble titles and of titles of office has dictated their shortening. A reference to Walpole, without any first name, is reference to Sir Robert Walpole and not to his brother Horace. Unless otherwise stated, the place of publication is London.

Abbreviations

Note: all books are published in London except where otherwise stated.

Add.	Additional Manuscripts in the British Library.
AE.	Paris, Quai d'Orsay, Archives du Ministère des Affaires Etrangères.
AG.	Paris, Vincennes, Archives de la Guerre.
AN.AM	Paris, Archives Nationales, Archives de la Marine.
Ang.	Angleterre.
ASG.	Genoa, Archivio di Stato.
ASM.	Modena, Archivio di Stato.
ASV.	Venice, Archivio di Stato.
Aut.	Autriche.
B⁷.	Pays Etrangères series.
BIHR	*Bulletin of the Institute of Historical Research*
BL.	London, British Library, Department of Manuscripts.
Bodl.	Oxford, Bodleian Library, Department of Western Manuscripts.
Bradfer Lawrence	Norwich, County Record Office, Bradfer-Lawrence Collection, Townshend State Papers and Letters.
Br.	Brunswick-Hanover series in AE.
CUL. CH.	Cambridge, University Library, Cholmondely (Houghton) manuscripts.
Chewton	Chewton Mendip, Chewton House, Waldegrave manuscripts, papers of James, first Earl Waldegrave.
Cobbett	W. Cobbett, *Parliamentary History of England from . . . 1066 to . . . 1803* (36 vols., 1806-20).
Coxe	W. Coxe, *Memoirs of the Life and Administration of Sir Robert Walpole* (3 vols., 1798).
CP.	Correspondance Politique.
Darmstadt	Darmstadt, Staatsarchiv.
Dresden	Dresden Hauptstaatsarchiv, Geheimes Kabinett, Gesandschaften.
Dunthorne	H. L. A. Dunthorne, The Alliance of the Maritime Powers, 1721-1740 (Ph.D., London, 1976).
Dureng	J. Dureng, *Mission de Théodore Chevignard de Chavigny en Allemagne* (Paris, 1912).
Eg.	Egerton Mss.
Egmont	Historical Manuscripts Commission, *Manuscripts of the Earl of Egmont, Diary of the First Earl of Egmont* (Viscount Perceval) (3 vols., 1920-3).
EHR.	*English Historical Review.*
EK.	Englische Korrespondenz.
Fonseca	Nachlass Fonseca.
GK.	Grosse Korrespondenz.
Hanover	Hanover, Niedersächsisches Hauptstaatsarchiv.

Hatton	R. Hatton, *George I* (1978).
Hervey	John, Lord Hervey, *Some Materials towards Memoirs of the Reign of King George II* (ed.) R. R. Sedgwick (3 vols., 1931, cont. pagination).
HHStA	Vienna, Haus-, Hof-, und Staatsarchiv.
HMC.	Historical Manuscripts Commission.
Hull	Hull, University Library, Hotham papers.
Hughes	M. Hughes, The Imperial Supreme Judicial Authority under the Emperor Charles VI and the crises in Mecklenburg and East Frisia (Ph.D., London, 1969).
Ilchester	Earl of Ilchester (ed.), *Lord Hervey and his Friends* (1950).
Ing.	Inghilterra.
Kart.	carton.
KB.	Kasten Blau.
KS.	Kasten Schwarz.
King	Peter, Lord King, 'Notes on Domestic and Foreign Affairs during the last years of the reign of George I and the early part of the reign of George II', in appendix to P. King, *Life of John Locke* (2 vols., 1830), II.
Knatchbull	A. N. Newman (ed.), *The Parliamentary Diary of Sir Edward Knatchbull, 1722-30* (1963).
LM.	Lettere Ministri.
Marburg	Marburg, Staatsarchiv, Bestand 4: Politische Akten nach Philipp d. Gr., England.
Marini	R. A. Marini, *La Politica Sabauda alla Corte Inglese dopo il trattato d'Hannover 1725-30 nella Relazione dell'ambasciatore piemontese a Londra* (Chambéry, 1918).
MD.	Mémoires et Documents.
Munich	Munich, Bayerisches Hauptstaatsarchiv.
Münster	Münster, Staatsarchiv, Deposit Nordkirchen, papers of the Plettenberg family.
Nancy	Nancy, Archives de Meurthe-et-Moselle, Fonds de Vienne, série 3F.
Osnabrück	Osnabrück, Staatsarchiv, Repertorium 100, Abschnitt 1.
PRO.	London, Public Record Office, State Papers.
RA.	Windsor Castle, Royal Archives, Stuart Papers.
Rawl.	Rawlinson Letters.
SRO.	Edinburgh, Scottish Record Office, Stair Papers.
sup.	supplément.
TRHS	*Transactions of the Royal Historical Society.*
Trevor	Aylesbury, Buckinghamshire Record Office, Trevor papers.
Varia	England Varia series in HHStA.
Wilson	A. M. Wilson, *French Foreign Policy during the Administration of Fleury, 1726-43* (Cambridge, Mass., 1936).
Wolfenbüttel	Wolfenbüttel, Staatsarchiv.

Contents

CHAPTER 1

Introduction − The Course of Policy

'Commonly all body politicks (I mean every nation) argue to their own purpose, and would have no remedys but such as are applicable to their particular distempers, no notice taken, nor no regard had, of their neighbours wants, etc, I ever remarked that our British politicians are of all others the most prepossessed this way, our islands would have the whole continent become in some measure subservient to their schemes tho' never so various or so inconsistent in themselves.'

Owen O'Rourke, Jacobite envoy in Vienna, 1728.[1]

'the sure way to prevent another man's knocking me down is by putting myself on my guard and having my stick up ready to give the first blow if I see him offering at it.'

Charles Delafaye, Undersecretary of State in the Southern Department, 1725.[2]

Space does not permit a detailed account of what Lodge termed the 'diplomatic mazes' of this period. An excellent recent work (D. McKay and H. M. Scott, *The Rise of the Great Powers*) deals with the European background.[3] British foreign policy in the reign of George I has been well covered, though 1721-4 still lacks sufficient attention.[4] Coverage of foreign policy is then patchy until the end of the Walpole ministry, when Anglo-Spanish differences and the outbreak of a major European war have been well covered. For the intervening period Vaucher's masterly study of Anglo-French (1731-42) and Dunthorne's excellent work on Anglo-Dutch (1721-40) relations throw light wider than their titles might suggest. Lodge's study of Anglo-Prussian relations is in need of replacement. Gibbs has written a series of important articles on themes in the 1710s and 1720s. The major gap in the literature is that there is no overall study of foreign policy in the years 1727-1733, for Vaucher's work does not begin in earnest until the outbreak of the Polish Succession War. This section cannot fill these gaps, but it will seek to chart the major developments in British foreign policy, largely paying attention to those areas that are poorly covered in the existing literature.[5]

The peace treaties of the period 1713-21, that ended the various wars then afflicting Europe, left many questions unsettled. Territorial and dynastic disputes affected large areas of Europe. In northern Europe the treaty of Nystad (August 1721), that ended the Great Northern War (1700-21), barely eased the anxieties aroused by the dramatic growth of Russian power under Peter the Great (Tsar, 1689-1725).[6] Further west the Peaces of Utrecht, Rastadt and Baden (1713-14), that ended the Spanish Succession War, left many questions unsettled. Philip V (King of Spain, 1700-46) was dissatisfied with the peace provisions relating to Italy, and anxious to maintain his claims to the French throne: he was the uncle of Louis XV (born 1710, King 1715-74), who remained without a son until September 1729. The dramatic revival of Spanish power under Philip V helped to

1

make his claims a source of international tension. The regent for Louis XV, Philip Duke of Orléans (1674-1723), was next in line in the French succession, provided that Philip V was forced to observe the renunciation of his rights that had been obtained in return for recognition of his claims to the Spanish throne.[7] The Austrian Habsburgs benefited from a spectacular growth in territorial power in the period 1683-1720, a growth only surpassed by Russia. Gains included Naples, Sicily, Mantua and the Milanese in Italy, Transylvania, Little Wallachia, much of Serbia and Hungary in the Balkans, and the Southern Netherlands. Accompanying this expansion was a growth in military strength and reputation, and a determination to enforce Austrian power and Imperial authority in every possible area. Within the Empire, Charles VI (hereditary Austrian Habsburg ruler and Emperor of the Holy Roman Empire, 1711-40) appeared as an insensitive ruler, determined to use the legal instruments of Imperial authority to enhance Austrian power. The Austrians felt that many German powers, such as Hanover and Prussia, were selfish and disloyal.[8]

In western Europe hostilities resumed in 1717: a Spanish invasion of the island of Sardinia was followed in 1718 by an invasion of Sicily. In northern Europe the coalition of Baltic powers (including Russia and Hanover) opposed to Charles XII of Sweden disintegrated. In late 1716 George I and his Hanoverian ministers fell out with Russia. The British Whig politicians divided in response to these two crises. Of the two Secretaries of State, Townshend, supported by his brother-in-law Walpole, was disinclined to support the anti-Russian moves desired by George I, whilst Stanhope, in alliance with the Earl of Sunderland, was ready to do so. George I determined to transfer Townshend from responsibility for foreign affairs, exacerbating the already bitter divisions over posts within the Whig ministry. Going into opposition in April 1717, the Walpole connection opposed British intervention in the developing Mediterranean conflict. In 1718 Walpole opposed the dispatch of the fleet that was to sink most of the Spanish fleet off Cape Passaro in Sicily that August. In December 1718 Britain and France declared war on Spain, a war that was to last until 1720.[9]

Stanhope's period of influence (he was George I's principal British adviser on foreign affairs from 1714 until his death in February 1721) was associated with war: war against Spain, and threatened war against Russia. Stanhope himself did not seek war. He was aware of the fiscal and political strains it would produce, and he hoped that the alliances he negotiated (the Quadruple Alliance – Britain, France, Austria and Savoy – of 1718 to coerce Spain, and the anti-Russian alliances of 1719-20) supported by British subsidies and seapower would intimidate other powers. Stanhope's foreign policy centred on the Anglo-French alliance he negotiated in 1716.

The 1716 treaty of mutual guarantees – important for Orléans, worried about Spanish interest in the French succession, and for George I and the Whigs keen to strengthen the Hanoverian succession – served as the basis for much of Stanhope's diplomacy: the Triple Alliance (1717, Britain, United Provinces, France), the Quadruple Alliance, French support for British policy in the Baltic, and a joint attempt to settle Austro-Spanish disagreements. Stanhope, interested in 'politics on a Europe-wide scale', produced grand peace plans based on mutual guarantees and the concept of collective security. He was an able diplomat, in no way duped by France and determined that the Anglo-French alliance should operate in accordance with British interests and wishes. [10]

Stanhope was a clever man. As such he has been generally praised. There is a strong historiographical bias towards clever men; a tendency in studies of eighteenth-century British foreign policy to favour Secretaries of State possessing diplomatic ability and an ability to concoct grand schemes. However, several of these Secretaries – Stanhope and Carteret are good examples – have been praised excessively. Fertility of diplomatic imagination was useless unless accompanied by an ability to create policies that could win political support within Britain. It is easy to see how diplomats (and diplomatic historians) attracted by the broad sweep of European problems could regard parliamentary management as a lesser, even vulgar, skill. And yet a policy that was not assured of domestic support and funding was dangerous, a Secretary of State unable to relate diplomatic and domestic requirements not fit for his post. It was not surprising to find diplomats urging policies that were not feasible: Horace Walpole, MP observed of one, 'St. Saphorin is a good Judge of the Court of Vienna, but not of the House of Commons'. [11] It was the Secretary's responsibility to reconcile diplomatic and domestic commitments. Stanhope, an MP who was a very bad parliamentary manager, was only too keen to get into the Lords. The interventionist policies associated with him produced grave difficulties for the ministry, limiting its room for political manoeuvre at a time when its parliamentary position was handicapped by the Whig Split and its contentious legislative programme was encountering much resistance. Furthermore, Stanhope was extremely lucky: the victory at Passaro, the bullet that removed Charles XII, the failure of Spanish attempts to overthrow the Regent were in no way predictable. Contemporaries were aware of the risks that were run, and the extraordinary good fortune enjoyed by the ministry. [12] Even so, Stanhope's policies were not a great success. Peter the Great was not intimidated into returning to Sweden some of the recently conquered Baltic provinces. Stanhope and George I bear much responsibility for the bad Anglo-Russian relations that were to continue until the early 1730s. The Quadruple Alliance settled few problems. When Spain joined the Alliance in January 1720, the issues that agreement could not be reached over were postponed for decision at a congress. This congress, expected to meet shortly, did not open (at Cambrai) until 1724. By then Stanhope's achievement of 1718 – Austro-French agreement – had been lost, whilst a host of issues had arisen or become more serious. Some involved Britain: Spanish claims to Gibraltar pressed with great energy until 1729, Austria's schemes for oceanic trade based on the Ostend Company. The most contentious issues involved Italy, particularly Spanish demands linked to the claims of Don Carlos (Philip V's eldest son by his second marriage, to Elisabeth Farnese) to the successions of Parma and Tuscany, claims recognised by the Quadruple Alliance. The Austrians, opposed to any challenge to their Italian hegemony, resisted such Spanish demands as garrisons in Parma and Tuscany to guarantee Carlos' succession.[13] The resumption of Franco-Spanish relations in 1720 weakened Britain's influence within the Anglo French alliance. By the time the Congress opened, British foreign policy was the responsibility of a new group of ministers. The two principal ministers, Walpole and Townshend (the latter reappointed to his Northern secretaryship) did not jettison the entire Stanhopian diplomatic inheritance, but their attitudes, particularly Walpole's, were different. Helped by an easier international situation (peace in the Baltic and the Mediterranean, Peter the Great busy on his Asian frontiers), the ministry was able to concentrate on domestic matters in the early 1720s: the restoration of fiscal and political stability after the South Sea Bubble, and the Atterbury plot of 1722, a Jacobite intrigue over which France provided Britain with valuable assistance.[14] The French alliance remained very important, though less close than it had been in the days of Stanhope and the French minister Dubois. Britain was suspicious of good Franco-Spanish and Franco-Russian relations.[15] Dubois and Orléans died in 1723, and the new French ministry, that of the Duke of Bourbon (1723-6), was keen to retain the British alliance but disinclined to follow the British lead.[16] Relations with Austria deteriorated. Hanoverian claims and the Ostend Company were major irritants, but the basic problem was that neither power was prepared to make the compromises and adjustments necessary to retain the friendship of the other. The British ministry did not appreciate Austrian sensitivity over Imperial authority in the Empire, nor Austrian fears that accepting Carlos in Italy would undermine their position there. British diplomats were increasingly hostile to Austria: Henry Davenant was sacked in 1722 for supporting Austrian views. The Austrians did not accept the reality of the Anglo-French alliance. They believed that Britain needed Austria as a safeguard against France. In 1718 the Austrian Chancellor Sinzendorf told the British representative in Vienna, St. Saphorin, that it was not in Britain's interest to permit Austrian lands to be gained by the Bourbons, and that even if there was no Anglo-Austrian alliance, necessity should lead Britain to oppose the French. Similar attitudes characterised Austrian policy towards Britain throughout Walpole's ministry, and were indeed voiced within Britain.[17]

Domestic concerns and a difficult though not pressing European situation help to account for the contrast between Stanhope's knight-errantry, his frenetic diplomacy, and the more circumspect policies of the years 1721-4. The British sought to extend the Anglo-French alliance to include Spain (achieved in 1721, though at the cost of a promise by George I to seek parliamentary approval for the return of Gibraltar), Prussia (George I's 1719 alliance with Prussia was confirmed by the treaty of Charlottenburg, 1723) and Russia (negotiations, partly through France, 1723-5). However, there was a lack of urgency and activity compared to the Stanhope years.[18] This owed much to the difficulties created by Britain's links with so many feuding powers. The British envoy in Berlin reported in 1724 a conversation with Frederick William I of Prussia who 'asked me twice what part I thought the King would take, if there should happen a rupture between the Emperor and the King of Spain'.[19] Possibly the British ministry did not think such problems through sufficiently, but the kaleidoscopic nature of European politics scarcely encouraged such analyses. If French policy did not change radically with Louis XV's majority and Orléans' death, the surprising abdication of Philip V in 1724 (he resumed the throne later that year after his eldest son Louis I died) and the changes in Russian activity produced by the death of Peter the Great in 1725, were reminders of the fragility of international arrangements in a dynastic age. This theme was frequently repeated in Britain in the 1720s.[20]

The failure of the Congress of Cambrai to settle problems (a failure that convinced some of the futility of the congress system) led Spain to attempt a bold move – an unexpected approach to Charles VI. This produced the First Treaty of Vienna (actually three treaties signed on 30 April-1 May (ns) 1725). The treaties stipulated little that was threatening to Britain – Austrian diplomatic support for the return of Gibraltar and Minorca, Spanish commercial concessions to Austria – but the British hastily organised a counter-alliance system, the Alliance of Hanover (Britain, France and Prussia, 3 September (ns) 1725).[21] Townshend, who played the major role in this negotiation (the French followed the British lead), has been criticised both then and since for over-reacting. Opposition publicists claimed that British interests were not really threatened and that Britain should have sought to mediate between the Alliance of Vienna and France. The ministry possibly took too seriously inaccurate reports that the Vienna Alliance had undertaken to support the Jacobites, but their fear was a reasonable one. It was understandable that they should seek to clarify and strengthen their alliances at a time when they were uncertain of Austro-Spanish intentions, fearful that the accretion of strength presented to Austria and Spain would lead them to increase their demands, and aware that it was best to negotiate from a position of strength.[22] A struggle by both powers to recruit allies began. The Vienna Alliance gained Prussia (1726) and Russia (1726). The Hanover Alliance lost Prussia, but gained the United Provinces, Sweden and Denmark. Both sides sought to intimidate the other and many feared war, though actual hostilities were restricted to an unsuccessful Spanish siege of Gibraltar in 1727.[23] In 1726 Frederick William I told the British envoy, 'your people in England imagine that they can bring about what they please with their pen, but the only way to prevent the ill designs of our enemies is to be ready with your swords'. In an impressive display of strength, British squadrons were dispatched in 1726 to Baltic, Caribbean and Spanish waters. Their impact is difficult to judge. Sinzendorf mocked naval power as useless, Horace Walpole feared the same. Ministerial publicists claimed that by preventing the movement of the bullion from Spanish America required to subsidise the Austrians, the navy wrecked the plans of the Vienna Alliance. Anxious to please, Brinley Skinner, Consul in Leghorn, wrote, 'The appearance of His Majesty's fleets abroad, and the great readiness the nation is in at home to resent and curb the growing ambition of foreign powers to the prejudice of the commerce of the King's subjects, will undoubtedly meet that glorious and constant success attending . . . the just and honourable measures of the Crown of Great Britain the lustre whereof must now dazzle the deepest and most distant politicks of the world, and whilst the key of peace is by heaven put into His Majesty's hand, no power I think will dare to break into war'.[24]

In fact heaven gave the key of peace to the new French first minister Fleury. Aided by Austro-Spanish mutual dissatisfaction, Fleury negotiated the Preliminaries of Paris of May 1727, a temporary settlement that arranged for the meeting of a new peace congress. George II, who acceded the following month, helped to preserve the Anglo-French alliance by retaining the Walpole ministry, whose retention Fleury supported.[25] Spanish unwillingness to accept the Preliminaries of Paris led the British to maintain a large fleet in Spanish waters that autumn. Dissatisfied at Fleury's failure to support British demands on Spain, George II considered diplomatic initiatives that would reduce Britain's dependence on France, including a secret approach to Austria via Saxony.[26] They came to nothing. Thanks partly to French pressure, Spain accepted the Preliminaries of Paris by the Convention of the Pardo (6 March (ns) 1728). This permitted the opening in June of the Congress of Soissons. The congress did not develop as the British had wanted. Fleury kept them largely in the dark, and, in place of the permanent diplomatic settlement sought by Britain, supported the idea of a provisional treaty. The unenthusiastic British, increasingly isolated, agreed with reluctance, only to find both Spain and Austria reject the settlement in late 1728. With royal anger and domestic criticism of the failure to settle British interests, there was increasing doubt about the value of the French alliance:[27] 'it is the unanimous voice of our people, whose interests as they are dearer to us than all other considerations we must consult in the first place, that we have been too long amused with fruitless negotiations, and that after all the moderation that has been shown on our part, and the endless chicanes and delays on that of the courts of Vienna and Madrid it would be entirely giving up the dignity of our Crown and the honour of the nation to suffer things to continue any longer in the same situation'.[28]

In early 1729 secret Anglo-Austrian discussions in London and Vienna failed to produce agreement.[29] Spain, dissatisfied with Austrian unwillingness to further her Italian interests and to arrange a marriage between Carlos and one of the Archduchesses, Charles VI's daughters (he had no sons), turned to France and Britain. Agreement proved difficult, as Spain was determined on Spanish garrisons in Tuscany and Parma to guarantee Carlos' rights. British anger at 'Spanish depredations', attacks on British commerce, led to the preparation of a large fleet in the summer of 1729 that some ministers wished to use against Spain.[30] Paying his first visit as Elector to Hanover, George II was nearly drawn into war (August-September) with Prussia, as a result of a confrontation over Prussian forcible enrolling for their army. French, Dutch, Danish and Hessian support for George discouraged Prussia.[31] Keen to tie Britain to their anti-Austrian alliance system, the French urged George II to sign treaties with the Wittelsbach Electors of Cologne, Bavaria and the Palatinate. Bavaria had claims on the Austrian inheritance, and the ministers in London warned of the danger of long-term commitments to the Wittelsbachs. The Wittelsbachs sought subsidies, and Townshend claimed that Walpole's opposition blocked these demands.[32]

On 9 November (ns) 1729 the Treaty of Seville was signed. The treaty settled outstanding differences between Britain and Spain (compensation for depredations was left to a commission) and committed Britain and France to support Spanish pretensions in Italy. Spanish garrisons were to be introduced, and if Charles VI did not consent, force was to be used.[33] Hopes that Charles would consent were dashed in early 1730, and Britain, France, Spain and the United Provinces (the Dutch had signed late) began active, and acrimonious, planning for war.

Anglo-French relations markedly deteriorated in the first half of 1730. Strain in the alliance was hardly novel, and from its inception in 1716 it had been criticised by British and French politicians and diplomats.[34] With time the initial pressures that had thrown the two powers together diminished. After Stanhope's death the British ministry was less eager to subordinate domestic to diplomatic concerns and less interested in the intensive and comprehensive diplomacy that required the French alliance. After the suppression of the Atterbury plot and the peaceful accession of George II, Jacobitism appeared less of a threat. France in the late 1710s had been politically and fiscally weak, recovering from a long period of fighting much of Europe single-handed, and with the French Regent Orléans badly worried by a pro-Spanish faction. During the 1720s France became stronger economically and politically, more independent and self-confident.[35] In a sense the Hanover Alliance had rebonded two powers who had been increasingly moving apart, but this proved only temporary. Fleury and Chauvelin (French foreign minister 1727-37) sought, with considerable success, to make Britain follow the French lead. This created tension, as neither George II nor Townshend was temperamentally prepared to take second place. In early 1730 the two powers clashed over the plans for war against Austria.[36] Britain resisted French pressure to settle with the Wittelsbachs, and France was suspicious of the Hotham mission, an unsuccessful British approach to Prussia. Longstanding parliamentary criticism of ministerial foreign policy, and in particular claims that British interests were being surrendered to France, finally struck home, when the issue of French repairs to the harbour of Dunkirk (prohibited by the Peace of Utrecht) gave them concrete form and political force.[37] The ministry secured a French promise to demolish all illegal works at Dunkirk, but French footdragging in the face of continued British pressure in the summer of 1730 worried British ministers, particularly Robert Walpole.[38] The importance of the Dunkirk issue in embittering Anglo-French relations cannot be underestimated, for, whatever the long-term weaknesses of the alliance, it was the short-term problems in 1730 that led Britain to turn to Austria. Far from being a 'little local difficulty', of no consequence for more general diplomatic developments, Dunkirk served to produce frustration and anxiety among the British ministers. It represented the manner in which the Anglo-French alliance was no longer producing any tangible benefits, but was instead threatening the parliamentary position of the British ministry. To the French it was a prime instance of the high-handed manner in which the British insisted on their interests (in this case dating from a humiliating peace) rather than devoting attention to securing the alliance.[39]

British concern about the French alliance was increased by growing fears for Hanoverian security. The failure of the Hotham mission, followed by justified Prussian suspicions of British connivance in the attempted flight of Crown Prince Frederick of Prussia, brought Anglo-Prussian relations to a new low.[40] Approaches to Saxony led to demands for British subsidies.[41] Russia had not collapsed into confusion after the accession of Anna (Tsarina 1730-40) as had been hoped. Furthermore, in the summer of 1730 the French made clear that they envisaged operations against Austria that would drive the Austrians from Italy.[42]

The Anglo-French alliance had therefore become, by the summer of 1730, the basis of a possible recasting of the European system. British foreign policy was to be tied to the abasement of Austria, which was to become a matter for action, not speculation. Such a situation had been advocated by various British ministers ever since the signature of the Treaty of Vienna,[43] but its practical implementation in the summer of 1730 was an entirely different matter. The Anglo-French alliance was no longer a defensive screen to protect Hanover, Gibraltar and British commercial privileges. Now it entailed projected subsidies to Sardinia and the Wittelsbachs and the conquest of Italy. The Anglo-French alliance that the British ministry decided to abandon in the summer of 1730 was being directed by the French towards goals very different from those that ministerial speakers had defended in Parliament over the previous five years. However difficult it had been to defend the alliance in those sessions, it would have been even harder to confront the new session with demands for fresh subsidies. Serious British soundings of Austria began in July 1730. The British proposed that Austria should satisfy Hanoverian demands in the Mecklenburg affair and accept the introduction of Spanish garrisons in Parma and Tuscany. In return the British were willing to guarantee the Pragmatic Sanction, Charles VI's scheme by which the entire Austrian Habsburg inheritance would be inherited by his eldest daughter, Maria Theresa. With the exception of the Hanoverian demands, this was the basis of the Anglo-Austrian alliance of 16 March (ns) 1731, the Second Treaty of Vienna. However, the negotiations were far from smooth. The Austrians refused to accept the Spanish garrisons. The British insisted, claiming that an Anglo-Austrian alliance would be useless to Britain unless Spain were satisfied over the garrisons, because without this, Anglo-Spanish relations would collapse, and Britain be forced to defend Gibraltar and her commercial concessions. The British informed the Austrians that, in regaining their friendship, they wished to do nothing to make Spain or France an enemy.[44]

Austrian firmness placed the British ministry in a difficult position. They were forced to abandon both the Hanoverian demands[45] and their hopes of finishing the negotiations before the session of 1731. Aware that France and Spain were also approaching Austria and that the Seville alliance was publicly disintegrating, the British ministry became more frenetic, as the Austrian diplomatic position became stronger.[46] The Austrian occupation of Parma in January 1731 increased diplomatic tension.

It was fortunate for the British ministry that the Austrians rejected the French and Spanish approaches and settled with them. The negotiation was closer run than many historians have realised. The treaty included a mutual guarantee of territories and rights, the permanent suppression of the Ostend Company and a proviso that the guaranty of the Pragmatic Sanction was to be considered void upon a Bourbon or Prussian marriage for Maria Theresa.[47] This last indicated the continuity of policy despite the resignation of Townshend (May 1730). It is often argued that Townshend's departure marked the replacement of anti- by pro-Austrian policies. In fact just as the ministry in the late 1720s, opposed as it was to Austrian policies, had resisted suggestions that would gravely weaken Austria, so, in the early 1730s, there was no unconditional support for Austria.

The treaty was proclaimed in Britain as a triumph for British diplomacy. Walpole was praised by Joshua Nun,

> . . . the Great Patriot whose propitious care,
> Averts the Horrors of all wasting war,
> And bids our Isle with peaceful pleasure crown'd
> Command the wonder of the world around.[48]

More prosaic ministerial writers asserted that Walpole had secured British national interests, whilst the Duke of Newcastle modestly stated that George II had 'singly given peace to all Europe'.[49] The ministry claimed that Spain would accede to, and France accept, the new treaty. However, far from being a triumphant diplomatic success, the treaty was to be a failure in the end, and in the short term it produced a very difficult diplomatic situation for Britain. Far from acceding 'with surprising alacrity',[50] the Spaniards hesitated for several months and war was feared. Simultaneous arming of the British, French and Spanish fleets,[51] and a burst of reports about possible Jacobite action,[52] produced a tense international position. France reacted to the treaty with fury, actively sought to dissuade Spain from acceding and attempted to create a party in the Empire and the Baltic pledged to resist the Pragmatic Sanction and Austrian power. In this situation of fear and uncertainty the news of a French military build-up along the Channel coast proved explosive. Fearing a British attack upon Dunkirk, the French moved troops towards the coast in June 1731, whereupon, fearing invasion, the British moved a sizeable portion of their army to the coast. War seemed imminent.[53]

The crisis finally blew over; Spain accepted the new treaty in July 1731. However, the crisis indicated the precarious state of Anglo-French relations after the new treaty. The Anglo-French treaty of mutual guarantees was still in force but it had lost all substance. Hopes that French agreement to the new treaty could be obtained had been lost. Thereafter, Anglo-French relations deteriorated. The French feared that the British would seek to force them to guarantee the Pragmatic Sanction, resented the new diplomatic configurations of 1731 and sought to undermine it.[54] The British saw France behind all the European difficulties they encountered, which was unfortunate because, despite growing colonial and commercial rivalries, there was a considerable degree of shared interest between the British ministry and Fleury (though not Chauvelin). Neither wished for war nor for any substantial alteration in the European system. Both were suspicious of Austrian and Spanish policy. Horace Walpole's mediation scheme in the Polish Succession War, his attempt to build on shared Anglo-French interests, was not as misguided, in theory, as might be thought.

The Anglo-Austrian treaty was to prove a disappointment for both states. Serious strains emerged in 1732, largely due to the efforts of both powers to reconcile their alliance with their ties with other countries. Britain sought in vain to settle Austro-Sardinian and Austro-Spanish disputes, Austria to settle Anglo-Prussian disputes and Anglo-Russian suspicions.[55] A major Spanish armament in the spring of 1732 led Sardinia and Austria (fearing invasion of her Italian possessions) to demand the dispatch of a British fleet to the Mediterranean. The British, claiming to be satisfied by Spanish assurances, refused, though they feared French connivance in Spanish schemes and were not unaffected by suggestions that Spain might attack Britain.[56] The refusal to send aid prefigured the British stance the following year when Spain attacked Austrian Italy. In 1732 the Spaniards attacked and captured Oran in North Africa.

Austrian failure to satisfy George II by abandoning Prussia led to tension. George suspected Austrian connivance in schemes for a Prusso-Russian dynastic link, and his failure to support Austrian schemes for settling Baltic problems led to his exclusion from the Treaty of Copenhagen of 1732, and from other Austrian diplomatic moves.[57] The Anglo-Austrian alliance was in a poor state long before it collapsed in late 1733.

The contrast between British foreign policy in the late 1710s and in 1731-3 is clear. As in the period of the Quadruple Alliance, Britain sent a fleet to the Mediterranean (1718 and 1731) and sought to expand the alliance, and to deal with tensions within it, by negotiations. However, in 1731-3 the ministry was more hesitant about committing itself abroad. The firm refusal to participate in the schemes to end the Holstein-Gottorp problem, which had plagued Baltic relations for so long, led to Britain's exclusion from the Treaty of Copenhagen. Willing to seek by negotiation to end Austro-Sardinian hostilities, the ministry was opposed to any formal British commitments, a break from the Stanhopian system of mutual guarantees. Charles Emmanuel III of Sardinia sought such British commitments. The British envoy in Turin was instructed that Charles Emmanuel 'has declared himself so desirous that the King should either become a party to this treaty, or make a separate one with him. Your Excellency will however manage this so, as that His Majesty may not be under any engagement to do either, but that it be left to the King's future determination to act as the circumstances of affairs may hereafter make it more or less agreable to His Majesty's interest'.[58]

The following year the efforts to involve Britain formally in a negotiation she supported, that of Austria and Saxony, were resisted.[59] The British stance was therefore defined well before the domestic complications associated with the Excise Crisis (spring 1733). Commitments were to be taken on with care, and only honoured if both feasible and in British interests. Furthermore, as the events of 1733-5 (the War of the Polish Succession) were to show, British interests were to be defined cautiously. The British ministry in the early 1730s was well aware of the fragile nature of the international system and the precariousness of their achievement in 1731. That year Lord Harrington (Secretary of State, Northern Department 1730-42, 44-6) wrote, 'there is no forming any sure judgment upon the future conduct of so capricious a court as that of Spain', whilst French conduct was seen to greatly depend upon the elderly Fleury.[60]

The international situation remained tense in 1731-3. Spain sought further Italian gains, France encouraged German opponents of Austria, particularly Bavaria which had claims of its own on the Austrian succession. War seemed imminent over German and Italian issues, but it was to be occasioned by a conflict over Poland. Poland was an elective monarchy, and Augustus II's death on 1 February (ns) 1733 produced two principal claimants, his son Augustus III of Saxony, and Stanislas Leszczynski, a former king, who was the father-in-law of Louis XV of France. The latter was elected in September 1733, but Russia, determined to prevent the spread of French influence in eastern Europe, invaded Poland the same month. Stanislas fled to Danzig and Augustus III, supported by Saxon and Russian troops, was elected king. These events touched off war. Accusing Austria of responsibility for the actions of her Russian ally, France declared war in October. Spain and Sardinia, anxious to acquire Austrian possessions in Italy, joined in.

The war was fought in three areas. Russian and Saxon troops conquered Poland, and a small French force failed to raise the siege of Danzig, which fell in the summer of 1734. In Italy the Austrian territories fell rapidly, and, after unsuccessful counter-attacks, only Mantua remained by the summer of 1735. Initial French successes in the Rhineland were never exploited.

The Austrians demanded British assistance under the terms of the Second Treaty of Vienna, and they pressed for the immediate dispatch of a fleet to western Mediterranean waters in order to help preserve their Italian possessions. Chancellor Sinzendorf 'bewailed Sicily as lost . . . for the want of the presence of 10 ships only, whether sent to act or not to act, in the Mediterranean'.[61] The British ministry argued that French claims that Austria had incited and abetted the Russian invasion of Poland required investigation; though there was no satisfactory reason why they should not have helped Austria against Spain and Sardinia. In fact the British ministry was clearly determined not to commit itself, either to war or to specific negotiating positions. In July 1733 Fleury had remarked to the British envoy in Paris, 'that His Majesty had very dexterously avoided to explain himself as to any future measures he should think fit to take; to which I made answer that those measures would probably be determined by other peoples proceedings, . . .'[62] Within the ministry differences existed as to the degree to which Britain should assist Austria. George II and both Secretaries of State, Newcastle and Harrington, adopted a more pro-Austrian stance than that of Walpole and, his principal adviser on foreign policy matters, his brother Horace. A number of policies were advocated, two in particular being intended to end the war by negotiation. It was suggested that Britain should attempt to arrange a separate Austro-Spanish settlement, Austria offering Don Carlos an archduchess and most of her Italian possessions as a dowry. Opinion in London was divided over this policy: it represented a reversal of that of 1725-31 when everything possible had been done to discourage such a union. Furthermore, the Spanish first minister Patino was distrusted. The second policy, that supported by Horace Walpole, was eventually followed. It was for the negotiation of the differences between all of the powers, rather than an attempt to split the Bourbon-Sardinian alliance. Horace placed great faith in the integrity of Fleury, with whom he had a confidential correspondence. Thanks to Horace's efforts, the winter of 1734-5 witnessed major negotiations at The Hague aimed at settling the conflict. Whether Fleury sincerely intended them to succeed is unclear, but their failure placed Britain in a difficult diplomatic position in 1735.

Horace Walpole's negotiations took place against the background of mounting Anglo-French tension, for, although the ministry would not support Austria, they did not fear her. Instead, it was France that was feared. Anxiety about possible French support for the Jacobites played a role in the preparation of large naval forces in 1734 and 1735. The British sought to prevent other powers supporting France. Particular efforts were devoted to keeping Sweden neutral, and to attempting to prevent the United Provinces from renewing their 1733 neutrality agreement with France. In 1734 the Anglo-Russian trade agreement was seen, correctly, as having political overtones; the following year Britain lent diplomatic support to the movement of a Russian army towards the Rhine. It was hardly surprising that Fluery questioned 'whether His Majesty was sufficiently in a state of neutrality to be a mediator, . . .'[63]

In London there were grave doubts about French intentions. The need for Britain to remain at peace was clear: the fiscal situation was alarming, Jacobitism was feared, there was a general election in 1734. The Austrians bewailed British selfishness; one Austrian envoy, Bishop Strickland of Namur, attempted to persuade George II to dismiss the Walpoles, and complained 'Ce n'est plus le regne de George premier, ni le Ministere de Mylord Stanhope . . .' Domestic factors stressed neutrality, but diplomatic fears led in a different direction. In October 1733 one British diplomat, the Earl of Essex, had hoped 'His Majesty will be able to keep himself free from all engagements whatever, till his taking any can be justified by the Liberties of Europe and the Balance of Power being threatened and immediately aimed at'.[64] In 1734-5 fears of French intentions led many to claim such a threat existed, and, within the ministry, not all shared Horace's relative confidence in Fleury. In October 1734 Harrington informed Horace,

> The King does not indeed himself expect such a reasonable scheme of pacification from the Cardinal and Mr Chauvelin in their present dispositions and is far from thinking that England and Holland can ever agree to see the armys of France in the heart of the Empire, and in the hereditary dominions of the House of Austria, or that any security that can be thought of, for her resisting so dangerous a temptation as that of making conquests there, would be sufficient, and satisfactory to the maritime powers, . . .[65]

Horace's failure, and fears that Bavaria and Prussia might declare for France, led to renewed diplomatic pressure for British aid to Austria. Indeed it is unclear what British policy might have been had the war continued for much longer. However, in the summer of 1735, whilst George was in Hanover, information of Austro-French negotiations was received. These produced a preliminary treaty, signed on 5th October (ns) 1735, that was finally to become the Third Treaty of Vienna. Under its terms Charles-Emmanuel received some of the Milanese, Don Carlos received Naples and Sicily but lost Parma and his rights to the Tuscan succession, Lorraine was given to Stanislas, who was to leave it to his daughter, the French Queen, and to her heirs (it thus passed to France in 1766), France guaranteed the Pragmatic Sanction, and the Tuscan succession was given to Francis III of Lorraine, who married Maria Theresa, the elder archduchess, in February 1736, and succeeded to Tuscany the following year. Poland was to remain with Augustus III.

Furious at the terms and at being excluded from the negotiations, Sardinia, and in particular Spain, sought British diplomatic assistance against the new agreement. The British, though they had sought in vain to be included in the negotiations, rejected these approaches and claimed, truthfully, that the terms were very similar to those Horace Walpole had proposed at The Hague. Nevertheless George II was no longer 'the umpire of Europe'.[66]

Aside from good work on Anglo-French and Anglo-Spanish relations, there is little available on British policy in the second half of the 1730s.[67] General views are unfavourable: Britain is held to have been excluded from European influence, her diplomacy aimless.[68] It is certainly true that Britain enjoyed less influence than France, that perception of a Bourbon threat was growing in Britain and that this led to criticism of the ministry. Pessimistic views were expressed by some members of the ministry, Horace Walpole writing in October 1736, 'our affairs abroad are in a most loose and shattered situation'. Deeply depressed by the European situation, Horace sought to create a northern alliance system for Britain, and, in particular, attempted to improve Anglo-Prussian relations, attempts thwarted partly by George II's intransigent stance on Hanoverian interests.[69]

It could be suggested that the international situation restricted British options and that the policies followed were not as misguided as contemporary and subsequent critics have suggested. Firstly, it is by no means clear that international relations after 1735 threatened Britain sufficiently to justify the construction of an alliance system to counter the new Austro-French alliance. The Duke of Newcastle had written in October 1735, 'We are all here in great joy upon the appearance of the peace being soon concluded between the Emperor and France, and that upon terms that can neither hurt the Equilibre nor our particular interests, and if it should be attended with a breach with Spain, which is most likely I think this war will have put things upon a better foot, than they were before'.[70] Newcastle was not simply indulging in wishful thinking. Franco-Spanish relations deteriorated rapidly, particularly after Chauvelin, the prime exponent of aggressive anti-Austrian policies in the French ministry, was dismissed, early in 1737. France took over from Britain the thankless task of preventing Austro-Spanish clashes in Italy. Far from being faced by a united Bourbon bloc, Britain was able to negotiate independently with each power, seeking unsuccessfully to improve Anglo-French relations in 1735-8, before settling, without French mediation, Anglo-Spanish commercial differences by the Convention of the Pardo (January 1739), a diplomatic triumph that could well have had important political consequences. Furthermore, it seems likely that the extent and detrimental consequences of Britain's exclusion from European affairs have been exaggerated. Britain played a major role in the mediation of Spanish-Portuguese differences in 1735-7, a role supported by the maintenance of a powerful fleet in the Tagus throughout this period. Such mediations were a mixed blessing. Britain's initial role in mediating in the Balkan war of the late 1730s was an unhappy one. As one perceptive British diplomat, Robert Trevor, pointed out, 'If we ask Oczakov of the Czarina, she may think us more Turbanised than his Eminency [Fleury] himself. On the other hand, should we make bold to ask it of the

Turks, may not Monsieur Villeneuve [French envoy in Constantinople] the very next hour get our nose damnably out of joint with the Musselmen by then declaring, that nothing was more reasonable, and equitable, than for the Czarina to restore that distant, unmaintainable acquisition to its old and natural master'.[71]

The British did not lose greatly when France gained the dominant role in Balkan negotiations; they were very sensible in rejecting Franco-Austrian attempts to involve Britain in the settlement of the Jülich-Berg question, attempts that they argued, correctly, would wreck Anglo-Prussian relations and expose Hanover to the threat of Prussian invasion. There was little to be gained by joining the Franco-Austrian collective security system, and Britain's exclusion from it should not be regarded as a failure. Neither power sought to aid the Jacobites (as the latter had hoped); the new alliance did not challenge British interests, and therefore Britain's failure either to join or to destroy it should not be condemned. British ministers argued correctly that the Franco-Austrian alliance would not last,[72] and that, when it collapsed, Britain would be able to improve her relations with Austria. They were surprised that the alliance did last as long as it did (until 1741), but they correctly analysed Austrian weakness, and the importance of preserving the Austro-Russian alliance as being a long-term rival to French interests, and thus in Britain's long-term interests, should European conflict resume. Britain attempted to lend diplomatic weight to the further-ance of the Austro-Russian alliance, Harrington writing of it, in 1739, that 'the King looks upon [it] to be so extremely important for the general good'.[73] The importance of the alliance during the War of the Austrian Succession (1740-8) was to bear out the accuracy of the British analysis.

Trevor claimed in 1736 that the British situation was 'rather a scene of observation, expectation, and speculation, than of deliberation, or action'.[74] The political nation in Britain, as represented in Parliament, concentrated their attention on domestic matters, with the sole exception of Spanish depredations, which became a major issue from 1737 onwards. Contentious religious legislation occupied a lot of attention, as did the quarrel of the Prince of Wales ('Poor Fred') with his father. Edward Weston, Under-secretary of State in the Northern Department, wrote, in 1737, that the latter 'engrosses everybody's attention so much, that little time is employed upon foreign business . . .'[75] Foreign policy played far less of a role in parliamentary debates. The opposition, which had for over a decade attacked the general direction of foreign policy, narrowed its sights to the specific issue of Anglo-Spanish commercial relations.

However, far from being quiescent and ignoring European affairs, considerable thought was devoted, particularly by the Secretaries of State and the diplomatic corps, to the European situation. Austria, weakened by the Polish Succession War, and defeated in her Turkish war of 1737-9, was seen as a broken reed. It was felt that her French alliance would soon dissolve, but that her effectiveness as an ally would be a limited one. The extraordinary resilience Austria was to display, in 1741-2, was not anticipated. The British envoy in Vienna, Thomas Robinson, noted, in 1739, that he had told Harrington

> that so notable a change, as is likely to be made in the relation, which the House of Austria has had for so many ages with the common interest of the rest of Europe, may, by being foreseen betimes, be provided against, by looking out, if possible, for a new weight, in the place of that which is lost, in the general Balance of Europe against the House of Bourbon; for this family cannot without a miracle be retrieved at all, or even with one, be entirely recovered under many years.[76]

The Anglo-Dutch alliance was in a poor way, the Dutch, in British eyes, heedless of European developments, 'dead asleep'.[77] The international system seemed to depend on Fleury's health. Born in 1653, he was a remarkably vigorous octogenerian, but his imminent death was widely anticipated, and a serious illness in 1738 exacerbated these fears. It was believed that after his death French policy would become more aggressive. This posed major problems for Britain for, under the energetic minister of the marine, Maurepas, France was rapidly developing as a naval and colonial power.[78] Commercial and colonial competition between Britain and France, already a problem during the alliance between the two powers, increased during the 1730s. The leading gloom and doom merchant on the British side was Horace Walpole. In 1737 he wrote that if anything 'should happen to the Cardinal [Fleury] I am afraid Europe would be undone too'; the following year, 'I foresee nothing but clouds big with darkness and destruction in Europe; if we can at last come to an agreement with Spain I must own I never saw an administration more at their ease than ours is at present with respect to domestick troubles, but the Cardinal's death will soon putt us into great confusion'.

Horace's letters to Trevor, of which much of interest was omitted in the Historical Manuscripts Commission edition of the correspondence, provide support for the view that Britain's position was a difficult one, but they also cast light on the problems facing attempts to negotiate new alliances:

> I never saw Europe in so dangerous a state as it is at present, and so much the more so because I see no remedy; which not only arises from the Emperors great distress, but from I'm afraid his resolution not to take one reasonable step to help himself or to induce others to help him.
> the general state of things is so confused and distracted, that I doe not see that we have anything to do at present besides expecting an eclaircissement of them from Providence, either by giving a better turn to events, or to the temper and humour of Princes; for though Europe is in so dangerous a condition, I could easily prescribe a remedy if the hearts of Princes were altered even so far only as to consult their own interest upon a great scale; . . .[79]

Prescribing a remedy became much more necessary in 1739, when the failure to maintain the peace with Spain, a failure that clearly indicated the primacy of domestic over diplomatic considerations, produced the War of Jenkins' Ear. This war was entered into enthusiastically by most of the political nation. It was widely believed that Spain's possessions in the western hemisphere would fall easily, and that the war would be profitable. This, the so-called Blue Water Strategy, was expounded eagerly by the opposition, and unrealistic expectations of success were engendered.[80] The ministry were more sceptical, for they feared French intervention: Newcastle wrote in August 1739, 'We take it for granted, that France will join Spain, and that we shall be attacked at home . . .', and, the following February, he stated that, though a French invasion was unlikely, Britain had to act as though war with France was possible.[81] Franco-Spanish relations were still far from perfect, but they had been improved by the marriage of Louis XV's daughter to Don Philip, the younger son of Philip V and Elisabeth Farnese, a move that seemed to suggest future French support for Spain's Italian schemes. More important was the French determination not to permit British gains in the West Indies, gains that would threaten French interests. In 1740 France sent a large fleet to the West Indies designed to support the Spanish position; 'so black a prospect I never saw,' commented the Lord Privy Seal, Lord Hervey.[82]

The deteriorating situation led the ministry to hasten their search for European allies. Attempts to gain Dutch support were rejected, approaches were made to Austria, but the main thrust of British foreign policy was towards northern Europe. In 1739, in response to Sweden's gravitation into the French orbit, and partly in order to end a troublesome confrontation with Hanover, Denmark was gained by means of a subsidy treaty. Urgency was lent to attempts to woo Russia, where no high-ranking British diplomat had been posted since May 1734. In 1740 Edward Finch was sent to St. Petersburg. His previous posting had been Stockholm, and his move symbolised a major alteration in Britain's Baltic policy. Hitherto Britain had sought to balance the two powers, and a major reason for limiting approaches to Russia had been the wish to avoid provoking Sweden. From 1740 onwards there was to be no doubt of the importance Britain attached to Russia. Finch's instructions claimed that an alliance of the two powers was 'one of the chief securitys which seem to remain for the preservation of the Balance of Power in Europe'.[83] The succession of Frederick II (the Great) of Prussia (31 May (ns) 1740) raised hopes of the possibility of an alliance, and attempts were made to negotiate one.[84]

Thus, by the autumn of 1740, before war had begun in Europe, the ministry was already actively seeking to construct an alliance system. A ministerial memorandum of early October claimed, 'If the powers now concern'd will not enter into any measures for the preservation of the Balance of Europe, which is now in immediate danger, His Majesty must be obliged to confine his care to the security of his own dominions and of the particular interests of his own subjects, without interesting or concerning himself, about the fate of Europe in general'.[85]

The following month the Lord Chancellor, Lord Hardwicke, informed the Lords of the danger of war with France, 'unless His Majesty can form such a confederacy upon the continent, as will make it dangerous for any power in Europe to disturb the tranquillity thereof'.[86] It is difficult to know what would have happened had Britain alone faced the Bourbon powers, but the speculation is not an idle one, for it was a danger the ministry was aware of. By October 1740 it was clear that it was going to be difficult to gain continental allies. That month, however, the European situation dramatically altered, for the Emperor Charles VI died, without any male heir, on 20 October (ns).

By 1740 most European powers had accepted the Pragmatic Sanction and the Austrian Habsburg inheritance should have descended, uncontested and undivided, to Maria Theresa. Charles Albert of Bavaria rapidly made clear that he intended to challenge this: he and Augustus III were married to the daughters of Charles VI's elder brother and predecessor, the Emperor Joseph I. However, the first military challenge to the Pragmatic Sanction was to come from Prussia: in December Prussian troops invaded Silesia, the most northerly and the most industrialised possession of Maria Theresa. The invasion was successful and it soon became clear that Frederick's action would be followed by other claimants: Spain, Sardinia, Saxony and Bavaria all had significant claims.

Maria Theresa's response was to call for assistance from the guarantors of the Pragmatic Sanction, a group including Britain and France. France, where the pacific Fleury was losing ground to a hawkish group of ministers, far from giving assistance, lent her resources and her troops to the anti-Habsburg powers. In the summer of 1741 French troops marched to the assistance of Bavaria. By the end of the year Bohemia and Upper Austria had been occupied, and in January 1742 Charles Albert was elected Emperor as Charles VII, the first non-Habsburg for three hundred years.

The British response was totally different from that of 1733. The ministry determined to support Austria with money and diplomatic assistance. On 13 April the Commons passed a motion granting £300,000, 'for preventing the subversion of the house of Austria; and for the maintaining the Pragmatic Sanction, and supporting the liberties and balance of power in Europe'. The proposer of the motion, Walpole, made it clear that aid to Austria was seen by the ministry as part of the strategy of constructing an anti-Bourbon coalition, in short a continuation of the policy that had been actively followed since 1739: 'the only power that can sensibly injure us by obstructing our commerce, or invading our dominions, is France, against which no confederacy can be formed, except with the house of Austria, that can afford us any efficacious support'.[87]

This strategy, of anchoring an anti-Bourbon European coalition on an Anglo-Austrian alliance, was to be followed until 1756. As with the approach to Russia, there was to be continuity between the Walpole and the post-Walpole years. In 1741 the strategy was handicapped by Austrian obduracy and by Hanover. The British ministry argued that the alliance could only be effective if Prussia was gained by Austrian territorial concessions in Silesia: 'the entering into a war, in support of the Austrian dominions, whether their dispute with the King of Prussia be accommodated or no, appears to His Majesty to be absolutely unavoidable . . . the true question is . . . whether we should have his Prussian Majesty, for a friend, or an enemy, in that war, and, in short, whether it should be undertaken, with an alliance capable of supporting the points it contends for, or upon a foot, which from the very beginning threatens the utter ruin and destruction of the whole . . .'[88]

Unwilling to yield to the Protestant Prussian aggressor, the Austrians argued that to yield Silesia would simply whet the appetite of other powers. This difference of interests was to bedevil Anglo-Austrian relations until the breach of 1756. For Britain the reconquest of Silesia would only serve to split two allies who ought to unite against France; Austria (and Hanover) feared Prussia most. In Vienna there was a disinclination to follow the British lead, and the anglophile Francis of Lorraine thought it necessary to press the British envoy in May 1741, 'to convince all the Austrian ministers, that the King's intention of forming a subsequent grand alliance, was not meant as an offensive one against France'.[89]

In 1741 the British forced Austria to settle with Prussia, arranging an armistice in October 1741. An Anglo-Austrian alliance, signed on 24 June (ns) 1741, promised British subsidies and 12,000 troops. Major diplomatic efforts promised the construction of a powerful anti-Bourbon coalition. These efforts were undermined by George II, as Elector of Hanover. Fearing French and Prussian attack, George negotiated (September-October 1741) a convention with Louis XV, under which Hanover was neutralised and George promised to vote for Charles Albert as Emperor, as he did in January 1742. This convention, made against the will of his British ministers, handicapped the latter in their attempt to create an anti-Bourbon coalition. The Sardinian envoy commented that it seemed as if the British ministry no longer had any system at all. Distinctions between George as King and as Elector convinced few. The Hanover convention increased tension within the ministry, sowed doubts in both Britain and Europe about

British policy, and helped to embitter discussion about foreign policy in Walpole's last session as first minister.[90]

The developments in Europe turned the attentions of Britain, France and Spain away from America. Spain sought Italian conquests, France recalled her fleet from American waters, Britain from 1741 onwards concentrated her resources in Europe. Partly this was a response to the difficulties and lack of success Britain had encountered in her Caribbean campaigns. Logistically they had proved a nightmare, indicating the limitations of eighteenth-century amphibious warfare and the dependence of naval operations on the wind. The fall of Porto Bello in November 1739 had raised expectations that were to be cruelly dashed by the 1741 failure to take Cartagena. However, the need to match Bourbon naval strength in European waters was the major reason for the downgrading of Caribbean operations. A large fleet had to be maintained in home waters, and assistance lent to Austria in the Mediterranean. In August 1741 Hardwicke wrote to Newcastle, 'I fear that now America must be fought for in Europe. It look'd last year, as if the old world was to be fought for in the new; but the tables are turn'd ... Whatever success we may have in the former [America], I doubt it will always *finally* follow the fate of the latter [Europe]; ...'[91] As the war progressed, Caribbean operations were largely forgotten, and this was reflected in the peace terms at Aix-la-Chapelle in 1748. The Anglo-Spanish conflict had become totally absorbed within the Anglo-French conflict.

By February 1742, when Walpole was forced to resign due to his disappearing Commons majority, the war was beginning to go well for the Anglo-Austrian alliance. The Austro-Prussian armistice enabled Austria to start driving back the Bavarians and the French. Bavaria was invaded, Bohemia regained, and the Hanoverian convention abandoned by George II. Walpole was replaced as most influential minister by Lord Carteret (Secretary of State, Northern Department, February 1742-November 1744). With Carteret British foreign policy reverted to the Stanhopian mould, for, though most policies were simply the continuation of those followed in recent years, the emphasis was entirely different. Carteret believed that Britain should play a dominant role in European affairs, and he came near to achieving this goal. Prussia and Austria were reconciled, a grand coalition constructed, George II defeated the French at Dettingen in 1743, and his minister negotiated a series of treaties that placed Britain at the centre of the diplomatic stage. An extraordinarily euphoric attitude can be discerned in the writings of ministers such as Carteret and the Earl of Stair. It was recaptured, several years later, by the writer Richard Rolt: 'this seemed to be the happy period in which the power of the oppressors of mankind might be for ever broken, in which universal liberty might be recovered; and a peace established in Europe, which it might never be the interest of any nation to interrupt or violate'.[92] Carteret failed: his anti-Bourbon alliance could not long contain the aspirations of both Austria and Prussia. Austrian success helped to lead Frederick the Great to invade Bohemia in August 1744, beginning the second Silesian War. Carteret's ministerial colleagues refused to support his policies, forcing his resignation in late 1744. As with Stanhope, Carteret had sought to dominate Europe, pursuing policies that had dangerous domestic repercussions, and that ultimately proved diplomatic failures.

It could be suggested that many of the problems faced by the British during the War of the Austrian Succession – Carteret's failure, the Jacobite invasion scare of 1744, the Jacobite invasion of 1745-6, the French conquest of the Austrian Netherlands, and the difficulty of alliance politics – do much to justify the foreign policy of the 1730s against the criticisms it faced then, and has done since. In a similar manner the political history of the period 1742-8 – Jacobitism, ministerial instability, the 'ratting' of most of the Patriots – did much to justify the Walpolean system against the assaults of its critics. Over-ambitious and unsuccessful participation in the European conflict led to fiscal strain, economic disruption, ministerial conflict, political strife and parliamentary difficulties. The debate over foreign policy in the Walpolean period will be examined later in this work. It is sufficient to note here that it is unfair to condemn the policies associated with the Walpolean period without considering the achievements and failures of subsequent administrations.

NOTES

1. O'Rourke to James Hamilton, Jacobite agent in London, 3 Ap. (ns) 1728, HHStA. Varia 8.
2. Delafaye to George Tilson, Undersecretary in the Northern Department, 21 July 1725, PRO. 43/74.
3. R. Lodge, 'The Treaty of Seville 1729', *TRHS* 4th series, 16 (1933) p. 32.
4. Hatton; J. F. Chance, *The Alliance of Hanover* (1923); G. C. Gibbs, 'Britain and the Alliance of Hanover', *EHR* 73 (1958); L. Wiesener, *Le Régent, L'Abbé Dubois, et les Anglais* (3 vols., Paris, 1891-9).
5. P. Vaucher, *Robert Walpole et la politique de Fleury, 1731-42* (Paris, 1924); Lodge, *Great Britain and Prussia in the Eighteenth Century* (Oxford, 1923); G. C. Gibbs, 'Parliament and Foreign Policy in the Age of Stanhope and Walpole', *EHR* 77 (1962); Gibbs, 'Newspapers, Parliament and Foreign Policy in the Age of Stanhope and Walpole', *Mélanges offerts à G. Jacquemyns* (Brussels, 1968), pp. 293-315; Gibbs, 'Laying Treaties before Parliament in the Eighteenth Century', *Studies in Diplomatic History*, edited by R. Hatton and M. S. Anderson (1970), pp. 116-37.
6. Chance, *George I and the Great Northern War* (London, 1909); W. Mediger, *Mecklenburg Russland und England-Hanover, 1706-21* (2 vols., Hildesheim, 1967); D. Aldridge, 'Sir John Norris and the British Naval Expeditions to the Baltic Sea, 1715-27' (Ph.D., London, 1971); H. Bagger, *Ruslands Alliancepolitik efter freden i Nystad* (Copenhagen, 1974), English Summary.

7. A Baudrillart, *Philippe V et la Cour de France* (5 vols., Paris, 1890-1901); Baudrillart, 'Les prétentions de Philippe V à la couronne de France', *Séances et travaux de l'Académie des sciences morales et politiques* 127 (1887); J. Shennan, *Philippe, Duke of Orleans* (1979).

8. A. Beer, 'Zur Geschichte der Politik Karl's VI', *Historische Zeitschrift*, new series, 19 (1886); M. Naumann, *Österreich, England und das Reich, 1719-32* (Berlin, 1936); M. Braubach, *Prinz Eugen von Savoyen* (5 vols., Vienna, 1963-5); D. McKay, *Prince Eugene* (1977); Hughes.

9. J. J. Murray, *George I, the Baltic and the Whig split of 1717* (1969); Hatton, pp. 193-202; W. Speck, 'The Whig Schism under George I', *Huntington Library Quarterly* 40 (1977); Hatton, 'New Light on George I', *England's Rise to Greatness, 1660-1763*, edited by S. Baxter (Berkeley, 1983), pp. 230-2; Black, 'Parliament and the Political and Diplomatic Crisis of 1717-18', *Parliamentary History Yearbook* 3 (1984).

10. B. Williams, *Stanhope* (Oxford, 1932); Lodge, 'The Anglo-French Alliance, 1716-31', *Studies in Anglo-French History*, edited by A. Coville and H. Temperley (Cambridge, 1935), pp. 3-18; O. Weber, *Die Quadrupel-Allianz vom Jahre 1718* (Vienna, 1887); Hatton, p. 191.

11. Horace Walpole to the Duke of Newcastle, Secretary of State in the Southern Department, 6 Feb. (ns) 1726, BL. Add. 32746.

12. Bonet, Prussian envoy in London, to Frederick William I of Prussia, 12 Aug. (ns) 1718, Merseburg, Deutsches Zentralarchiv, Rep. XI, 41.

13. E. Armstrong, *Elisabeth Farnese 'the Termagant of Spain'* (1892); M. Martin, 'The Secret Clause, Britain and Spanish ambitions in Italy, 1712-31', *European Studies Review* 6 (1976); G. H. Jones, 'Inghilterra, Granducato di Toscana e Quadruplice Alleanza', *Archivio Storico Italiano* (1980); Jones, 'La Gran Bretagna e la destinazione di Don Carlos al trono di Toscana 1721-32', *Archivio Storico Italiano* (1982); G. Quazza, *Il Problema Italiano e l'equilibrio europeo, 1720-38* (Turin, 1965).

14. G. V. Bennett, *The Tory Crisis in Church and State, 1688-1730* (Oxford, 1975).

15. Whitworth, envoy in Berlin, to Tilson, 1 Ap. (ns) 1721, PRO. 90/13; Destouches, French envoy in London, to Dubois, 9, 30 Ap. (ns) 1722, 4 Jan. (ns) 1723, Chammorel, French Chargé d'Affaires in London, to Dubois, 29 Nov. (ns) 1722, 15 Nov. (ns) 1723, AE. CP. Ang. 341, 344, 343, 346; Townshend to St. Saphorin, representative at Vienna, 4 July, 12 Aug. (ns) 1723, PRO. 80/48; Newcastle to Robert Walpole, 3 Sept., Horace Walpole to Newcastle, 20 Nov. (ns) 1723, BL. Add. 32686; *The Loyal Observator or, Collins's Weekly Journal*, 10 Aug. 1723.

16. J. Dureng, *Le Duc de Bourbon et l'Angleterre, 1723-6* (Paris, 1911); Horace Walpole to St. Saphorin, 9 July (ns) 1724, Hanover Hann. Des 91, St. Saphorin, Nr. 2; Chammorel to Morville, French foreign minister, 10 Feb. (ns) 1724, AE. CP. Ang. 347; Horace Walpole to Lords Polwarth and Whitworth, Plenipotentiaries at Cambrai, 5 May (ns) 1724, BL. Add. 37394.

17. St. Saphorin to George I, 6 July 1718, Hanover, Calenberg Brief Archiv 11, Nr. 1619; St. Saphorin to Townshend, 21 Feb. 1722, PRO. 80/46.

18. Harris, secretary at Berlin, to Tilson, 2 Sept., (ns) Whitworth to Townshend, 10 Oct. (ns) 1721, PRO. 90/15; Scott, envoy in Dresden, to Whitworth, 23 Feb. (ns) 1722, BL. Add. 37388; Chammorel to Morville, 15 Feb. (ns) 1723, AE. CP. Ang. 344; Robert Walpole to Newcastle, 25 July (os) 1723, BL. Add. 32686.

19. Du Bourgay to Townshend, 12 Aug. (ns) 1724, PRO. 90/18.

20. Black, 'The theory of the balance of power in the first half of the eighteenth century', *Review of International Studies* 9 (1983).

21. G. Syveton, *Une cour et un aventurier au XVIIIe siècle: le baron de Ripperda* (Paris, 1896) and review by Armstrong, *EHR* 12 (1897), pp. 796-800.

22. Horace Walpole to Newcastle, 26 June (ns) 1726, BL. Add. 32746; extract of despatch of Keene, Consul in Madrid, 15 June (ns) 1726, CUL. CH. papers 26/23; Townshend to Diemar, Hesse-Cassel Envoy Extraordinary in London, 4 Jan. 1727, PRO. 100/15; *The Occasional Writer* I (London, 1727), p. 26; John Barnard, MP. London, Robert Walpole, 29 Mar. 1734, Cobbett, IX, 595, 597; J. Ralph, *A Critical History of the Administration of Sir Robert Walpole* (1743), p. 408; Hervey, I, 58; P. Fritz, *The English Ministers and Jacobitism* (Toronto, 1975), p. 134.

23. Wilson, pp. 151-67; Lodge, review of Chance's *Alliance of Hanover, EHR* 39 (1924), pp. 293-7.

24. Du Bourgay to Townshend, 17 May (ns) 1726, PRO. 90/20; Sinzendorf to Fonseca, Austrian Chargé d'Affaires in Paris, 4 Feb. (ns) 1727, HHStA. Fonseca 11; Horace Walpole to Newcastle, 26 June (ns) 1726, BL. Add. 32746; Skinner to Delafaye, 4 May (ns) 1726, BL. Add. 41504.

25. Broglie, French Ambassador in London, to Morville, 30 Nov. (ns) 1724, AE. CP. Ang. 349; Fleury to George II, 2, 11 July (ns) 1727, PRO. 100/7; Atterbury to James III, the Pretender, 20 Aug. (ns) 1727, RA. 109/87; Hervey, I, 30-1, 49.

26. Instructions for Le Coq and Hoym, Saxon Plenipotentiaries to Congress of Soissons, 24, 30 June (ns), Le Coq to Augustus II of Saxony, 28 July (ns), 11 Aug. (ns) 1728, Dresden, 2733.

27. Townshend to the Earl of Chesterfield, Ambassador at The Hague, 6 Sept. 1728, PRO. 84/301; Newcastle to Horace Walpole and Stanhope, Plenipotentiaries at Soissons, 6 Nov., Stanhope to Newcastle, 9 Dec. (ns) 1728, BL. Add. 32759; Tilson to Waldegrave, Ambassador in Vienna, 8 Nov. 1728, Chewton; Broglie to Chauvelin, French foreign minister, 19 Dec. (ns) 1728, AE. CP. Ang. 363; *Mist's Weekly Journal,* 17 Aug. 1728; Zamboni, Saxon agent in London, to Count Manteuffel, Saxon minister, 10 Dec. (ns) 1728, Bodl. Rawl. 120.

28. Deleted section of undated draft instructions to Plenipotentiaries at Soissons, early spring 1729, PRO. 103/110.

29. Count Philip Kinsky, Austrian Envoy Extraordinary in London, to Charles VI, 18, 25, 28 Jan. (ns) 1729, HHStA. EK. 65; Kinsky to Prince Eugene, Austrian minister, 8, 25 Feb. (ns) 1729, HHStA. GK. 94(b); Townshend to Waldegrave, 16, 25, Mar. Waldegrave to Townshend, 18, 19, 26 Mar. (ns) 1729, PRO. 80/64.

30. Newcastle to Townshend, 13 June 1729, PRO. 43/77; King, 17 June 1729, pp. 90-1; Townshend to Horace Walpole, 1 July (ns) 1729, BL. Add. 48982; P. S. Cady, 'Horatio Walpole and the making of the Treaty of Seville, 1728-30' (Ph.D., Columbus, Ohio, 1976).

31. Townshend to Newcastle, 25 Aug. (ns), 6 Sept., Newcastle to Townshend, 29 Aug. 1729, PRO. 43/80; H. Schilling, *Der Zwist Preussens und Hannovers, 1729-30* (Halle, 1912).

32. Dureng; Account of Council meeting, 11 Aug. 1729, PRO. 43/80.

33. Treaty, PRO. 108/490.

34. Dodington, envoy in Spain, to the Earl of Stair, Ambassador in Paris, 29 June (ns) 1716, SRO. GD. 135/141/6; Stair to James Stanhope, 7, 10 July (ns) 1717, Maidstone, Kent CRO., Chevening Mss. U1590 0145/24; Stair to James Craggs, 7 Mar. (ns) 1718, BL. Stowe Mss. 246; Craggs, Secretary of State for the Southern Department, to Stair, 29 Nov. 1718, SRO. GD. 135/141/13A; Molesworth, envoy in Turin, to Craggs, 25 Jan. (ns) 1721, PRO. 92/30.

35. Wilson, pp. 42-90, 149-50.

36. Newcastle to Keene, 16 Mar. Newcastle to Stephen Poyntz and Lord Harrington (the ennobled William Stanhope), envoys at Paris, 14 Ap., Harrington to Newcastle, 10 Ap. (ns) 1730, BL. Add. 32766.

37. Chammorel to Chauvelin, 22 Feb. (ns), Broglie to Chauvelin, 27 Feb. (ns) 1730, AE. CP. Ang. 369; Knatchbull, pp. 104-6; Egmont, I, 34-8.

38. Robert Walpole to Newcastle, 3 July 1730, BL. Add. 32687; Journal of Waldegrave, Ambassador in France, 28 Aug. (ns) 1, 2 Sept. (ns) 1730, Chewton; Delafaye to Newcastle, 4 Aug. 1730, PRO. 36/20; Horace Walpole to Fleury, 21 June (ns) 1730, AE. MD. France 459.

39. Waldegrave Journal, 12 Aug. (ns) 1730, Chewton; Horace Walpole to Newcastle, 10 Sept. (ns) 1730, BL. Add. 32769.

40. Count Seckendorf, Austrian envoy in Berlin, to Duke Ferdinand Albrecht of Brunswick-Bevern, 14 July (ns), 9 Sept. (ns), 14 Oct. (ns), 4, 14 Nov. (ns) 1730, Wolfenbüttel, 1 Alt 22, Nr. 585 (e); Hotham to Harrington, 11 July (ns) 1730, PRO. 90/28.

41. George Woodward, envoy in Dresden, to Newcastle, 16 June (ns) 1730, BL. Add. 32768.

42. Waldegrave Journal, 7 Aug. (ns) 1730, Chewton; Horace Walpole, Waldegrave and Poyntz to Keene, 2 Aug. (ns) 1730, BL. Add. 32770.

43. Townshend to Du Bourgay, 29 Oct. (ns) 1725, PRO. 90/19.

44. Account by Sinzendorf of conference with Thomas Robinson, envoy in Vienna, 25 Oct. (ns) 1730, HHStA. England, Noten, 2; Robinson to Harrington, 28 Oct. (ns), 14, 18 Nov. (ns) 1730, PRO. 80/69; Harrington to Chesterfield, 6, 10 Nov. 1730, PRO. 84/304.

45. Harrington to Robinson, 5 Dec. 1730, BL. Add. 23780; Harrington to Robinson, 28 Jan. 1731, Coxe, III, 87.

46. Frederick Prince of Wales to Hervey, undated, Bury St. Edmunds, West Suffolk CRO., Hervey Mss. 941/47/1; Newcastle to his brother Henry Pelham, 24 Oct. 1730, PRO. 63/393.

47. Treaty of Vienna, PRO. 103/113.

48. *The Flying Post or Post Master*, 22 Ap. 1731; *Hyp-Doctor*, 1 June 1731.

49. Newcastle to Waldegrave, 26 Mar. 1731, BL. Add. 32772.

50. J. H. Plumb, *Sir Robert Walpole. The King's Minister* (1960), p. 229.

51. Newcastle to Waldegrave, 24 Ap. 1731, BL. Add. 32772; Waldegrave to Newcastle, 12, 16 June (ns) 1731, BL. Add. 32773.

52. Newcastle to Waldegrave, 1, 15 Ap. 1731, BL. Add. 32772; Chesterfield to Harrington, 10 Ap. (ns) 1731, PRO. 84/312.

53. Chauvein to Chammorel, 10 Ap. (ns) 1731, AE. CP. Ang. sup. 8 f.196; Baudrillart, *Philippe V*, IV, pp. 72-3, 86-91; Thomas Pelham, Secretary of Embassy at Paris, to Delafaye, 16, 21, 30 July (ns) 1731, PRO. 78/198; Duke to Duchess of Newcastle, 2 July 1731, BL. Add. 33073.

54. Waldegrave to Newcastle, 15 Mar., Broglie to Chauvelin, 9 Ap. 1731, BL. Add. 32772; Keene to Newcastle, 20 May 1731, PRO. 94/107.

55. G. Quazza, 'I negoziati austro-anglo-sardi del 1732-3', *Bolletino Storico Bibliografico Subalpino* 46-7 (1948-9); Black, 'The Development of Anglo-Sardinian Relations in the first half of the eighteenth century', *Studi Piemontesi* 12 (1983), p. 54; Black, '1733 – Failure of British Diplomacy?', *Durham University Journal* 74 (1982).

56. Sinzendorf to Kinsky, 29 Mar. (ns) 1732, PRO. 100/11; Ossorio, Sardinian Envoy Extraordinary in London, to Charles Emmanuel III of Sardinia, 17, 31 Mar. (ns), 7, 14, 21, 28 Ap. (ns) 1732, AST. LM. Ing. 39; Robinson to Edward Weston, Undersecretary in the Northern Department, 8 Ap. (ns) 1732, PRO. 80/87; Newcastle to Edward Allen, Chargé d'Affaires in Turin, 31 Mar. 1732, PRO. 92/84.

57. Walter Titley, envoy in Copenhagen, to Harrington, 2 Feb. (ns) 1732, PRO. 75/59 f. 60-1; Harrington to Robinson, 11 Feb. 1732, PRO. 80/85.

58. Newcastle to the Earl of Essex, 4 Aug. 1732, PRO. 92/34.

59. Robinson to Harrington, 16 May (ns) 1733, PRO. 80/96. For British opposition to giving a guarantee in the Jülich-Berg succession dispute, Degenfeld, Prussian envoy in London, to Frederick William I, 17 Mar. (ns) 1733, PRO. 107/10.

60. Harrington to Robinson, 14 May 1731, PRO. 80/74.

61. Robinson to Harrington, 28 Mar. (ns), 2 July (ns) (quote) 1734, PRO. 80/105, 108.

62. Waldegrave to Newcastle, 12 July (ns) 1733, BL. Add. 32781.

63. Waldegrave to Newcastle, 24 Feb. (ns) 1734, BL. Add. 32784; Vaucher, *Walpole;* Lodge, 'English Neutrality in the War of the Polish Succession', *TRHS* 4th series, 14 (1931); D. Reading, *The Anglo-Russian Commercial Treaty of 1734* (New Haven, 1938).

64. Strickland to the Austrian minister Bartenstein, 16 Nov. (ns) 1734, HHStA. Varia, 8; Essex to Newcastle, 22 Oct. (ns) 1733, PRO. 92/35.

65. Harrington to Horace Walpole, 8 Oct. 1734, PRO. 84/333.

66. *B. Berington's Evening Post,* 11 Oct. 1733.

67. Vaucher, *Walpole;* J. O. McLachlan, *Trade and Peace with Old Spain, 1667-1750* (Cambridge, 1940).

68. McKay and Scott, *Great Powers,* p. 153.

69. Horace Walpole to Trevor, 28 Oct. (ns) 1736, Trevor, vol. 5.

70. Newcastle to Waldegrave, 20 Oct. 1735, Chewton.

71. Trevor to Weston, 27 Dec. (ns) 1737, PRO. 84/359; K. A. Roider, *The Reluctant Ally: Austria's Policy in the Austro-Turkish War, 1737-9* (Baton Rouge, 1972).

72. Horace Walpole, memorandum, 28 Nov. (ns) 1736, BL. Add. 9131 f.158; Tilson to Robinson, 18 Dec. (ns) 1736, BL. Add. 23799.

73. Harrington to Robinson, 20 Feb. 1739, PRO. 80/133.

74. Trevor to Weston, 21 Sept. (ns) 1736, PRO. 84/359.

75. Weston to Titley, 25 Feb. 1737, BL. Egerton Mss. 2684.

76. Robinson to Harrington, 19 Aug. (ns) 1739, PRO. 80/136.

77. Horace Walpole to Trevor, 2 Jan. 1739, Trevor, 16.

78. Wilson, pp. 71-86.

79. Horace Walpole to Harrington, 8 Nov. (ns) 1737, PRO. 84/368; Horace to Trevor, 29 Sept., 24 Oct., 22 Dec. 1738, Trevor, 14, 15, 16; HMC., *Manuscripts of Earl of Buckinghamshire* (1895).

80. H. Temperley, 'The Cause of the War of Jenkins' Ear 1739', *TRHS* 3rd ser., 3 (1909); R. Pares, *War and Trade in the West Indies, 1739-63* (Oxford, 1936).

81. Newcastle to Hardwicke, c.11 Aug. 1739, BL. Add. 35406; Newcastle to Waldegrave, 27 Feb. 1740, Chewton.

82. Hervey to Stephen Fox, 9 Sept. 1740, BL. Add. 51345.

83. Instructions for Finch, 29 Feb. 1740, PRO. 91/24.

84. U. Dann, Hanover and Great Britain, 1740-60 (D. Phil., Oxford, 1981), pp. 29-46.

85. Memorandum, 7 Oct. 1740, BL. Add. 32993 f. 108-9.

86. Hardwicke, 18 Nov. 1739, Cobbett, XI, 677.

87. Robert Walpole, 13 Ap. 1741, Cobbett, XII, 168.

88. Harrington to Robinson, 31 Mar. 17 Ap. (quote), 1741, PRO. 80/144, 145; Horace Walpole to Trevor, 24 Apr. 1741, Trevor, 27.

89. Robinson to Harrington, 25 May (ns) 1741, PRO. 80/145.

90. Dann, *Hanover,* pp. 70-85; Ossorio to Charles Emmanuel, 9 Oct. (ns) 1741, AST. LM. Ing. 47; Villettes, envoy at Turin, to Trevor, 18 Nov. (ns) 1741, Trevor, 29.

91. Hardwicke to Newcastle, 17 Aug. 1741, BL. Add. 32697; H. Richmond, *The Navy in the War of 1739-48* (3 vols., Cambridge, 1920).

92. Rolt, *The Conduct of the Several Powers of Europe engaged in the late General War* (4 vols., 1749-50), III, 10.

Hanover and the Crown

'two principal and fatal errors yt have prevailed from the accession of the present royal family, that prevail still, and that will continue to support and strengthen one another till they ruine the family, or the nation, or both, unless they are eradicated, are these, that the foreign interests of Britain must be conducted in a certain subordination to those of Hanover, and that the domestick interest must be submitted to those of a party.'

Bolingbroke, 1741[1]

The role of Hanover in eighteenth-century British foreign policy was a matter for bitter contemporary controversy. Many commentators and politicians did not doubt that British foreign policy was being distorted to serve Hanoverian ends.[2] This was a view by no means restricted to opposition elements: many ministers and diplomats bewailed the impact of Hanover.[3] This section will seek to assess these claims and to consider in addition what the Hanoverian role revealed about royal power.

Hanover was a recently formed state, the product of the amalgamation of the territories of all but one (that of Brunswick-Wolfenbüttel) of the branches of the House of Brunswick. The major acquisition, that of the Duchy of Celle, had occurred as recently as 1705, whilst the prestigious, though largely empty, honour of being one of the Electors of the Holy Roman Empire, had been gained in 1692. The first two decades of the eighteenth century witnessed impressive territorial gains by the new Electorate. The acquisition of the territories of the Duke of Sachsen-Lauenburg in 1689 was followed by many years of negotiation in order to achieve recognition. Possession of Lauenburg, which fortified the Hanoverian position on the Lower Elbe, and dragged Hanover further into the concerns of the neighbouring duchies of Mecklenburg and Holstein-Gottorp, was recognised in the early 1700s, though Imperial recognition of the Hanoverian gain of part of the inheritance – the county of Hadeln – was delayed until 1731. Expansion was partly by purchase: in 1700 the district of Wildeshausen, in 1711 that of Delmenhorst. The biggest acquisitions were the duchies of Bremen and Verden, Hanover's spoil from the collapse of the Swedish Empire in the Great Northern War (1700-21). These duchies gave Hanover a coastline – on the North Sea – but Imperial delay in the 1720s in investing George I and George II with them produced tension.[4] Furthermore the duchies were acquired through some complex diplomacy that committed the Hanoverians to supporting the Danish acquisition of the duchy of Sleswig. The dispossessed ruler, the Duke of Holstein-Gottorp, found support for his claims from various sources during the first half of the century, including Sweden, Austria and, most seriously of all, Russia.

27

Thus, the role of Hanover in British foreign policy must be set against a background of rapid territorial expansion and consolidation that provoked hostility from neighbouring powers, particularly Prussia, and the territorial instability of this area of north Germany, known as the Lower Saxon Circle. Hanoverian aspirations were matched by Prussian and Danish expansionism, the collapse of the Swedish empire led to increased opportunities, whilst the irruption of Russia into European diplomacy had particular impact in this area. Russian striking power was indicated by the deployment of Russian troops in Jutland and Mecklenburg in 1716, whilst the marriage in April 1716 of Peter the Great's niece Catherine to Charles-Leopold Duke of Mecklenburg-Schwerin, then engaged in a bitter conflict with his nobles, both represented and accentuated Peter's interests in the Lower Saxon Circle.

The need to retain acquisitions, the desire for more, particularly in Mecklenburg and later in the Westphalian bishoprics, such as Hildesheim and Osnabrück,[5] and the anxiety over security in the face of powerful military rivals, meant that Hanover required allies. Turning to Britain was hardly novel – William III had provided support against Denmark during the Sachsen-Lauenburg conflict – but the accession of the Hanoverian dynasty pushed the issue to the fore in both British and Hanoverian thinking, and made it one of the most divisive in British public debate about foreign policy. Historians of British foreign policy during Walpole's ministry have tended to underrate the issue. Massive destruction of the archives, by bombing and flood, in the 1940s has furthermore made it difficult to study. Hanover plays very little role in the works of Lodge and Vaucher; in particular, Hanoverian fears of Prussia during the War of Polish Succession tend to be ignored in discussion of British policy during the war. Hatton in her works on George I has robustly denied that British interests were 'sacrificed' to Hanover. The major exception to this downplaying of Hanoverian distortion is the recent work of Dann, who, in a significant study of Hanoverian diplomacy in the period 1740-60, indicated the divergences between Hanoverian and British foreign policy goals, and the attempt by George II to use British strength for Hanoverian ends.[6]

One of Dann's most important points is to draw attention to the divergence of views between Hanoverian ministers and the Elector. 'Hanover' too often serves as a term of analysis that denies the disputes over policy that existed. Furthermore, the Hanoverian ministers themselves could, at times, be bitterly divided. There are few signs of such divisions in the 1730s, but the correspondence between Friedrich Wilhelm von der Schulenburg, a Hanoverian courtier in London who was the half-brother of George I's mistress, and Friedrich Wilhelm von Görtz, President of the Hanoverian Chambers of War and Finance, reveals bitter divisions for the years 1717-19. Schulenburg presents a picture of Hanoverian ministers in London who were bitterly divided and seeking to increase their authority vis-à-vis the divided ministers in Hanover. Not all Hanoverians approved of the costly confrontations produced by the acquisitions of Bremen and Verden.[7]

The issue of Hanoverian distortion is therefore intertwined with that of royal influence on the conduct of foreign policy, as it was thus that Hanoverian concerns largely influenced British foreign policy. Furthermore, it is difficult to separate (and it was well nigh impossible for contemporaries to do so) the commitment to European affairs produced by the Hanoverian connection, from that which had developed following the Glorious Revolution and which played such a role in Whig thinking. Debate over the latter, both within ministerial circles and in the political nation, was affected greatly by the former. Whig ministers, such as Walpole in the 1710s, unhappy about the extent of British commitments to European quarrels, were placed in a difficult position when seeking to limit them, by the royal interest that stemmed partly, though not entirely, from Hanoverian concerns. Tories criticising widespread British commitments that stemmed partly from Hanoverian concerns could end up criticising the Hanoverian succession.

The history of Hanoverian foreign policy in the period 1714-40 remains to be written. Whilst the work of Hatton and others has thrown much light on the period 1714-21, there is extremely little material on the last years of George I's reign and a large void for the first thirteen years of that of George II. There is no doubt, as Dann has shown, that the British connection could distort Hanoverian policy. It has been suggested that this was the case in 1725-7, when the armed confrontation between the Alliances of Hanover and Vienna exposed Hanover to the risk of Austrian, Prussian and Russian attack.[8] However, we are concerned to consider the issue from the British viewpoint, and the premise of this section is that policy was distorted for Hanoverian ends, that this was largely due to the crown, that it posed major problems for the British ministry, and that it justified much of the opposition propaganda.

In the last decades of the seventeenth century the principal diplomatic problem for those who advocated an interventionist foreign policy was that of devising an alliance system that could hold its own against the Bourbons and their allies. The principal developments of the European international system in the first half of the following century — the rise of Russia and Prussia — might seem to have solved this problem. Gaining their alliance would tilt the military balance, whilst fears of a threatened or actual invasion of Hanover, as was to happen in 1741, could be alleviated by the prospect of Prussian and Russian aid. Solving the difficult problem of

Hanoverian security, an alliance with these powers would also provide the political and military weight to underpin the interventionist schemes of those, such as James Stanhope, who believed in a significant British role in Europe. Some politicians and diplomats were well aware of the need for Britain to gain the alliance of both these powers. Thomas Robinson, envoy in Vienna, castigated George II in 1732 for failing to realise this, whilst Horace Walpole grounded his schemes of 1739-40 for a new European system on such an alliance.[9] Other European powers realised that harnessing these two new powers was of crucial importance, and diplomatic competition to do so was very great. It led high-ranking diplomats, such as the Spanish Duke of Liria in 1727-30, to Berlin and St. Petersburg. France made major efforts to win a Russian alliance in the early 1720s and early 1740s, and raised British fears by approaching Russia in 1733. Austrian efforts were rewarded by an Austro-Russian alliance of 1726 that remained the basis of Austrian policy in eastern Europe for several decades.

The development of good Anglo-Prussian and Anglo-Russian relations was, without any doubt, hampered by commitments and interests directly resulting from the Hanoverian accession. There were common Hanoverian-Prussian interests, particularly in 1719-21 in protecting the position of Protestants in the Empire, in 1719-20 in fearing Russian strength, and in the early 1720s in resenting the attempt of the Imperial Vice-Chancellor Schönborn to impose Imperial authority (and often to thus further Austrian interests) upon the Princes of the Empire. These interests were outweighed by family strife and territorial conflict. George I's daughter, Sophia Dorothea (1687-1757) had married Frederick William I of Prussia (1688-1740) in 1706, whilst Frederick William's father had married George I's sister. George II was therefore brother-in-law and first cousin to Frederick William I, and uncle to his eldest son, Frederick the Great (II) who succeeded in 1740. Whilst Frederick William seems to have respected George I, he hated George II and envied his British realm. The feeling was reciprocated, and George II's attempts to protect his sister and his nephew from the worst excesses of Frederick William's quixotic and violent conduct were, rightly, resented as meddlesome and self-serving. It had long been envisaged that dynastic links would be further enhanced by the double marriage of George II's son Frederick Prince of Wales to Wilhelmina, the Prussian Princess Royal, and of Frederick of Prussia to one of George II's brood of daughters. This issue, a reminder of the importance and unpredictability of dynastic factors in eighteenth-century international relations, bedevilled Anglo-Prussian relations. Anger about George I dragging his feet over the issue was one motive for Frederick William's leaving the Alliance of Hanover in 1726. In 1730 Sir Charles Hotham's important mission to Berlin, the most significant attempt to improve Anglo-Prussian relations between 1725 and 1740, was fatally identified with the double marriage scheme.[10] In 1732-3 George II was infuriated, with unhelpful consequences for Anglo-Austrian and Anglo-Prussian policy, by the betrothals and marriages of Wilhelmina, to the Prince of Bayreuth, and Frederick, to a Princess of Brunswick-Bevern, a move he blamed on the Austrians.[11] George II's fond hopes that the accession of his nephew Frederick, whom he had secretly provided with money, would lead to an alliance were destroyed by the Prussian invasion of the Austrian province of Silesia in December 1740. Frederick's action and subsequent success aroused fury and anger in his uncle, and George's hostility greatly complicated British policy to Prussia in the 1740s.

These factors were dynastic, a product of the influence of the Hanoverian succession. They were complicated by a long series of territorial disputes and by a general competition for primacy in north Germany. In a sense Hanover and Prussia were a couple of bullies, who having benefited from the collapse of Sweden's empire and her traditional influence, fell out over the spoils. Border quarrels were serious. Frederick William's aggressive forcible recruiting in the territory of his neighbours infuriated George I and George II and played a large role in provoking the Hanoverian-Prussian war panic of 1729. Both powers vied for influence in Mecklenburg, a dispute, never resolved satisfactorily in this period, that helped to poison relations. It was particularly serious in the winter of 1733-4 when the revival of conflict in the duchy limited George II's willingness to send his Hanoverian forces to assist the Austrians on the Rhine against the French invasion. Both Hanover and Prussia claimed the succession to the Duchy of East Friesland. Although the succession did not become open until 1744, endemic civil war in the Duchy throughout the 1720s made this a serious issue, further complicated by Dutch and Danish intervention. Under Frederick William I, Prussian hopes for territorial expansion were centred on the succession to the Rhenish duchies of Jülich and Berg, a succession contested by the Wittelsbachs on behalf of the Sulzbach branch of their family. Though British ministers were willing at times to consider support-ing Prussian acquisition of these duchies as part of an Anglo-Prussian alliance, the crown tended to oppose such schemes. Aside from these specific disputes, Prussia upset Hanover by contesting her influence, offering aid or mediation in issues affecting Hanover directly such as her quarrel with the Bishop of Hildesheim in 1730 or that with Denmark over the contested possession of the area of Steinhorst in 1739-40, or where George I and George II were attempting to exert their influence, as in the quarrels between Hamburg and Denmark over the Elbe navigation in 1720 and 1733-5. The list could be greatly extended; the point is that few of these issues had any great importance to Britain and none were crucial for British interests. And yet British ministers and diplomats found British resources, including diplomatic effort, devoted to dealing with these problems; few of them were under any illusion about the distortion of British interests. An instance of the pressure of supporting Hanoverian interests can be taken from the correspondence of Charles Whitworth, envoy in Berlin, in the first months of 1720, a period of good Anglo-Prussian relations. This is a good example, for not only do Whitworth's despatches to the British ministry survive, but also his correspondence with Görtz, then effectively regent of Hanover. Whitworth received instructions from three different sources, the Secretary of State in London, James Stanhope, George I and the Hanoverian Chancery in London (these were countersigned by Hattorf) and the Regency in Hanover. He was instructed to deal with a rich variety of problems: forced enrollments of Hanoverian subjects in the Electorate of Hanover, the cession of fiefs and presentations to churches situated in Wolfenbüttel and Bevern, a border territorial quarrel, Prussian support for George I's brother Ernst August of Osnabrück in his quarrel with papal procedure, Prussian policy in Hamburg and the concerting of a strategy to obtain from the Emperor investitures for Frederick William I and George I of territories obtained from Sweden. Whitworth argued that these instructions harmed Anglo-Prussian relations and his wider purpose of retaining Prussian support for an anti-Russian diplomatic coalition. Writing to Görtz about the Hamburg affair, he bluntly suggested that the Hanoverian ministry was overcommitting George I's credit in an issue that did not merit it. Görtz was informed that the Finkenholf border dispute, complicated as it was by differing maps, should be settled by civil process in a court of justice, not by negotiation. Whitworth argued that issues such as the Wolfenbüttel fiefs would make it difficult to establish good relations, claimed that he was made 'disagreeable by such commissions', and wrote, with respect to instructions from the German Chancery in London, 'I cannot comprehend the reasonings in the two orders directed to me . . . except they designed to create jealousies at this court and overthrow all we have been doing . . .'[12]

The first three months of 1720 are by no means untypical. Similar cases can be found throughout the period, and their cumulative effect was very serious. British envoys were placed in an impossible situation, receiving contrary instructions and ordered to pursue approaches they knew to be harmful. At least such a problem was avoided in the 1720s with Russia: diplomatic relations had been ruined by the contrary Baltic policies of Peter I and George I, and they were broken off in 1719, to be resumed in 1730. In the 1730s British envoys in St. Petersburg were instructed to follow policies many of which originated in Hanoverian goals: opposing schemes for a Prusso-Russian marriage alliance in 1731-3, urging Russia to avoid intervention in

Mecklenburg, and, in 1733-5, to intimidate Prussia over her Mecklenburg policies.[13] Thus, the Anglo-Russian negotiations of the 1741-56 period, with their schemes for Russian pressure on Prussia, originated in the 1730s. They conflicted with the views of several British diplomats who sought, as in 1740, an Anglo-Prusso-Russian pact.

The intervention of Hanoverian factors was not restricted to Anglo-Prussian and Anglo-Russian relations. They also confused Anglo-Austrian relations. In the negotiations leading to the Quadruple Alliance of 1718, when the British ministry under Stanhope, in alliance with the French, were pressing Austria to accept Spanish claims in Tuscany and Parma, the Hanoverian ministers in London provoked anger by supporting the Austrian reluctance to do so. In February the French envoy Dubois complained bitterly of Hanoverian support for Austria, and James Craggs, Secretary of State for the Southern Department (Mar. 1718-Mar. 1721) suspected secret Hanoverian assurances to the Austrians. Indeed Bothmer, one of the leading Hanoverian ministers in London, certainly had a confidential correspondence with the Austrian government in the mid-1710s.[14] Hatton has suggested that after 1718 the interests of the electorate were not pushed as hard as they might have been. This is true, but it would be mistaken to claim that British interests, such as opposition to the Austrian schemes for oceanic trade, based on the Ostend Company, caused as much tension in Anglo-Austrian relations as policies associated with George I's position as Elector:[15] his zealous, often intemperate, championing of the Protestant cause within the Empire,[16] his suspicion of Austro-Russian links, his incessant demands for investiture with Bremen and Verden and his pressure over Hadeln. The Hanoverian stance in the crisis of 1725-7 is obscure. George I's Chamberlain Fabrice pressed George to abandon his anti-Austrian policy, but Fabrice had only entered Hanoverian service in the late 1710s, and he appears to have pursued his views in headstrong independence.[17]

With the accession of George II in 1727, the role of the Hanoverian ministers and diplomats, already much weakened with the relative disgracing of Bernstorff in 1719, was further diminished.[18] No Hanoverian minister in the 1720s or 1730s wielded the influence that Bernstorff and Bothmer had enjoyed in their heyday. Though Bothmer survived until 1732, he did not enjoy George's confidence. Fabrice failed to obtain the diplomatic post he sought in late 1727 and returned to Hanover. The principal officials of the German Chancery in London, Jobst and Andreas von der Reiche and Johann Philipp von Hattorf, were credited with little power, though Hattorf was to play a role in the attempt to bring Britain into the War of the Polish Succession. Foreign envoys, sensitive to the sources of influence, felt that the Hanoverians lacked that influence. The Sardinian envoy D'Aix, accompanying George II on his first royal trip to Hanover, reported that the German ministers were excluded from important negotiations. The same year the French envoy Chavigny noted opposition by some of the Hanoverian ministers to Townshend's negotiations with the Wittelsbachs, and George's support for Townshend. In 1730 Augustus II of Saxony-Poland instructed his new envoy in London, Count Watsdorf, to attach himself to the English ministers because their influence was paramount even in what concerned Hanoverian influences, whilst George ignored his Hanoverian ministers.[19]

Until the partnership in the late 1740s and early 1750s of the Duke of Newcastle and Münchhausen, the leading Hanoverian minister of the time, there was very little cooperation between Hanoverian and British ministers. In crucial negotiations, such as the attempt to end the War of the Polish Succession in 1733-5, or the negotiations with the Wittelsbachs in 1728-30, the British did not consult the Hanoverians, even though German issues were often involved. When the Hanoverian diplomat Reck was sent to the Congress of Soissons in 1728, Townshend ordered the British plenipotentiaries to tell him nothing about the negotiations for a Wittelsbach alliance, and wrote, 'He has no powers nor anything to do at the Congress, and was sent by the King with no other view but to inform and assist your Ex.cies in the affairs of the Empire'. Horace Walpole, always suspicious of Hanoverian interests, urged that the negotiations with the Wittelsbachs be kept a secret from the Hanoverians, and angered George II in the late 1730s by his views over Jülich-Berg and East Friesland.[20] Relations between British and Hanoverian envoys were not always bad — Waldegrave and Saladin enjoyed good relations in Paris in the early 1730s[21] — but there was often tension and differences, particularly at Vienna.[22]

If the Hanoverian ministers of the 1720s and 1730s lacked influence, this did not mean that Hanoverian concerns were not of great importance, for George I and George II did not require advice from Hanover in order to support Hanoverian goals. The basic goal in this period was security. The heady expansionism of the early years of the century, their highpoint the acquisition, for the dynasty, of the British throne, was replaced by a consciousness of vulnerability. The fact that Hanover was not in the first rank as a military power mattered less in the 1690s and 1700s, when northern Germany was not a battlefield for the great powers, than it did from the mid-1710s. The sudden awareness of vulnerability, produced by the temporary Russian occupation of Mecklenburg, was sustained by a series of scares, that did not end until 1730, of Russian troops being deployed against Hanover.[23] Confrontation with Austria, in 1725-30, and with Prussia, from 1726 onwards, exacerbated the situation. Townshend, Secretary of State for the Northern Department (1721-30), wrote, in 1729, of 'the exposed situation and extent of his Majesty's frontiers, and that, as he has no fortifications to defend it, if he be not supported by a considerable body of his allies, there will be great danger from the first impression'.[24]

Foreign diplomats shared this awareness, the French envoy in London in 1738 reporting that Hanover could not hope to resist successfully a Prussian invasion.[25] Given this situation, the defence of Hanover became a top priority for George I and George II; precisely because defensive arrangements are less contentious than their offensive counterparts, this has received inadequate attention, particularly in its relationship to the Anglo-French alliance of 1716-31. The defence of Hanover became as much a purpose of this alliance as the defence of the Hanoverian Succession in Britain had played a major role in its inception. George I and George II actively planned in 1725-30 for the deployment of French troops in the Empire in order to protect Hanover from attack.[26] Furthermore, in moments of tension British envoys were instructed to request French pressure on powers threatening Hanover. This occurred in the case of Prussia in 1729 and 1730.[27] Furthermore this vulnerability was exploited by French envoys, Chavigny in Hanover in 1729, Broglie in London in January 1730, in an attempt to influence British policy in directions favourable to France. Broglie reported that he lost no opportunity, when he saw George II, to press him on the vulnerability of Hanover and the absence of British popular support for its preservation.[28]

Royal concern for the defence of Hanover is understandable and was defended by the ministry as perfectly natural. The safest answer to the question of how far this distorted British policy is to note that it created an atmosphere in which ministers and diplomats, ever aware of the need for royal favour, had to be aware of Hanoverian interests. This awareness has to be elicited from the documents, as for obvious reasons care had to be taken about expressing preference for Hanoverian interests in British diplomatic correspondence. Occasionally the impact of Hanover was brutally clear: 'His Majesty's thoughts upon the points of Mecklenburg and Sleswig, on which he is very earnest and would not suffer the least delay to be made . . . I never saw the King more displeased in my life than he was upon reading what was said in this project and your despatches upon those two articles. . . . For God's sake, Dear Horace, do your best, both your reputation and mine are at stake'.[29] More often, careful questioning of the purposes of subsidy treaties, particularly with Denmark, Hesse-Cassel and Brunswick-Wolfenbüttel, or consideration of the anti-Austrian war planning of 1725-7 and 1730, is required. The question of the role of Hanover finally resolves into one of the most interesting issues for current eighteenth-century study: the role of the crown.

There was a period when scholars could write about eighteenth-century British politics as though Britain was not a monarchy. The closet had been stormed, Kings were forced to accept the position and views of ministers who could control Parliament. Such a view is no longer tenable. In recent years a series of important works – Gregg's biography of Queen Anne, Hatton's work on George I, Owen's essay on George II, and Clark's work on British politics, 1754-7 – have reinterpreted the position of the crown, re-establishing the monarch as the principal political actor. Some of this work, in particular Blanning's article on the Fürstenbund of 1785 and the writings of Hatton, have identified foreign policy as the crucial field of royal concern and intervention, and Hanoverian interests as a major issue.[30] It might seem that the age of Walpole would be an exception: a minister securely in control of Parliament, George I 'obliged to conform in every-thing to their [his English ministers'] will', according to the Austrian envoy Count Palm in April 1726; George II a 'King in toils'. The relationship between crown and first minister in the age of Walpole is certainly a very difficult matter to assess. In a recent essay Roberts has argued that 'in later Stuart England the power of party overwhelmed the power of patronage', that the room for manoeuvre enjoyed by the monarchs of the period was severely limited, and, in particular, that the failure to sustain mixed ministries of Whigs and Tories gravely weakened the monarchy.[31] The applicability of such an analysis to the Walpole years has to be limited by the fact that during this period neither monarch ever seriously envisaged a mixed ministry. Employing one or two prominent Tories, such as Harcourt and Trevor, in the 1720s did not represent an attempt to gain Tory support by forming a mixed ministry. Certainly, for the years of Walpole's ascendancy, both monarchs envisaged only a Whig ministry. In a sense they were clearly 'in toils'; had either monarch, for example, attempted to bring the practices of the Church of England into line with those of the Lutheran Church of their native Hanover, they would have got nowhere. However, what is striking about the Walpole years is that after 1721 (and this contrasts strongly with the position under the later Stuarts) most of the issues that King and ministers differed over did not involve parliamentary legislation. The 1710s had seen several major attempts at far-reaching legislative change, particularly in the ecclesiastical field. These became less frequent after 1721. Neither monarch sought to persuade Parliament to endorse major legislative changes. The relationship of Parliament to foreign policy, a complex issue dealt with elsewhere, was important to the issue of the crown's freedom of manoeuvre, but Walpole's undoubted control of the House of Commons did not lead to his being able to dictate policy. Showdowns between monarch and minister were avoided, most clearly during the War of the Polish Succession, and, just as Walpole did not prefigure the Pelhamite attempt in 1744 to force George II's hand by the threat of resignation, so George did not provoke his parliamentary manager, Walpole, as he was to do the Pelhams.

The constitutional basis of the royal position in foreign policy was admirably summarised by a leading London ministerial paper, the *Daily Courant* in its issue of 1 October 1734: 'In the military Part of the domestick indeed, and in both the military Branches of our foreign policy or Government, which regulates our Leagues and Treaties, our Wars or Peace with other States, the King has a greater Latitude; for, as they are almost all of them individual points or cases, which admit of very few, or no invariable general Rules, and do also require the utmost Dispatch, and the greatest secrecy, he is therein invested with the intire power of determining both what shall be done, and who shall execute those Determinations; subject nevertheless to the Regulation of the Legislature as to the Expense which the Publick shall furnish towards those Transactions; and by which subjection it usually becomes necessary to the Crown to consult their Inclinations, in a general Manner at least, in most of the momentous undertakings of that sort'.

Royal power was increased by the fact that diplomats were personally appointed by the crown and paid from the Civil List, the monarch's personal finances, whilst Secretaries of State were not only royal appointees but also, due to the absence of the practice of collective ministerial responsibility, willing often to support the views of the monarch in defiance of ministerial colleagues. The pliancy of Secretaries of State varied greatly: few were as passive in the face of the royal will as William Stanhope, Lord Harrington (Northern Department 1730-1742, 1744-46), and yet he could not stomach the Hanover neutrality of 1741, when, as Elector, George II unilaterally concluded a neutrality convention with the French, thus undermining British attempts to create an anti-French coalition.

Pliant or not, Secretaries of State could not ignore royal wishes. Through the Hanoverian Chancery the monarch could, and did, instruct British envoys without the Secretary's knowledge. This was widely practised by George I, particularly for the British envoys whose posts involved Hanoverian interests: Berlin, Vienna, St. Petersburg, Stockholm, Copenhagen. In addition Hanoverian ministers maintained a personal correspondence with British envoys, for example Bothmer with Whitworth when he was at The Hague, Robethon with Stair at Paris. This provided George I with an additional channel for instructions and information: Robethon communicated Stair's letters to George I and transmitted George's orders. In April 1716, for example, Stair was ordered to support in Paris the Alsatian claims of the Count of Hanau. It was understandable that the Hanoverian diplomatic network shrank when the monarchs could use British diplomats for their ends.[32]

There is much evidence for George II's detailed interest in the drafting of instructions. He also used audiences with foreign and British envoys to gather information and further his own views.[33] Thus George II exerted influence both formally and informally, usually towards the same end: the furtherance of Hanoverian interests, as construed by George. In August 1727 Horace Walpole was made aware of the impact of George's accession: 'Your Excy. will perhaps think us too full of ye scheme for taking care at ye Congress of the Libertys of the Germanick Body, as being pretty strong meat for the Cardinal's digestion: But Mylord Townshend ordered me to tell you that it arises from the King himself, who sees with regret ye Emperor gaining such an absolute Influence throughout Germany as may make him an overmatch for us and France too . . .'[34]

Other envoys were speedily made aware of George's role in the conduct of foreign policy. Townshend informed Baron Diescau, the Hanoverian representing British interests in Sweden, 'I must tell you once for all, that I receive no letters from any foreign minister, which I don't lay immediately before His Majesty'.[35] Other ministers acted otherwise: Newcastle and Horace Walpole, when he accompanied George to Hanover in 1736 and acted as Secretary of State, kept letters secret, and the Spanish envoy, Montijo, believed in 1733 that the British ministry deliberately kept George in the dark by concealing independent correspondences.[36]

Equally George II had his own channels of information. In 1727-8 he worried British ministers by taking advice from the former envoy in Vienna, St. Saphorin, and using him in a secret attempt to develop an understanding with Saxony. In 1728 William Stanhope was sent to Soissons with secret instructions to negotiate with the Austrians.[37] During the War of the Polish Succession George maintained a correspondence with the leading Austrian minister, Prince Eugene, via the Hesse Cassel envoy in London, Diemar.[38] Furthermore George used his trips to Hanover − 1729, 1732, 1735, 1736 and 1740 in this period − to conduct much diplomacy in person. Whilst in Hanover he maintained, through the accompanying Secretary of State, a correspondence with British envoys independent of theirs with the Regency in London. This gave him many opportunities to affect policy. In 1729 George transferred the handling of Anglo-Wittelsbach negotiations from his envoys in Paris to his court at Hanover. The same year he thwarted the bellicose desire of the London ministers for naval action against Spain.[39] In 1732 and 1735, accompanied by Harrington, he did exactly as he wished: in 1732 pressing Austria hard over Mecklenburg and, in the view of Robinson, endangering Anglo-Austrian relations, in 1735 transferring the handling of British attempts to end the War of the Polish succession from Horace Walpole, at The Hague, to Hanover.[40]

The view of George I and George II 'in toils' over their foreign policy in the period 1721-42 stems from four major issues: the resignations as Secretaries of State of Carteret in 1724 and Townshend in 1730, both apparently against royal wishes, the decision to defer Hanoverian pretensions during the Anglo-Austrian negotiations in early 1731, and British neutrality in the War of the Polish Succession. George I certainly respected Carteret, a distinguished diplomat who had served him well and whose knowledge of German clearly did him no harm. Much about the ministerial rivalries of 1722-5 is unclear, and it is still probably the most obscure period of British political history in the eighteenth century. It is not clear that George I put up much of a fight to keep Carteret. Cooperation between Carteret and his fellow Secretary Townshend had broken down, Carteret could be honourably transferred to the Lord Lieutenancy of Ireland, and George, angered and embarrassed by the consequences of Carteret's meddling in internal rivalries within the French peerage, appears to have viewed Carteret's pro-Austrian stance with less favour than Townshend's firmer stance towards Austria.[41] In 1729-30, faced with a rift between Townshend and Walpole, George II made major efforts to keep the ministry united. They failed, but it is important to note that George obtained a pliant replacement, Harrington, and that George was not forced to dismiss Townshend. Townshend resigned partly because of ill health, partly because of policy differences with Walpole, differences over Anglo-Wittelsbach relations and Anglo-Prussian relations and over Britain's foreign policy stance. It was generally agreed that George favoured many of Townshend's views. Townshend's Undersecretary, George Tilson, sent Poyntz, envoy at Paris, a paper containing Townshend's private thoughts 'as to what is to be done in the present situation of affairs, his Lop. bid me let you know at the same time . . . that the King has seen them, and approves of them . . .' George shared Townshend's suspicion of Prussian policy, at a time when Walpole and Queen Caroline appear to have been pushing for a major effort to win the alliance of Prussia.[42]

These differences were clear by January 1730. Neither Townshend's quarrel with his fellow Secretary Newcastle nor his differences with Walpole were new. And yet he held office till May. As in 1733, when Walpole was unable to persuade George to dismiss Harrington and Scarborough, so in 1730, Walpole had to wait for Townshend to resign. He did so still enjoying the confidence of the King, though the ministerial quarrels were making the administration of foreign policy difficult. George was certainly thwarted in his wish to keep Townshend in the ministry, though it is by no means clear how much of an effort he was making to keep him there by the spring of 1730. A detailed study of the ministerial crisis of 1729-30 is required, but it is likely that it will do little more than add to the accumulation of conjectures the present archives permit. The court was an intensely personal sphere of politics, where discussions took the place of memoranda, so that the significance of court developments is frequently elusive, as indeed it was to contemporaries. 'The German affairs . . . have been the chief clog to this negotiation', noted Thomas Pelham when commenting upon the role of Hanoverian interests in hindering the Anglo-Austrian negotiations that produced the Second Treaty of Vienna of March 1731.[43] George's demand that the 'Electorial points' should be satisfied clashed with Austrian claims that these demands, which included such old favourities as Hanoverian claims in the Hadeln, Mecklenburg, and Bremen and Verden questions, were diametrically opposed to the Imperial constitution and would offend Austria's ally, Prussia. In December 1730 Harrington wrote that it was the '. . . highest injustice that those vexations and injuries done to H.M.'s Electoral rights, and interests purely on account of difference, and animosities unhappily arisen betwixt the Empr. and the crown of Great Britain, should not, upon the renewal of the ancient good understanding and friendship betwixt those two powers, be at the same time removed and redrest'.

The Austrians saw no reason to capitulate to Hanoverian demands. Walpole noted of one of Robinson's dispatches: 'Prince Eugene makes the distinction between the King and the Elector, and appeals to Robinson as an English minister . . .' The Austrians, helped by British fears of Spanish and French approaches, succeeded, and the consideration of the Electoral points was postponed until after the signature of the treaty. Had George chosen to insist upon the points he would have found himself in a very weak diplomatic position, and this is the probable reason why they were postponed; the extent to which King and ministers quarrelled over the issue is unclear.[44]

When France attacked Austria in 1733, invading the Empire in the process, George II was one of the German princes who voted for the Empire's declaration of war on France, and sent his contingent to the Imperial army. As King he ruled a state that ignored clear treaty obligations, under the Second Treaty of Vienna, to aid Austria against the attack of France, Sardinia and Spain. The traditional historiographical position, found in Coxe, Vaucher, Lodge and Plumb, is that George wished to aid Austria and was only prevented from doing so by the Walpoles, aided, albeit after some difficulty, by Caroline, who persuaded him to attempt to settle the war by negotiation. This view can be found in several contemporary sources: the despatches of Diemar, and his Austrian and Saxon colleagues, Kinsky and De Löss, as well as the memoirs of Lord Hervey. None of these sources can be lightly dismissed.[45] Diplomats could be misled and could fail to appreciate the nature of British politics, but they had regular contacts with British ministers, and as such are an important source. Hervey's reliability has been attacked – 'on the whole vindictive nonsense', according to one recent writer – but there is no better guide to the Court in the 1730s, and therefore his memoirs should be used, albeit with care. Hervey was a perceptive commentator upon human nature whose opinions are of importance as coming from an insider.[46]

There was no doubt of George's emotional commitment to the Austrian cause, of his detestation of the French and of his concern at their success in the war. He was quite open in showing his preference, and it was this that foreign envoys and Hervey noted. Thus they ascribed to Walpole the fact that George's preference did not result in military action. In fact George's response was more ambivalent. It is necessary to distinguish George's outbursts from his considered response. In the period 1727-30 the Austrians had been the victim of such outbursts; in September 1729 he had told Chavigny that he would have his revenge on them for their conduct; the previous year Prince Eugene had written that George was the prime cause of Anglo-Austrian conflict.[47] George's anger was nevertheless compatible, as in early 1728, with attempts to improve relations. Again George's undoubted animosity to Frederick William had not prevented the Hotham mission; rather George ensured that Hotham carried instructions framed according to his wishes, just as Hanoverian demands were an essential part of the British approach to Austria in early 1729.

A good guide to George's conduct in the War of the Polish Succession was his conduct as Elector, where he was free from the constraints of British circumstances. As Elector George was most concerned with the situation in north Germany, not with the French invasion of the Rhineland. Attempts in 1731-3 to settle the Mecklenburg question had failed: in the autumn of 1733 civil war resumed, leading to Hanoverian and Prussian movements of troops into the duchy. George was determined to remove the Prussian troops, and the resources of the British diplomatic service were used to this end. Foreign envoys, such as Diemar, noted that George was extremely concerned about Mecklenburg. The British pressed the Austrians and the Russians to persuade the Prussians to withdraw their forces. The Prussians broke a promise to do so, and George, in order to obtain further Austrian pressure upon Prussia, delayed the departure of the Hanoverian contingent earmarked for the Rhine as part of the army of the Empire. Furthermore, the mobilisation of a large part of the Prussian army in late 1733 had transfixed the Hanoverians with fear, and George refused to send his troops until he received an assurance that the Prussians would also march to the Rhine at the same time. Prussian suggestions that their troops should march to the Rhine through territories bordering Hanover increased George's fears, whilst further delay was created by an Austro-Hanoverian dispute over the conditions of service of the Hanoverian troops.[48]

Far from George being eager to serve the Austrians, his troops did not join Eugene's army until early June 1734. Furthermore the order to march at once had been dispatched from London on 20 April (ns) in response not to Austrian pressure but to two letters from Prince William of Hesse-Cassel. The successful beginning of Marshal Belle Isle's campaign on the Moselle and the rapid fall of Trarbach led to fears that Belle-Isle would seize the Rhine crossing points at Coblenz and at the Hessian fortress of Rheinfels. George II was well aware of the strategic significance of Rheinfels: in 1727 the British had argued that its early seizure would be essential so that the French could cross the Rhine to protect Hanover from the Austrians and the Prussians. In 1734 it was feared that Belle-Isle would cross the Rhine and march on Saxony via Hesse-Cassel.[49]

Thus, George II's policies as Elector in the War of the Polish Succession were closely linked to Hanoverian interests, rather than to any selfless dedication to Austria. Poor Austro-Hanoverian relations in 1732-3 must take much of the blame for this; in addition, despite his German loyalty, George II had never conquered his fundamental distrust of Austrian intentions, Austrian ministers and Austria itself. Despite innumerable complaints Austrian policy in north Germany was still directed by Count Seckendorf, with the aid of Ferdinand Albrecht of Brunswick-Bevern, and George blamed Seckendorf for much of Prussia's hostility to Hanover. As a proud Protestant prince George II was intensely suspicious of the Austrian interpretation of Imperial authority and the Austrian championing of the Catholic cause.[50]

George's concern at the threat of war in the Lower Saxon circle persisted throughout the Polish Succession War. It was fortified in 1734-5 by Prussian threats to intervene with troops in the quarrel between Denmark and Hamburg, and in 1735, by fears that Prussia would enter the war on the French side. George's particular interests go far towards explaining his attitudes. He was particularly concerned that the French claimant to the Polish throne, Stanislas Leszczynski, should be defeated by the Saxons and Russians and showed great interest in the issue. Similarly, in 1733, he had exerted diplomatic pressure to help Austro-Saxon negotiations. George's purpose was clear. An alliance of Saxony, Austria and Russia was to deny Poland to French influence and to intimidate Prussia. This alliance would be linked to Hanover by the Hanoverian-Saxon alliance of 1731, and, if George could not rely on Austria to coerce Prussia, he would hope to do better with Saxony-Poland and Russia. To a certain extent George's policy prefigured his 1744 alliance with the same powers against Prussia.[51]

In eastern Europe the War of the Polish Succession went well for George. Poland was conquered for Augustus III of Saxony, Prussia failed to thwart the Russian siege of Danzig in 1734 and gained no Polish territories, and

French influence was defeated. Had the Russians and Saxons failed it is probable that George's stance would have been different, but their success guaranteed Hanoverian security against Prussia until 1741.

Overall George followed a middle path during the War. In the winter of 1733-4 he rejected separate Wittelsbach and Prussian approaches that would, by means of joint mediations, have left Hanover neutral. Hanover did support the Empire's declaration of war and did send troops to the Rhine. The Austrian Chancellor Count Sinzendorf told Robinson that George's conduct as Elector 'was of the greatest importance towards giving a good example to the other Princes of the Empire'. The Spanish first minister Patino told the British envoy Benjamin Keene that George II's 'proceedings in his Electorate . . . are lookt upon as prognosticks of the part England will take in favour of the Emperor'.[52]

And yet George, as Elector, did not go as far as the Austrians wished. Austrian suggestions for more extensive Hanoverian support were rejected. The Austrians had been keen on a Hanoverian-Russian agreement, 'a more extensive alliance than that of mutual friendship and reciprocal good offices', but George was careful to limit his commitments.[53]

A variety of considerations, principally concern about Prussia, helped to make George's attitude much more complex than a simple desire to aid the Emperor. Furthermore, George's stance changed during the war, as indeed did that of British ministers. The fears of the first half of 1734 when the Spaniards successfully invaded Naples, Belle-Isle's army threatened to invade Hesse and Berwick's French army dislodged the Austrians from their positions further up the Rhine, diminished in late 1734: the French attempt to aid the Poles had clearly failed, the Rhine front was stable, the Austrians had mounted a powerful counter-attack in northern Italy. In 1735, despite Austrian reverses in Italy, Poland was relatively quiet under Saxon-Russian occupation, the Rhine front was stable, and the movement of Russian troops into the Empire quelled fears of Bavaria and Prussia declaring for the French. It was therefore in early 1734 that George was most concerned about the situation. On 20 April (ns) 1734 the Dutch statesman Slingelandt told Horace Walpole 'that an universal notion was entertained here, as if H.M. on account of his being Elector of Hanover, and of his interest and engagements with the Emperor in that quality, had been induced to give too great encouragement to the Impl. court to hope, that the Maritime Powers might be drawn into the present war; . . .'[54] Judging from what George told the envoys of the anti-Bourbon powers, there was truth in this claim. However, it is entirely different to state that George wanted war and was thwarted by his ministers. Hervey's *Memoirs* are insufficient evidence. George doubtless complained of his British ministers and of the need to consider Parliament, but this was hardly novel.

He had done the same in 1729 during negotiations with the Wittelsbachs when the latter demanded a subsidy. It could serve as an excuse, just as ministers excused themselves with reference to the need to placate Parliament. The relationship between King and ministers during the crisis is an important one, but it is impossible at present to state definite conclusions on the matter. It is certainly wrong to state that George's hand was forced by Walpole.

Contempories ascribed great influence to George II's wife Caroline. It was generally argued that she knew how to manage her husband. Horace Walpole recorded being told by George, soon after her death in 1737, 'that her presence of mind often supported him in trying times, and the sweetness of her temper and prudence would moderate and aswage his own vivacity and resentment; that incidents of state of a rough difficult and disagreeable nature would, by her previous conferences and concert with that able Minister Sir R. Walpole, be made smooth easy and palatable to him'. Others held a less favourable view. Sarah Marlborough wrote in 1727, 'she never means anything that she says, but she loves to talk and thinks that everybody will be pleased with words'. Robert Walpole's youngest son, Horace Walpole, who scarcely knew her, claimed that she fomented 'jealousies between the Ministers that each might be more dependent on herself'.[55] She certainly played a role in diplomacy, engaging in confidential discussions with foreign envoys. She was aware of St. Saphorin's secret diplomacy in the winter of 1727-8, and she pressed the Saxon envoy Le Coq on the need for an Anglo-Saxon alliance without France. In early 1729 Caroline urged the Austrian envoy Kinsky to revive negotiations for an Anglo-Austrian alliance.[56] The general trend of Caroline's views is clear. Despite bitterly criticising Austrian policy, as in 1733, she was generally pro-Austrian and possessed little of the interest in Hanover displayed by her husband. Caroline's impact is difficult to assess. She certainly played a large role in the episodic Anglo-Prussian marriage negotiations of 1728-33, but her care to avoid angering George by appearing to adopt a prominent role leaves little evidence of her role. She corresponded with St. Saphorin during the late 1720s and with Horace Walpole during his mission to The Hague in 1734-5. She regularly discussed international relations with foreign envoys. When George was in Hanover she certainly read draft instructions to British envoys, though there are no signs that she altered them.[57]

Caroline was clearly able, less able perhaps than suggested by Hervey and others who wished to theatrically contrast her with her husband, but far abler than the general run of eighteenth-century queen consorts. She enjoyed far less influence than Elisabeth Farnese, Queen of Spain, however. The political role of eighteenth-century women who were not rulers was generally limited; Caroline did not push her role to the limits.

In foreign affairs the King not only had to be heeded; he often directed foreign policy, particularly when the Secretaries of State were pliant (1732, 1736-8, during Townshend's illness in the winter of 1727-8), or when internal matters occupied the attention of the ministry. The royal role varied. Neither George I nor George II displayed much interest in British maritime difficulties with Spain. Neither was terribly interested in Anglo-Spanish relations, except insofar as Spanish claims in Italy affected international relations. It was Baltic and German affairs that concerned them most. There they enjoyed most influence, particularly when, as in the 1730s, their ministers had no strong views in these areas. The regular royal role in foreign policy – giving audiences to foreign envoys and reading draft instructions to British envoys – gave them great influence, particularly when ministers' attentions were directed elsewhere. The availability of a Hanoverian diplomatic service, the possibility of giving British diplomats secret orders, and the personal links, direct or indirect, of George I and George II with foreign rulers and statesmen further increased their influence. Clearly royal influence was greatest in areas of little public concern or parliamentary interest. Had George II, in the spring of 1730, instructed his ministers not to press the French on their repairs to Dunkirk because he did not wish to endanger French support for Hanover, then his ministers would doubtless have told him that the parliamentary crisis over Dunkirk made this impossible. George I's promise to return Gibraltar could not be honoured for similar reasons. The King had to operate within the parameters of what was politically possible. These parameters were more institutionalised in Britain (and Sweden and Poland) than other European monarchies. However, much of eighteenth-century politics was a matter of personalities, and the weak nature of contemporary institutions, traditional respect for the monarch and the tradition that foreign policy was particularly the sphere for royal activity helped to ensure that a strong monarch could do much. George I and George II did not control Britain's foreign policy as completely as Victor Amadeus II and Charles Emmanuel III did Sardinia's or Peter I Russia's or Frederick II Prussia's, but compared to the indolent Louis XV or the harassed Frederick I of Sweden, they were in control. Their influence was also more purposeful than that of the idiosyncratic Philip V of Spain and the indecisive Charles VI of Austria. Royal wishes could not be ignored; British ministers had to consider them and could rarely thwart them. Much royal interest was directed to ensuring the security of Hanover. This not only created diplomatic problems for British foreign policy. It also helped to make foreign policy a more sensitive issue of debate and increased the difficulties for ministers of coping with parliamentary agitation.

46   British Foreign Policy in the Age of Walpole

NOTES

1. Bolingbroke to George Lyttelton, 4 Nov. 1741, *The Lyttelton Papers*. Southeby's catalogue for sale of 12 Dec. 1978, p. 115.

2. Tory M.P. Sir John Hynde Cotton, 17 Jan. 1734, Cobbett, IX, 190; *London Journal* 27 July 1728; *Fog's Weekly Journal* 12 Oct. 1734; *Common Sense* 31 Oct. 1741; 'Safety and Tranquility – an excellent new ballad', Hertford, County Record Office, Panshanger MSS, D/EP F240.

3. Tilson to Whitworth, 16 Feb. 1722, BL. Add. 37388.

4. Townshend to St. Saphorin, 5 Aug., 7 Sept., 6 Nov., 14, 18 Dec. 1722, 8 Feb., 4, 24 July (ns), 27, 31 Oct. (ns) 1723, 30 June 1724, PRO. 80/47-8; St. Saphorin to Bernstorff, 26 Mar. (ns), St. Saphorin to George I, 17 Nov. (ns) 1723, Hanover, Calenberg Brief Archiv 24, Nr. 4921; Townshend to Waldegrave, 26 Oct. (os) 1727, PRO. 80/62.

5. Chavigny to Chauvelin, 19 Sept. (ns) 1729, AE. CP. Br- Han. 47; Hughes, pp. 368-9, 376-7.

6. Dann, Hanover and Great Britain; Hatton; Hatton, 'New Light', pp. 238-9.

7. Schulenburg-Görtz correspondence, Darmstadt, F23 A 153/6, e.g. Schulenburg to Görtz, 19 Feb. (ns), 11 May (ns), 20 Aug. (ns) 1717.

8. Gibbs, 'Britain and Alliance of Hanover', *EHR* 73 (1958); Horace Walpole to Newcastle, 20 Sept. (ns) 1726, BL. Add. 32747.

9. Robinson to Newcastle, 30 Sept. (ns) 1732, BL. Add. 32778; Horace Walpole to Lord Chancellor Hardwicke, 10 Oct. 1740, BL. Add. 35586.

10. DuBourgay to Townshend, 19, 21 Feb. (ns) 2, 16 Mar. (ns), Townshend to DuBourgay, 22 Feb. 1726, PRO. 90/20; Count Albert, Bavarian envoy in Paris, to Count Törring, Bavarian Foreign Minister, 12 Aug. (ns) 1726, Munich, KS. 17091.

11. Wachtendonck, Palatine envoy in London, to Karl Philipp, Elector Palatine, 3 July (ns) 1733, Munich, KB. 84/40.

12. PRO. 90/11-12; Whitworth-Görtz corresp., Darmstadt, F23 A 159/9. quotes, Whitworth to Tilson, 13, 20 Jan. (ns) 1720, PRO. 90/11.

13. Kinsky to Eugene, 16 Feb. (ns) 1734, HHStA. GK. 94(b); Robinson to Harrington, 26 Mar. (ns) 1734, PRO. 80/105; Eugene to Kinsky, 15 Dec. (ns) 1734, CUL. CH. corresp. 2375.

14. Schulenburg to Görtz, 23 Nov. (ns) 1717, 22 Feb. (ns) 1718, Darmstadt, F23 A 153/6; Dubois to Orléans, 16 Mar. (ns) 1718, AE. CP. Ang. 316; Craggs to Stair, 11 May 1718, SRO. GD. 135/141/13B; Mémoires du Marquis de Torcy', French Minister, Paris, Bibliothèque Nationale, nouvelles acquisitions françaises, III, 3; Tilson to Whitworth, 1 Oct. (os) 1721, BL. Add. 37386.

15. Hatton, 'New Light' p. 239.

16. Albert to Baron Malknecht, Bavarian foreign minister, 29 June (ns) 1721, Munich, KS 17076; K. Borgmann, *Der deutsche Religionsstreit der Jahre 1719-20* (Berlin, 1937). George's role was praised in the Lords' Address of 8 Dec. 1720 and in the ministerial press, *Flying-Post: or Post Master* 19 Sept. 1719; *London Journal* 13 Jan. 1722; *St. James' Journal* 12 July 1722.

17. Palm, Austrian envoy in London, to Charles VI, 17 Dec. (ns), Riva, Modenese envoy in London, to Duke of Modena, 27 Dec. (ns) 1726, CUL. CH. corresp. 1382, 1389.

18. Bernstorff continued to be of some influence until his death in 1726, Townshend to St. Saphorin, 6 Mar. 1724, DuBourgay to Tilson, 6 Dec. (ns) 1725, PRO. 80/48, 90/19. However, his influence was much less than in the 1710s: Destouches to Dubois, 9 July (ns) 1722, Chavigny to Morville, 17 Nov. (ns) 1723, AE. CP. Ang. 342, 346.

19. D'Aix to Victor Amadeus, 23 June (ns) 1729, AST. LM. Ing. 35; Chavigny to Chauvelin, 19 Sept. (ns) 1729, AE. CP. Br.-Han. 47; Augustus to Watsdorf, 12 Oct. (ns) 1730, Le Coq, Saxon Envoy Extraordinary in London, to Augustus, 15 Aug. (ns) 1727,

Dresden, 2676; Anon., 'Mémoire sur l'Etat présent de la Grande Bretagne' 31 Dec. (ns) 1728, AE. CP. Ang. 364 f. 391.

20. Townshend to British Plenipotentiaries at Soissons, 12 Sept. 1728, Horace Walpole to Delafaye, 12 Sept. (ns) 1728, PRO. 78/189, 188; Horace Walpole to Tilson, 28 May (ns), Horace Walpole to Newcastle, 28 May (ns) 1727, BL. Add. 48981, 32750; Horace Walpole to Tilson, 2 Nov. (ns) 1728, Bradfer Lawrence.

21. Robinson to Harrington, 12 Aug. (ns) 1733, PRO. 80/98.

22. St. Saphorin to Townshend, 8 Feb. (ns), Townshend to St. Saphorin, 6 Mar. 1724, PRO. 80/52, 48; Titley to Tilson, 3 May (ns) 1729, PRO. 75/52; Horace to Robert Walpole, 11 Oct. (ns) 1734, CUL. CH. corresp. 2349.

23. Whitworth to Tilson, 15 Nov. (ns) 1721, PRO. 90/15; Tilson to Whitworth, 13 Ap., Whitworth to Bothmer, 14 Ap. (ns) 1722, BL. Add. 37388; Edward Finch, envoy in Warsaw, to Townshend, 21 Dec. (ns) 1726, PRO. 88/33; Townshend to DuBourgay, 22 Ap. 1726, PRO. 90/20.

24. Townshend to Richard Sutton, on special mission to Denmark, 2 Sept. (ns) (quote), Townshend to Chesterfield, 2 Sept. (ns) 1729, DuBourgay to Townshend, 27 Aug. (ns) 1729, PRO. 81/123, 84/305, 90/25; Anon. travel account, Bodl. Rawl. 72 f. 2; Dickens, envoy in Berlin, to Harrington, 21 June (ns) 1738, PRO. 90/44.

25. Cambis to Amelot, French foreign minister, 27 Mar. (ns) 1738, AE. CP. Ang. 397; Chavigny to Chauvelin, 12 Aug. (ns), Chauvelin to Chavigny, 21 Aug. (ns) 1729, AE. CP. Br.-Han. 47; Boissieux, French envoy in Cologne, to Chauvelin, 13 Sept. (ns) 1729, AE. CP. Cologne 70; Ossorio to Charles Emmanuel, 9 Jan. (ns), 6 Feb. (ns), 3 Ap. (ns) 1741, AST. LM. Ing. 47.

26. Newcastle to Horace Walpole, 17 May 1726, BL. Add. 32746; Townshend to DuBourgay, 31 May 1726, PRO. 90/20; Chambrier, Prussian envoy in Paris, to Frederick William, 4 Mar. (ns) 1727, AE. CP. Prusse 83; Newcastle to Horace Walpole, – Ap. 1727, BL. Add. 32750; Townshend to Richard Sutton, envoy in Cassel, 5 May 1727, PRO. 81/122.

27. Plenipotentiaries to Townshend, 21 Aug. (ns), Horace Walpole to Delafaye, 31 Aug. (ns) 1729, PRO. 78/192; Newcastle to Harrington and Poyntz, 23 Ap. 1730, BL. Add. 32767.

28. 'Mémoire pour servir d'instruction au S. de Chavigny allant a Hanovre', 26 June (ns) 1729, AE. CP. Br.-Han. 47; Broglie to Chauvelin, 2 Jan. (ns) 1730, AE. CP. Ang. 369.

29. Townshend to Horace Walpole, 31 July 1728, 21 Aug. (os) 1727, Bradfer Lawrence, BL. Add. 48982; King, 17 Aug. 1729 p. 107.

30. E. Gregg, *Queen Anne* (1980); J. Owen, 'George II Reconsidered', *Statesmen, Scholars and Merchants*, edited by A. Whiteman, J. S. Bromley and P. Dickson (Oxford, 1973); J. Clark, *The Dynamics of Change* (Cambridge, 1982); T. Blanning, '"That Horrid Electorate" or "Ma Patrie Germanique"? George III, Hanover, and the *Fürstenbund* of 1785', *Historical Journal* 20 (1977); Black, 'George II Reconsidered', *Mitteilungen des Österreichischen Staatsarchivs* 35 (1982).

31. Palm to Charles VI, 23 Ap. (ns) 1726, Coxe, II, 498; J. D. Griffith Davies, *A King in Toils* (1938); C. Roberts, 'Party and Patronage in Later Stuart England', Baxter (ed.), *England's Rise* p. 16.

32. Robethon, secretary of George I, to Stair, 16 Ap. (ns) 1716, SRO. GD. 135/141/7.

33. De Löss to Augustus III, 6, 20 Oct. (ns), 27 Nov. (ns) 1733, Dresden, 638 I.

34. Delafaye to Horace Walpole, 8 Aug. 1727, PRO. 78/187.

35. Townshend to Diescau, 16 Jan. 1728, PRO. 95/50.

36. Chavigny to Chauvelin, 13 July (ns) 1733, AE. CP. Ang. 381; Newcastle to Waldegrave, 11 Ap. 1740, Chewton; Horace Walpole to Trevor, 19 Aug. (ns) 1736, Trevor, 6.

37. Horace Walpole to Tilson, 3, 21 Oct. (ns) 1727, BL. Add. 48928; Le Coq to Augustus II, 28 July (ns), 11 Aug. (ns), 18 Sept. (ns) 1728, Dresden, 2733.

38. Diemar-Eugene correspondence, HHStA. GK. 85a.

39. Townshend to Chesterfield, 1 July (ns), Townshend to Horace Walpole, 1 July (ns) 1729, BL. Add. 48982; King, 17 June 1729, pp. 90-1; Albert to Plettenberg, 9 Aug. (ns) 1729, Münster, NB 33[1].

40. Robinson to Newcastle, 20 May (ns) 1732, BL. Add. 32777.

41. Destouches to Dubois, 26 Ap. (ns), Chavigny, French envoy at Hanover, to Morville, 5 Sept. (ns), 17 Nov. (ns) 1723, Broglie to Morville, 20 July (ns) 1724, AE. CP. Ang. 344, 346, 348; Gibson, Bishop of Lincoln, to Nicolson, Bishop of Derry, 12 Ap. 1724, Bodl. A. 269; Walpole to Newcastle, 1 Sept., Newcastle to Horace Walpole, 26 Sept. 1724, BL. Add. 32687.

42. Tilson to Poyntz, 20 Jan. 1730, BL. Add. 48982; Horace Walpole to Poyntz, 21 Jan. 1730, Coxe, II, 667; Reichenbach, Prussian envoy in London, to Prussian minister Grumbkow, 31 Mar. (ns), 7 Ap. (ns) 1730, Hull, DDHO 3/3.

43. Pelham to Waldegrave, 23 Mar. 1731, Chewton.

44. Harrington to Robinson, 4 Dec. 1730, PRO. 80/69; Walpole, CUL. CH. papers 26/39a.

45. Black, 'George II Reconsidered'.

46. Baxter, 'The Conduct of the Seven Years War', Baxter (ed.), *England's Rise* p. 323; H. Gerlg, *Die Memoiren des Lord Hervey als historische Quelle* (Freiburg, 1936).

47. Chavigny to Chauvelin, 4 Sept. (ns) 1729, AE. CP. Br.-Han. 47; Eugene to Kinsky, 2 May 1729, HHStA. GK. 94(b). In 1734 it was claimed that George had a natural aversion to the very name of France, Gansinot to Törring, 16 Ap. (ns) 1734, Munich, KS, 17326.

48. Diemar to Frederick I of Sweden, 27 Nov. (ns) 1733, Marburg, 203; De Löss to Augustus III, 30 Oct. (ns), 17 Nov. (ns) 1733, Dresden, 638, I; Ulfeld, Austrian envoy at The Hague, to Kinsky, 30 Ap. (ns) 1734, Vienna, Palais Kinsky, papers of Count Philip Kinsky, Kart. 2d.

49. Waldegrave to Newcastle, 16 Ap. (ns) 1734, BL. Add. 32784; Diemar to Eugene, 20 Ap. (ns) 1734, HHStA. GK. 85(a); Diemar to Frederick I, 23 Ap. (ns) 1734, Marburg, 203.

50. Robinson to Harrington, 29 Mar. (ns), Harrington to Robinson, 7 Ap. 1732, PRO. 80/86, 87; Chesterfield to Robinson, 15 Jan. (ns) 1732, BL. Add. 23784; Black, 'British Neutrality in the War of the Polish Succession', *International History Review* (forthcoming).

51. De Löss to Augustus III, 22 Feb. (ns) 1735, Dresden, 638 IIIa.

52. Robinson to Harrington, 24 Aug. (ns) 1733, PRO. 80/98; Keene to Newcastle, 24 Mar. (ns) 1734, PRO. 94/119.

53. Robinson to Harrington, 28 Oct. (ns) 1733, 26 Mar. (ns) 1734, PRO. 80/100, 105.

54. Horace Walpole Journal, 20 Ap. (ns) 1734, BL. Add. 9140 f. 127.

55. Horace Walpole, 'Apology', BL. Add. 9132 f. 37; Sarah Marlborough to Captain Fish, 'Bearleader' of her grandsons, 31 July 1727, BL. Add. 61444; Horace Walpole the younger, Reminiscences, *The Letters of Horace Walpole*, edited by P. Cunningham, I (Edinburgh, 1906) cxxxvii.

56. 'Lettre de Mr Le Coq.' 12 Dec. (ns) 1727, Dresden, 2676; Kinksy to Eugene, 8, 25 Feb. (ns) 1729, HHStA, GK. 94(b).

57. Diemar to Landgrave Karl, 4 July (ns) 1727, Marburg, 175; Diemar to Eugene, 31 Dec. 1734, HHStA., GK. 85a; King, 2 Sept. 1729, p. 111; Newcastle to Caroline, 4 Aug. 1732, BL. Add. 32778; Horace Walpole to Walpole, 29 Mar. 1730, CUL. CH. corresp. 1706.

Ministers, Secretaries of State and Diplomats

'our Principals at home are too much occupied with the House of Commons to attend to what passes on the Continent; and, if any good is even done there, it must be effected through the King's ministers abroad, and not by those about his person. Long experience has taught me this; and I never yet received an instruction that was worth reading.'

Sir James Harris.[1]

'The orders, which your Excy. will receive by this messenger, for your talking to the Cardinal upon the subject of the secret negotiation, some of your friends think can be of little use, and therefore wish your Excy. would be tender in the execution of them. They hope you will take this as a mark of their particular confidence in your Excy., and that your answer to the letter, containing the said orders, will be such, as not to occasion any suspicion of your having had this hint given you'.[2]

Sir James Harris' pungent comment of 1785 summarised, albeit unfairly, the situation in the 1760s and 1770s when for many years a series of ill-informed Secretaries of State devoted insufficient attention to British foreign policy. This chapter seeks to examine the machinery for the formulation and execution of foreign policy that existed in the age of Walpole. Three groups command attention: the Secretaries of State, the diplomats, and those who exerted direct influence even though their formal position did not encompass responsibility for foreign policy. These groups were not exclusive. Walpole, the leading member of the third group, acted as Secretary of State in 1723; his brother Horace was a member of all three groups, a leading diplomat who served as Secretary of State in 1736 and possessed influence even when he lacked formal responsibility, as in 1731-2; Harrington was a long-serving diplomat before he became a Secretary of State. Important studies exist both for the eighteenth-century diplomatic service and for the Secretaries of State.[3] I shall concentrate on assessing the influence of those who played a role in the formulation and execution of policy.

'Employments of extraordinary trust and multiplicity' was oow a pamphlet described the Secretaryships of State in 1727, and the bewildering variety of tasks for which the Secretary was responsible was described ably by Thomson. With the exception of the short-lived Secretaryship of State for Scotland, there were two Secretaries: for the Northern and the Southern Departments. Aside from their multifarious domestic tasks, they were responsible for conducting foreign policy, both by instructing envoys abroad and by handling negotiations with foreign envoys in London. There was a clear and constant geographical delimitation of responsibility. The Northern Department handled the United Provinces, Russia, Scandinavia, Poland, and the German-speaking lands; the Southern Department, Turkey,

Italy, France and Iberia. If either Secretary was absent or ill, the other was expected to handle his correspondence, and his interviews with foreign envoys. From the accession of George I the Northern Department was held to be the more important, although there was no subordination, and the Secretaries were equally servants of the crown. During Walpole's ministry, in contrast to the rapid changes of the preceding decade, only four men held the Secretaryships: Lord Carteret (southern, 1721-4), Viscount Townshend (northern, 1721-30), the Duke of Newcastle (southern, 1724-1748), Lord Harrington (northern, 1730-1742). The operation of the Secretaryships owed much to the policies and personal relationships of these men.[4]

John Lord Carteret had served with considerable success in 1719-20 as Ambassador Extraordinary and Plenipotentiary in Stockholm during the negotiations to end the Great Northern War and to create an anti-Russian alliance. Of Tory background, he was a protégé of Sunderland and an opponent of Walpole. When he was appointed Secretary, it was seen as a blow to Walpole. Carteret was talented: in 1720 his diplomatic colleague, Charles Whitworth, noted, 'Myld. Carteret is a perfect man of business, he acts and writes clearly and consequentially, and gives a mighty agreeable turn to everything that passes thro' his hands'.

Greatly knowledgeable about European affairs, and the only Secretary of the period who understood German, Carteret was sociable and cultured. In no doubt of his own ability, he was very ambitious and possessed a reputation for self-serving. His colleague in opposition, William Pulteney, was to describe him in 1735 as false and malicious; the following year a French memorandum, noting his ambition, claimed that he was neither Whig nor Tory, but simply seeking a post. He had no experience of the Commons, had sat in the Lords since May 1709, and was an experienced and cogent debater. He had defended the Quadruple Alliance in the Lords. His political following was scanty. In 1728 Hervey claimed he had 'many admirers and not one adherent', Basil Williams wrote, 'Carteret . . . carried on the Stanhope tradition of looking on Europe as a whole and taking no insular or pettifogging view of England's interests and responsibilities'; which, phrased differently, meant that he arrogantly sought to define England's interests in terms of his views of the European situation and did so with no concern for domestic political realities.[5]

The political legacy of the 1710s was of great importance. Just as the Whig-Tory split of 1710-14, represented in foreign policy terms by the Treaty of Utrecht, played a major role in defining attitudes in the subsequent period, so to with the Whig split of 1717, represented in foreign policy terms by the Stanhopian diplomatic legacy and, in particular, the Quadruple Alliance of 1718. Walpole was determined to remove former supporters of Stanhope and Sunderland – Cadogan, Carteret, Roxburgh,

Macclesfield – and his success in doing so in 1723-5 dramatically altered the nature of Whig politics. Carteret, despite his lack of political strength, maintained himself in office through royal favour. In 1723, however, he threatened to compromise the Anglo-French alliance by meddling in French court politics, and this was used to discredit him. Furthermore, he was weakened by being more closely associated with Austrian interests than Townshend at a time when the logic of the Anglo-French alliance was leading to steadily worse Anglo-Austrian relations. Ultimately he had to go, for the same reason that a change was to be essential in 1730: the division of authority between two Secretaries demanded their cooperation for the efficient execution of foreign policy. Bishop Gibson of Lincoln noted, 'the quarrels between them were grown to such a height that it was next to impossible to go on longer together'.[6]

Charles Viscount Townshend (1674-1738) was a prominent Whig politician who had served at The Hague in 1709-11, negotiating the Anglo-Dutch Treaty of Barrier and Succession of 1709 which stipulated Dutch military assistance if the Hanoverian succession was endangered. His reward was to be appointed Northern Secretary on George I's accession. In 1716-17 he had differed with George and Stanhope over the latter's determination to shape foreign policy to suit Hanoverian ends. Replaced by Stanhope in December 1716, he went into opposition in the spring of 1717. The Whig split ended in 1720 and Townshend regained his old post on Stanhope's death in February 1721. Townshend is the major ministerial figure of the early eighteenth century to lack a biographer, and further difficulties are created by the scanty nature of his surviving papers. Various assessments of his character exist. To some he was honest and uncorrupt, to others headstrong, arrogant and impetuous, 'Charlie Bluster' in one pamphlet.[7] Insufficient attention, as often with eighteenth-century political figures, has been paid to his health. Ill health in the 1720s culminated in a very serious illness in 1727-8 that nearly killed him, and his two remaining years as Secretary were marred by recurrences.[8] Townshend was able and well-informed about European affairs, though Frederick William I of Prussia claimed in 1728 that he knew little about those of northern Europe. His views are difficult to summarise. A longstanding proponent of close Anglo-Dutch relations – he corresponded with leading Dutch politicians including Slingelandt – he had less time for the other pillar of the Grand Alliance, Austria. Personally he had little sympathy for Austria, distrusted Austria's religious policies and regarded her as an ungrateful ally who had repaid past English assistance with ingratitude and obstinancy, a view shared by several British diplomats. The Austrians held him responsible for bad Anglo-Austrian relations, blaming him for the Alliance of Hanover of 1725 and for the subsequent dominance of anti-Austrian ideas in

British foreign policy, and their view has been generally accepted by historians. There is no doubt that Townshend strongly disapproved of Austrian policy in the 1720s and believed that it threatened the European system. However, he should be seen as a 'short-term hawk' in Anglo-Austrian relations. Townshend believed that Austria had to be coerced into abandoning provocative policies, such as her oceanic schemes, her stance towards Hanover and her support of Spanish opposition to British interests, but he was certain that the territorial stability of Austria was essential to Britain's long-term interests. He believed that a British alliance was in Austria's interest and argued that it was best for Charles VI 'to put an end to the present disturbances as soon as possible, and by doing so put the Maritime Powers in a condition to renew their ancient friendship with him'. Townshend was aware of the need to regain Austrian cooperation, because he was well aware of the fragility of the Anglo-French alliance.[9] He was suspicious of French policy – in 1722 the French envoy Destouches had thought him more pro-Austrian than pro-French – and argued that Britain should avoid being dragged into a war with Austria that might serve to upset the balance of power and enable France to acquire territory in Flanders and the Rhineland. In 1728 he stressed the precariousness of the Anglo-French alliance, dependent as it was on the life of the elderly French first minister, Cardinal Fleury.[10] Townshend's policies were therefore not as out of step as has been suggested with those that were to be followed after his resignation in May 1730. It has been argued that British policy became isolationist after Townshend resigned, a view that ignores a considerable continuity of policy. Though Townshend negotiated far and wide to gain accessions to the Alliance of Hanover, his views represented a conscious rejection of Stanhope's attempts to use British diplomacy, money and seapower to settle European problems. Townshend lacked Stanhope's confidence in a system of collective security involving reciprocal guarantees and did not display Stanhope's enthusiasm for solving problems by means of congresses. In August 1727 he wrote to Horace Walpole, 'I do in my own opinion think, that if we can have peace upon good and honourable terms, the fewer obligations we put ourselves under to other powers towards obtaining it, the better. This you know was always my principle . . . I did not care to how narrow a compass the things to be treated of at the Congress were confined if . . . the points in which we and the Dutch are concerned should be adjusted to our minds; and secondly that nothing should be done in relation to Sleswick, or any other point in which the King may be concerned as Elector, but what should be agreeable to his Maty . . . I shall not care one farthing for any more accessions, nor in truth for engaging in any new scheme, or with any more powers. . . .'[11]

Townshend was aware of the fundamental transience of international affairs, the shifting nature of alliances, and he wrote in 1728, 'there is more of name and sound, than of substance and reality between a definitive treaty, and a provisional and suspensive one . . . Treatys commonly last, and are interpreted according to times and circumstances'.[12] Aside from intelligent scepticism about international affairs, Townshend was aware of the need to win parliamentary approval for foreign policy. He was well aware of the political difficulties of persuading Parliament to grant peace-time subsidies to foreign powers, displaying this in 1726 over discussions about offering Bavaria such subsidies, and the Hesse-Cassel envoy Diemar found him very firm in negotiations over subsidies and concerned about parliamentary attitudes. Claims that Townshend, an experienced debater in the Lords, was unconcerned by parliamentary and popular opinion are inaccurate. The French envoy Chammorel, pressing Townshend in 1726 against a projected tax upon French cloth imports, reported that the minister was very concerned about the possibility of the opposition exploiting the issue. In 1728 he wrote to Horace Walpole of the need to conduct matters so as to win public support. Townshend, like George II, did not take Parliament for granted.[13]

As Northern Secretary Townshend had the sensitive task of attempting to satisfy the Hanoverian interests of the monarch. He won royal favour by his support for these interests, though he was far from pliant, and clashed with George II over diplomatic strategy in 1727-8.[14] Support for Hanover posed major difficulties for British foreign policy, though Townshend in the 1720s did not encounter the difficulties he had faced in 1716. A good instance of the impact of Hanoverian interests on Townshend's department are the instructions be sent to Waldegrave at Vienna, in February 1729, when a negotiation of Anglo-Austrian differences had been proposed: 'If the court of Vienna is sincerely desirous to renew the perfect friendship and harmony, which so long subsisted between them and us, they will of themselves see the necessity of doing H.M. as Elector justice upon several points, upon which the King, and his father, have so long, and with so much reason, complained. These are matters of so little importance to the Emperor, and his Imperial Majesty has them so entirely in his own power, that it will be impossible for him ever to convince us that he sincerely desires our friendship, unless he does explain himself clearly and explicitly to the King's satisfaction upon those several articles'.[15]

Townshend's willingness to support the consequences of George II's Hanoverian interests played a large role in the crisis of 1729-30, but behind the differences over policy, important as they were, was a struggle for power between Walpole and Townshend.[16] The Anglo-Wittelsbach negotiations served to crystallise Walpole's suspicions that Townshend was not consulting his ministerial colleagues. Relations between Townshend and his fellow-Secretary Newcastle were very bad,[17] a matter largely not of policy

differences, but of Newcastle no longer being willing to accept the
subordination to Townshend he had displayed in 1724-8.[18] Tension and
suspicion meant that a change was necessary as ministers were no longer
able to work together. Coxe claimed that Townshend was resolved to form
'a new administration', and sought to replace Newcastle by Chesterfield.
Given the fact that negotiations with the Wittelsbachs only became a
divisive issue in the second half of 1729, whilst Townshend had been
actively sponsoring Chesterfield and Newcastle opposing Townshend from
before this period, it is clear that these negotiations were not the original
cause of division.[19] As in 1716-17 and 1723-4, ministerial differences over
power and place were readily linked to policy issues, and the absence of a
defined governmental hierarchy, and in particular of any clear overall
responsibility for foreign policy, made it very difficult to solve these
differences. In the absence of collective ministerial responsibility ministers
followed contrary policies. The political consequences were to stress the
importance of the royal attitude, but also to make it very difficult for the
king to maintain a ministry comprising different groups. In Austria it was
suggested that Charles VI deliberately encouraged competing ministers to
pursue contrary policies in order to maintain his own freedom of political
manoeuvre. This created chaos in Austria, and there is no sign that George
I and George II favoured such a policy.

Townshend's successor William Stanhope (c. 1683-1756), ennobled as
Lord Harrington in February 1730, was a cousin of James Viscount
Stanhope. After military service during the War of the Spanish Succession
he followed a diplomatic career of which the principal features were three
missions to Spain (1717-18, 1720-7, 1729) and being one of the British
Plenipotentiaries at the Congress of Soissons (1728-30). Neither in the
Commons nor in the Lords did he play much of a role in Parliament,
though he called meetings of ministerial peers prior to the sessions of 1731,
1732 and 1738. He acquired a good reputation, which some felt he did not
deserve, by his missions to Spain.[20] His position in 1727-30 indicated the
interrelationship of foreign policy and ministerial factions. Appointed Vice-
Chamberlain of the Household in 1727, he was used often for confidential
diplomatic overtures. In 1728 he received secret orders from George II as
part of George's scheme for an approach at Soissons to the Austrian
Chancellor Sinzendorf. Stanhope told the Saxon diplomat Le Coq that
Townshend knew nothing of these secret instructions.[21] The following
January Stanhope took part in secret negotiations with the Austrian envoy
in London, Count Kinsky, negotiations of which Townshend was aware,
whilst at Soissons Stanhope had a secret correspondence with Newcastle.[22]
Stanhope was clearly regarded as being less pro-French and more pro-
Austrian than other ministers. The Austrian envoys in Paris certainly held

this view and distrusted Horace Walpole. According to Zamboni, the Saxon agent in London, when in January 1729 on their return for the parliamentary session George II asked whether France would, in case of necessity, act vigorously and sincerely to support Britain, Horace Walpole said yes, but Stanhope refused to commit himself. Zamboni, uncorroborated, is never a reliable source, but it is interesting to note what it was possible to believe. In 1730 sources as varied as the Emperor Charles VI and the French foreign minister Chauvelin were to write of their belief that Harrington, as was by then, was pro-Austrian; Harrington himself made clear his increasing impatience with the French alliance. His important role in the negotiation of the second Treaty of Vienna, and the approach to Austria following shortly after his return to England, suggest that he was partly responsible for the decision to approach Austria.[23]

Stanhope's relation to the British ministers altered in the late 1720s. According to Newcastle, Stanhope was unanimously chosen by the ministry in 1727 as their representative at the forthcoming Congress. He was one of the names suggested as a possible replacement for Townshend that winter.[24] However, Stanhope's relationship with Townshend was a poor one, and in 1728 he blamed Walpole for his failure to receive a peerage and the absence of favour enjoyed by his brother.[25] His promotion to the Secretaryship in 1730 probably owed much to longstanding royal favour and much to Newcastle, who reconciled Stanhope and the Walpoles. In May 1730 Harrington could write of Walpole, 'I am unalterably attached to his interests and determined to live in the same confidence and friendship with him, as I should have done with Ld. Stanhope were he still alive. I have long looked upon Horace as my brother . . .' Reality was to prove otherwise.[26] Bad relations between Harrington and the Walpoles swiftly became well known. Harrington's independence was no secret, and he did not trouble to hide continued close social links with members of the opposition. He was particularly close to two favourites of George II who fell out with Walpole in 1733-4, his cousin Philip Stanhope Earl of Chesterfield, and the Earl of Scarborough. Harrington's stance led to innumerable reports, throughout the 1730s, that he would be dismissed or transferred to less powerful positions, usually to be replaced by Horace Walpole. It is unclear if any serious effort was ever made to remove him. He was helped by the fact that he enjoyed royal favour; though in 1736 when Horace Walpole instead of Harrington accompanied George to Hanover, a loss of favour (albeit temporary), ill health and Walpolean pressure were blamed. There was never any question of Harrington aiming for the position of first minister; he did not display the pretensions or enjoy the political influence of Newcastle in the late 1730s.[27]

Harrington's is one of the least studied of all eighteenth-century Secretaryships. The contrast between the scanty surviving evidence of his thoughts and the profusion for those of Newcastle is partly responsible, but so too is Hervey's dismissal of him. Thomson's low view of him appears not to have been based on any examination of diplomatic sources. In part Harrington suffers from the tendency in work on British foreign policy in their period, such as that of Lodge and Vaucher, to concentrate on relations with states in the Southern Department.[28]

Contemporary diplomatic views of Harrington varied. He was widely held to be circumspect, honest, reserved, capable, flexible and temperate.[29] He was also accused by a wide variety of diplomats, such as the Sardinian Ossorio in 1732, and the Dane John and the Dutch envoy in 1733, of being indolent, whilst Chavigny thought him nonchalant. Accusations of indolence stemmed from his inaccessibility to foreign envoys;[30] there are no suggestions that he was lax in his diplomatic correspondence, and indeed his instructions are impressive: crisp and clear. His inaccessibility owed much to ill health: he had frequent crippling attacks of gout.[31] Opinions differed as to how much he took the initiative, Newcastle complaining in 1734, 'Lord Harrington is, as usual, very fond of his own plan'.[32] Judging from accounts of conversations with him recorded by foreign envoys, Harrington was a perceptive commentator on European affairs, well-informed, open-minded and free of the fixed ideas of his co-Secretary.

Naturally reserved, Harrington left fewer indications of his views than Newcastle. He was blamed, particularly by Horace Walpole, for the marked deterioration in Anglo-Dutch relations in the 1730s. Harrington did not cultivate Dutch politicians as Townshend and Horace had done, and he rarely stayed long in Holland on his way to or from Hanover.[33] Harrington's stance matched a general shift in British attitudes towards the United Provinces, so that Whig politicians, such as Chesterfield in the early 1730s, bewailing the selfishness of and difficulty of dealing with the Dutch, sound at times like Tories of the early 1710s.[34] Furthermore, Harrington's stance matched that of George II, who lacked his father's care for Dutch interests, and, by actively supporting the 1734 marriage of his eldest daughter Anne to William IV of Orange, angered the Dutch political establishment.[35]

Opinions of Harrington's stance in the Polish Succession War varied. Chauvelin and Hervey accused him of being pro-Austrian, Newcastle of insufficiently considering Austria.[36] Excluded from control of the negotiations at The Hague that sought to settle the conflict, Harrington handled well the efforts to prevent Sweden from joining France and successfully achieved the desired balance in Anglo-Russian negotiations: commercial gains without political guarantees. Closely associated with George II, he was criticised in 1732 by Thomas Robinson, envoy in Vienna, for failing to persuade George to overcome his reluctance to improve Anglo-Prussian and Anglo-Russian negotiations. Robinson wrote to Newcastle complaining of the changeability of Harrington's instructions, although possibly he should rather have blamed George.[37] In 1741 Newcastle criticised Harrington for subservience to Hanoverian interests: 'It is very easy for my Lord Harrington to act and talk agreeably to the King at Hanover; but we must think how we can serve the King in Parliament and defend there what is done elsewhere'.[38] Newcastle was unfair – Harrington was in a difficult position and took care to dissociate himself from the Hanoverian neutrality – but he did possibly capture the essence of Harrington's Secretaryship. Harrington was very much George's man. Lacking both great estates and the arrogant self-confidence in their own indispensability of the Whig Lords, Harrington, through necessity and by inclination, conformed to the royal will.

Newcastle (1693-1768) is the only Secretary of the period of whom there is a recent scholarly biography.[39] Devoid of diplomatic experience, he knew little of Europe and was very reluctant to travel there. In his early years as Secretary he anxiously sought support and reassurance from Townshend and the Walpoles, and was closely united with them. Allowing for eighteenth-century conventions, one may note a letter he received from Horace Walpole in 1727: 'ye case between friends so cordially united, as our familys are ... is like that of Lovers; ...' In the late 1720s the position changed. Townshend's growing ill health, the difficulties encountered by the Alliance of Hanover and the fact that Townshend clearly enjoyed less favour with George II than he had with his father, helped to make the situation more volatile, and Newcastle became increasingly ambitious. He became notoriously sensitive about other ministers discussing matters with foreign envoys or corresponding with British envoys in his Province. Newcastle resisted suggestions from others as to the drafting of dispatches, and played a major role in provoking the ministerial crisis of 1729-30.[40]

Thereafter Newcastle was the Secretary with the most political influence. Opinions of his ability varied. It was fashionable to mock, the Prince of Wales writing of him that ... 'with a great deal of comical ministerial formality, [he] has acquired the prettiest mixture of a negligent one, with a busy body, which two excellent qualitys never before this great man could be reconciled'.[41] Over recent years it has become usual to stress his political shrewdness and agility.[42] However, it is fair to say that these abilities rarely extended to foreign policy. The leading Tory London weekly, *Fog's Weekly Journal*, in its issue of 21 March 1730, claimed 'that politicks consisted in the knowledge of the different Interests of all the Governments in the World, the open and secret Views of those that presided in their councils, and the Manners of treating with them; ...' Such a definition is an acceptable contemporary one for foreign policy, and Newcastle met none of the criteria. In addition he was a classic instance of one of the major problems confronting the eighteenth-century Secretaryship, the absence of any differentiation between domestic and foreign duties, and between political and administrative responsibilities. This was particularly marked during parliamentary sessions, when he was often inaccessible to foreign envoys and seriously in arrears in his diplomatic correspondence, and at election times.[43] As election preparations took nearly a year, this was particularly serious, as the 1734, 1741 and 1747 elections fell during times of grave international tension. In December 1733 his distant cousin and Secretary of Embassy at Paris, Thomas Pelham, wrote from London, 'As his Grace will not himself think of any other business here but what relates to the Elections he permits nobody else to do otherwise'. British diplomats, such as the Earl of Essex at Turin, complained frequently of Newcastle's delay in writing.[44]

In the 1720s Newcastle had supported the French alliance. The French envoy Chammorel reported in 1724 that he was a firm supporter of the alliance. In 1727 in a draft dispatch Newcastle wrote of France 'where the present administration appears to act upon different maxims from those which may have been produced in a former reign'.[45] However, in 1728-30 Newcastle became increasingly disillusioned with the French alliance and the interminable, expensive and politically vulnerable armed confrontation between the Hanover and the Vienna allies. He supported reconciliation with Austria, although he appears to have played no significant role either in the successful negotiations of 1730-1 or in their abortive predecessors of 1728 and 1729. In the 1730s Newcastle displayed keen support for the Austrians: 'I pass here, as I really am, 'pour bon Imperialiste', and . . . I never neglect any occasion that offers of promoting, if possible, a closer and better correspondence'.[46] Newcastle's support for Austria was not uncritical. In the summer of 1733 the Prussian envoy Count Degenfeld reported a conversation he had heard between Newcastle and the Austrian envoy Count Kinsky at Hampton Court, Newcastle saying, 'you Imperialists are too active; were you to be left to yourselves, you would make yourselves arbitrators over all the world . . . But, said Count Kinski, if France attacks us, we must defend ourselves, upon which the Duke of Newcastle answered, then one must not talk of attacking, but see who gave occasion to it, and wait the event . . .' Newcastle shared the British anger over Austrian policies and conduct in 1732-3, but his commitment to Austria became clear once the Polish Succession War began. He urged a pro-Austrian British line, and it was understandable that the ministry held the key negotiations with France in early 1735 at The Hague and not in his Province at Paris.[47]

The principal issue agitating Newcastle in the late 1730s was Spanish depredations upon British commerce. He urged a tough stance and was less averse to the prospect of war with Spain than the Walpoles.[48] He appears to have given little attention to the consequences for British foreign policy of the war, for Britain had no allies who could be relied upon against the Bourbons. Newcastle was well aware of the political capital the opposition made out of Spanish depredations, and urged ministerial action on the issue largely because he feared the domestic political implications. 'A little yielding to Times', he urged, and throughout the negotiations his was a forceful and aggressive stance, culminating in his pressure for hostilities in the second half of 1739, because he feared domestic and particularly parliamentary criticism.[49] Differences with Walpole, which owed much to policy disagreements and much to a struggle for power, symbolised by Walpole's determination to make Hervey Lord Privy Seal, produced a marked deterioration in ministerial relationships, and an absence of confidence and of consultation. In January 1740 Newcastle wrote complaining that he did not enjoy Walpole's confidence, and by July 1740 Newcastle and Harrington were conducting a confidential correspondence exclusive of Walpole.[50]

Newcastle's response to the Prussian invasion of Silesia in December 1740 was wholehearted support for British aid to Austria. It was from this background that he criticised the Hanoverian neutrality convention, just as he had criticised and listened to criticism of Hanoverian interests in the past. By late 1741 Newcastle was eagerly constructing a pro-Austrian, anti-Bourbon alliance, prefiguring the work of Carteret. Relations with Walpole, who had little sympathy for the revival of interventionist policies, were poor. Enthusiastic for his policies, Newcastle gave few thoughts to the domestic costs, political, fiscal and economic, of war.

Dividing official responsibility between two Secretaries was far from ideal. The French solution was better: separate departments within a single ministry. Relations between the two Secretaries were usually a sensitive issue, and the geographical delimitation of responsibilities was not very successful. When Britain was conducting negotiations involving powers in both provinces – seeking to solve Austro-Spanish differences in 1731-3 or Austro-Sardinian quarrels in 1732-3, attempting to end the War of the Polish succession – there were major difficulties.[51] Secretaries could and did jointly meet foreign envoys, but drafting instructions presented a problem. In October 1728 Townshend complained of 'the difficulties that arise often with the D. of Newcastle upon forming the draughts of orders'.[52] Confidential correspondence between ministers and envoys was common, serving the useful purpose of clarifying policy to envoys and explaining to them what was going on elsewhere. In 1739 Keene informed Walpole that the latter's letters 'always explain the loose general expressions office letters are usually composed of'.[53] And yet this correspondence could produce considerable confusion. Of the three Plenipotentiaries at the Congress of

Soissons, Newcastle was in correspondence with Stanhope, and Townshend corresponded secretly with Poyntz and Horace Walpole separately. George II approved of Townshend corresponding with Horace without Newcastle's knowledge, but the situation produced distrust and confusion.[54] After Townshend's fall there was less secret Secretarial meddling in the affairs of the other Province. Newcastle's correspondence with Robinson, though significant, was irregular, Harrington's intervention in the Southern Province only occasional.

More trouble was created in the 1730s by the activities of the Walpole brothers, who enjoyed no formal responsibility for foreign policy. Horace (1678-1757) had an extensive background in foreign policy. He had been an Undersecretary of State (1708-10, 1714-15), had served in Spain (1706-7), The Hague (1709-11, 1715-16, 1722, 1734-7, 1739) and Paris (1723-30), and acted as Secretary of State in 1736. Whilst abroad he exercised great influence in negotiations with other courts. From Paris he played a large part in Anglo-Spanish relations, particularly in the mid-1720s and in 1729. He regularly returned to London from diplomatic posts in order to be one of the principal ministerial speakers in the Commons, specialising in foreign affairs. In 1730 he was appointed Cofferer of the Household and thereafter had no formal diplomatic responsibility for several years. Nevertheless, whether in London or abroad, he played a major role in the conduct of foreign affairs. In London he regularly discussed matters with foreign envoys who believed he was important to cultivate, and he maintained an extensive correspondence, both with foreign politicians such as the French first minister Fleury, and the Swedish envoy in Paris, Gedda, and with British diplomats. Several diplomats were his protégés: Robinson at Vienna, Robert Trevor at The Hague, to a certain extent Waldegrave at Paris.[55] Horace argued that he was not seeking to influence policy. Criticising pressure on Austria to provide information on her negotiations with France, he wrote to Robinson in 1735, 'You will understand that what goes before is only to be considered as the private thoughts of a friend and intended for your own particular information and no ways to influence your conduct'. Trevor was informed in 1741, 'I should be sorry if any friendly hints that I should give you at any time should have any effect upon your conduct one way or other, you must be governed by your orders . . .'[56]

Secretaries of State and the Crown were also the recipients of Horace's thoughts: 'I am afraid, if besides giving a relation of my own ministry, I should presume to tell my sentiments, and doe it in extenso either to ye King or ye Queen; I may be thought, as I was last year sometimes to dictate too much, or to encroach upon ye department of one or other of ye Secretary of States; . . .'[57] Though other envoys corresponded extensively and often advanced their own views, none was as comprehensive and assertive as Horace. Horace appeared to challenge the position of the Secretaries, was frequently indeed reported to be being considered for a Secretaryship, and was believed to possess great influence with his brother. His activities were viewed with suspicion by ministerial colleagues, and he received a tremendous amount of criticism from the opposition. Until his eclipse in the late 1730s, the Spanish Convention of 1739 (for which Keene received the diplomatic blame), and the revival of Hanoverian interests as an issue of public debate in 1741, Horace was the principal figure whom the opposition attacked over the conduct of foreign policy. Townshend was rarely mentioned, and Newcastle and Harrington were largely ignored, but Horace was accused of being the dupe of France and the negotiator of useless treaties, as well as being stigmatised for his manners and appearance: 'Clumsy is a near relation of Sublimate's and by him employ'd as his agent to Doctor Ballance. The poor fellow has the misfortune to be born a blockhead, and to be bred a clodhopper . . . a certain awkward, heavy, slovenly, but assuming Equilibrist . . . we hear that a certain ancient Crown-Jewel, called the Ballance of Europe hath been missing some Time; and that it is supposed to have formerly stolen out of the Hands of a certain person in France, who was entrusted to carry it Abroad with him, . . .'[58]

Horace was closely associated with the French alliance, and had particularly good relations with Fleury (French first minister, 1726-43). Colleagues suspected and opponents claimed that he was duped by Fleury and unnecessarily responsive to French suggestions, and he does not emerge well from Vaucher's detailed account of his relationship with Fleury during the War of the Polish Succession. It is certainly true that Horace was a keen proponent of the French alliance, and in 1730 defended it in the face of ministerial critics keener to settle with Austria. The Austrians thought Horace 'inviolably attached to France',[59] but Horace was not an uncritical supporter of the French alliance. In 1723 he argued that it was important for Britain to have links with Spain, independent of France, in 1728 criticised a lack of French vigour in opposing the Vienna powers, and in 1729 argued against Britain so committing herself to French schemes as to be unable to guarantee the Austrian succession. Horace was aware of the precariousness of the Anglo-French alliance and the difficulty of relying upon Fleury.[60] To a certain extent he was misled by Fleury during the War of the Polish Succession, although the decision to negotiate with France was understandable, given the unreliability of Spain and the diplomatic dangers presented by the scheme to end Austro-Spanish differences by a marriage of one of the archduchesses to Don Carlos, second in line to the Spanish throne, a scheme supported by Robert Walpole and opposed by Horace.[61] Horace was a keen supporter of the Dutch alliance, though well aware of the difficulties of obtaining Dutch diplomatic support. Despite the claims of the Sardinian envoy Ossorio, Horace was not a keen supporter of Austria. Austrian diplomats regarded him as opposed to their interests, and during the War of the Polish Succession, Horace sought to keep Britain an impartial mediator. In July 1734 he told the French envoy Chavigny that he resented the arrogance of Austrian policy, was not an Imperialist and sought only to maintain the balance of power.[62] This remained his attitude in the late 1730s. In 1737 he claimed, 'the Imperiall Court has a most unfair and unalterable principle in endeavouring to create jealousys and suspicions between other courts, and particularly with regard to England and France . . .' The following year he wrote that Austria 'deserves noe favour'.[63] Austrian defeats in the Balkans in the late 1730s and a feeling that Austria was not a reliable or a powerful enough ally for Britain to centre her alliance system on, led Horace to argue that Britain, instead of seeking to regain the friendship of Austria (allied with France from late 1735 to early 1741), should turn elsewhere. A wide variety of schemes for alliances with Northern European powers had been suggested from 1735 onwards. Horace supported the idea of an alliance system based on Prussia and Russia.[64] He was a keen supporter of better Anglo-Prussian relations, views, thwarted by Hanoverian interests, that led to a loss of George II's favour. By 1738 he was disillusioned, and though he continued to expound his views and was consulted by the ministry, his influence diminished. His last mission, an attempt to win Dutch support in 1739, failed.[65]

It was widely believed that Robert Walpole took his views on foreign policy from Horace, and relied greatly upon him, or, in the early and mid-1720s, upon Townshend.[66] Walpole had no diplomatic experience and was bad at languages.[67] Foreign policy was neither his first concern nor his ministerial responsibility, nor was it his prime interest. Nevertheless, he played a role in the drafting of instructions, read despatches, conducted a confidential correspondence with Waldegrave at Paris, had frequent discussions with foreign envoys, and participated actively in Council discussions of foreign affairs. His correspondence and accounts of discussions with him leave no doubt that he possessed considerable knowledge and an ability to make perceptive points.[68]

Mocking him in the guise of a doctor, the *Craftsman*, the leading opposition London weekly, claimed, 'when he found himself absolute master of the profession here, nothing would satisfy his ambition, but the same arbitrary dominion over all the Physicians abroad . . .'[69] Such a view was inaccurate, for Walpole was totally opposed to an interventionist foreign policy. He had bitterly opposed Stanhope's Baltic and Mediterranean policies, and in 1736 told Chavigny, the French envoy, that he was at last free from the system that Stanhope had left him and that he had been obliged to follow hitherto.[70]

Walpole displayed an acute sensitivity, born of long parliamentary experience, to the interrelationships of foreign and domestic politics. He was well aware of the political and fiscal costs of interventionist policies, and feared that they would provoke foreign support for Jacobitism. In March 1718 in the Commons, attacking proposals to grant funds that would permit an anti-Spanish naval commitment, he spoke of the need to attempt to avoid war, the dangerously high level of the national debt, and the political dangers presented by levels of wartime taxation. In 1723 he acted with success as Secretary of State during the absence of the two Secretaries in Hanover. He wrote then to Newcastle of his opposition to 'very rash engagements' and, in the context of foreign policy, that 'my politicks are in a narrow compass . . . foreign disturbances . . . alone can confound us here'.[71]

Walpole was less keen on the French alliance than Horace and readier to subordinate diplomatic to parliamentary considerations: in the summer of 1730 he pressed a disagreeing Horace to be firm over Dunkirk.[72] In the first two years of his ministry Walpole's concern with foreign affairs was subordinated to the need to reintroduce fiscal and political stability after the South Sea Bubble, but thereafter it increased. Foreign policy was pushed to the fore by political struggles, both ministerial (with Carteret in 1723-4, Townshend in 1729-30), and with the opposition, which concentrated on foreign policy in the sessions in the second half of the 1720s, culminating in that of 1730 when the ministry was in danger of falling. Walpole was not responsible for the alliances of the 1720s: they stemmed, as with so much of that period, from the previous decade. His role in foreign policy increased in the 1730s. He met foreign envoys more frequently, and clearly dominated the two Secretaries for much of the decade. He was particularly, though in no way wholly, responsible for neutrality in the Polish Succession War and for the non-interventionist policy in subsequent years, both of which he believed to be in Britain's interests; for, in his eyes, it was impossible to separate domestic and foreign interests.[73]

In the last years of his ministry Walpole enjoyed less influence in foreign policy, though he continued seeing foreign envoys. He played a large role in the negotiation of Anglo-Spanish commercial differences in 1737-9 (Geraldino the Spanish envoy contrasted his ability favourably with that of other ministers),[74] but his policy, temporarily successful with the negotiation of the Convention of the Pardo and its passage through Parliament, failed as Britain drifted into war with Spain. Spain did not seek war either, but the compromises necessary to settle outstanding differences and to implement the Convention proved impossible, partly because of a lack of effort on the part of Spain which hoped for French support, partly because of the impact on British policy of ministerial differences against a background of popular and parliamentary pressure.

Opposed to conflict with Spain, Walpole did not wish to fight Prussia over Silesia, and the Austrians distrusted him. After Walpole's fall, Horace Mann, envoy in Florence, wrote, 'I am represented as an enemy to the Queen of Hungary and a disapprover of all strong resolutions to support her ... because I am a Walpoliano who was the greatest enemy she had. Is not this the most vile ingratitude to him, as all the steps in her favour were set on foot by him, and a large supply given while he was at the head of affairs, so that all that has been done since has only been a continuation of what he began?'[75]

In fact Walpole did not play a large role in foreign policy in the years 1740-2. He was responsible neither for the attempts in 1741 to settle Austro-Prussian differences nor for the negotiations for an anti-Bourbon alliance. The interventionism of these years, which was further stressed by the ministry that followed Walpole, was alien to his views, though there are no signs that he resisted policy developments. There was a major difference between the interventionism of the late 1720s and that of the early 1740s. In the latter case Britain was already at war with Spain, with the threat of France joining in on the Spanish side. Therefore a search for allies had a definite purpose, and Britain could hope to divert Bourbon attentions elsewhere.

In 1728 Britain was described as being ruled by a triumvirate: Walpole, Townshend and Newcastle.[76] The impact of other ministers on foreign policy was limited. Much discussion of policy appears to have taken place in *ad hoc* ministerial meetings and in meetings between ministers and the King, rather than in formal Councils. The latter were particularly important when the King was in Hanover. Reports of their views were sent to Hanover and are preserved in State Papers Regencies. Unfortunately they do not specify the views of individual ministers. Evidence for other periods is sparse. In a recent article Jubb has concluded, 'Nomenclature is clearly no guide to the status of a meeting under George I, and constitutional practice appears to have remained fluid ... The development under the early Hanoverians of the Cabinet and of the various committees of the Privy Council and of councillors. remains hazy'. It is clear from the surviving records – and the *Notes* kept by the Lord Chancellor Lord King are particularly useful – that Jubb's comments apply equally to the early years of George II's reign.[77] Commentators agreed in reporting that Councils were not of great importance. In 1718 the Prussian envoy Bonet reported that the 'Conseil de Cabinet' met only very rarely, and that all was handled in communications between King and ministers. A French memorandum of 1736 reported that the Privy Council was only consulted for form, whilst the French politician Villars, writing in 1729 of the project for peace with Spain, claimed that it had been concerted between George II and 'le Conseil d'Angleterre, c'est-a-dire proprement avec le Comte de Townshend ... et Robert Walpole. ...'[78]

The principal ministers took care to restrict discussion. In 1723 Walpole and Newcastle kept the Lord Justices, those responsible for administration in George I's absence, in the dark. In 1725, whilst Townshend was in Hanover, the 'only proper persons to be trusted' for discussing foreign affairs were a very small group: Lord King, the Duke of Devonshire (Lord President of the Council, 1725-9), the Earl of Berkeley (First Lord of the Admiralty, 1717-27), and the Earl of Godolphin, besides Newcastle and Walpole.[79] On 10 March 1726 a discussion of the arrangements for a subsidy treaty with Hesse-Cassel involved Townshend, Newcastle, Walpole, Devonshire, King and the Duke of Argyle, presumably for his military knowledge; those present on 21 June 1728, when James III's reception at Parma was discussed, were Walpole, Newcastle, Townshend, Devonshire, Godolphin and Lord Trevor (Lord Privy Seal, 1726-30). A small but varying group (not all of whom held ministerial office) emerges from the records, and no-one's presence appears to have been essential. Clearly composition was a sensitive issue. King recorded that Newcastle told a meeting on 16 May 1729 'that we would not tell anyone . . . of this, or of any other meeting that we should have, because there were some others that might expect, to whom it was not fit that everything should be known'. He named no-one, but it is possible he meant Wilmington and Carteret. Clearly Councils could witness discussions. King recorded a debate on 16 November 1730 over instructions for Waldegrave, and an Austrian agent in London claimed in January 1728 that Argyle and Walpole had differed over the retention of Gibraltar and the issue of war with Spain. However, the general picture is obscured by the absence of detailed records for council meetings.[80]

It is clear that the influence of ministers owed much to their personalties. Of the Lord Chancellors, Talbot (1733-7) appears not to have been involved in important discussions of foreign policy, King (1725-33) was involved but enjoyed little influence, whilst Hardwicke (1737-1756), a member of the inner circle of ministers who discussed policy, enjoyed great influence, particularly with Newcastle. Horace Walpole was important in the early 1730s though only Cofferer of the Household; the Duke of Grafton a frequent attender of important meetings though Lord Chamberlain (1724-57). Administrative hierarchies and delimitation were well developed in some areas of government, but not at all the highest levels. This was particularly so with foreign policy, an area of administration both inseparable from politics and subject to the unpredictabilities of royal control and intervention. The system of two Secretaries of State was defective, however valuable it might be in enabling one Secretary to go to Hanover or to cultivate his political interests, and in increasing the ministry's chances of finding able parliamentary defenders of foreign policy. Too often Secretaries complained of not knowing what was transpiring in the other office, and felt it necessary to engage in secret correspondence with British envoys. These were serious faults, particularly when the two Secretaries clashed, but they were merely part of a more general problem of administrative organisation at the highest political levels. The importance of personal ability and influence rather than simply of office was and is common to political systems. It is easy reading the disciplined diplomatic series to forget the more complex situation that produced them.

In October 1733 British ministers were able to read an intercepted report that claimed there were serious deficiencies in the British diplomatic service. The Danish envoy in London claimed that Britain was very badly informed of European events, and blamed this on her foreign service, asserting that when diplomats were appointed, no attention was paid to their merit or ability, but simply to the influence they, their friends and their relations possessed in Parliament. Furthermore, good service was not rewarded, a discouraging factor, and the ministry was unwilling to spend the necessary sums to create 'correspondances secrètes'. The following year the Tory leader in the Commons, Sir William Wyndham, bitterly attacked Walpole in Parliament: 'ignorant of the true interest of his country . . . in foreign affairs trusting none but such whose education makes it impossible for them to have such knowledge or such qualifications as can be of service to their country, or give any weight or credit to their negotiations'.[81]

Five years later the *Craftsman* attacked Keene, noting, 'in former times it was always usual, upon such important occasions, to employ men of the highest rank and eminence; who, by their dignity, might add a weight to their negotiations abroad; and, by their fortunes, give a pledge to their own country for the integrity of their conduct – this was certainly a wise precaution, which ought always to be observ'd; for a man of mean birth, and low fortune, may be tempted to sacrifice the publick interest to his own; or, at least, become the subservient tool of a minister, by whose indulgent hand he was rais'd'.[82]

In addition, individual diplomats were attacked: Keene for surrendering British interests during the Anglo-Spanish commercial negotiations in 1738-9; Horace Walpole for being duped by the French both in the late 1720s and during the War of the Polish Succession, and Waldegrave for being duped by the French.[83] When combined with those diplomats found wanting by the ministry, the list becomes an impressive one: William Finch a poor representative at The Hague who failed to note the Dutch move into neutrality in 1733;[84] the Earl of Essex (Turin, 1732-6) found Turin boring, constantly sought leave for travel, and complained about a lack of attention from London;[85] St. Saphorin (Vienna, 1718-27) played a major role in the deterioration of Anglo-Austrian relations;[86] Lord Tyrawly (Lisbon, 1728-41), whose intemperance had to be restrained frequently; Isaac Leheup (Stockholm, 1727), recalled in disgrace for being rude to the Prince of Wales; the Earl of Kinnoull (Constantinople, 1729-35), recalled after reiterated complaints that he was pro-French;[87] Du Bourgay (Berlin, 1724-30), reprimanded on several occasions for exceeding orders.[88] Furthermore envoys quarrelled, particularly with consular officials or others in the same post: Titley (Copenhagen) with the Consul at Elsinore; Tyrawly with Admiral Norris during the latter's stay in Portuguese waters (1735-7); Tyrawly's predecessor Dormer (1725-7) was recalled after a dispute with the Consul led to violence; Essex had a bitter feud with Edmund Allen, Secretary in Turin. Envoys also criticised the failure of their colleagues to keep them informed: 'I should, I think have done more service, if I had been once informed by Lord Hyndford. Egotisms are not enough in business', complained Robinson.[89]

One must add the problems inherent in eighteenth-century diplomacy. Poor communications meant not only that the arrival of letters was unpredictable as well as often late but also that envoys could only rarely return to Britain for discussions. The absence of distinct unpolitical foreign policy institutions and the close relationship in most countries of foreign policy and domestic politics meant that diplomats in many countries, including Britain, had to face difficult questions. Should they seek to lend support to domestic opponents of governments following antagonistic policies? Edward Finch ended his Swedish mission (1728-39) disastrously through so doing. Should they seek to gain the support of the reversionary interest? Instructions were often ambiguous and outdated.[90]

Diplomats were rarely career civil servants. Many were MPs, a few were Peers; most hoped that foreign service would earn them promotion, usually at home. William Stanhope, MP, was a classic success story, gaining a Secretaryship as other diplomats did – Methuen, Craggs, Carteret, Robinson, Townshend – and sought to do – Chesterfield. Promotion, however, was often to posts where diplomatic experience was of no value. Edward Finch, MP, returned from Russia to become Groom of the Bedchamber, Abraham Stanyan returned from Constantinople to become a Commissioner of the Privy Seal. Diplomats were royal servants who owed their promotion often to ministers other than the Secretary with whom they corresponded: Keene, Mann, Robinson and Leheup were Walpole connections, Essex and Waldegrave royal favourites. Relations could be poor: Newcastle and Waldegrave did not get on, and Newcastle's cousin, Thomas Pelham, was appointed Secretary of Embassy at Paris, a move Waldegrave resented.[91] Sometimes envoys had to be recalled or dismissed for failing to follow ministerial policy: Kinnoull from Constantinople, Henry Davenant (Envoy Extraordinary to several Italian states, 1714-22) for supporting Austria. Pay was often insufficient and in arrears; many diplomats felt neglected and were worried about their promotion prospects, and whether they would ever be 'quiet and snug in Vatterlandt'.[92]

The use of foreigners, Germans, Swiss and Huguenots, had been common under George I. It aroused some criticism, but ceased to be an issue by the late 1720s. The two powerful Swiss diplomats, Schaub (Paris, 1718, 1721-4) and St. Saphorin, lost their postings and thereafter enjoyed less influence. Plans in 1727 to give several Hanoverians responsibility for British and Hanoverian interests only materialised for the Stockholm posting, where Baron Diescau, the Hanoverian envoy, represented Britain from late 1727 until October 1728. Subsequently Diescau fell foul of Edward Finch and was recalled in 1730 partly due to Finch's complaints.[93]

Enthusiasm for a diplomatic career was not widespread in Britain, and this seriously limited the choice of diplomat available. It was widely held in Europe that senior posts should be given only to those of high social rank, a view apparently shared by George II who, to show his friendship and regard for Charles Emmanuel III, sent Essex to Turin in 1732, the first British envoy to the court with the rank of Ambassador. Choosing aristocrats did of course limit the field.[94]

Aside from Horace Walpole (and James Stanhope in the late 1710s, who acted as a diplomat whilst Secretary), no diplomat of this period enjoyed the independence that was to be claimed by Harris. Partly this was due to ministerial stability and experience, both of which were in shorter supply later in the century, partly possibly to firmer royal control. Obstreperous diplomats were disciplined: the Earl of Stair (Paris, 1715-20) was removed because his criticisms of French policy were held to be endangering the alliance.[95] Clearly domestic commitments and awareness of the problem of distance led the Secretaries to allow much independence to the diplomats. The Undersecretary in the Northern Department, George Tilson, wrote, 'I don't see by your relations that you wanted any instructions. You on the spot with those just notions of the true state of affairs will always act better than we can bid you from hence, unless something new should arise'.[96] This was certainly true for unimportant postings, and for periods when the ministry had no particular policy to advance. In opposite cases supervision was close. A courier could easily go to Paris or The Hague from London and return in a week.

What was termed later in the century 'the English plan' of diplomacy, negotiating through British envoys abroad rather than foreign envoys in London, had clear attractions: it was usually easier for ministers to control negotiations and to limit the impact of British domestic politics on them. However, it did lead to more reliance being placed on British envoys, and not all were equal to the task. The 'English plan' was not followed fully in this period: the British negotiations in 1733 to end Austro-Spanish differences were handled in London, while the British attempts to end the War of the Polish Succession were negotiated primarily in London and The Hague, not Vienna, Turin, Paris and Madrid.

The criticisms advanced by the Danish envoy in 1733 must be qualified. Patronage played a major role in appointments, hardly unusual in eighteenth-century British or continental governments. Success was at times richly rewarded: Robinson and Harrington would probably never have risen to senior ministerial positions but for their diplomatic services. Most diplomats filed regular and comprehensive reports. If they tended to concentrate on court and ministerial factions, this was both something they shared with other diplomatic services, and an understandable response to the sources of power and policy. Most British and European diplomats devoted little attention to broader social and political developments; they lacked the resources to do so, the information was not readily available, and it was generally believed to be of slight significance. Many years' reading in all the diplomatic series in the Public Record Office leads one to the conclusion that most British diplomats in the period were conscientious reporters and worthy, rather than brilliant, negotiators. Lapses occurred, but on the whole London was well informed of the policies of other governments. Warnings or advance information were given about many of the surprising international moves of the period: the Sardinian alliance with France of 1733, the Austro-French peace of 1735. The ministry was also prepared to spend to create 'correspondances secrètes'. The attempt to develop one with the French foreign minister Chauvelin failed, but the French diplomat and foreign office official Bussy provided much reliable information. The excellent British postal interception and decyphering system yielded much information. The diplomatic service was no professional entity but it served reasonably well.[97]

In 1713 Abraham Stanyan, a career diplomat, wrote to Secretary of State Bolingbroke, 'I have long been of opinion that our management of foreign affairs has been very loose and negligent, and that no part of our civil administration had greater need of redress'.[98] Aside from the abortive attempt to train diplomats at Oxbridge,[99] things were no different by the time of Walpole's ministry, nor were they altered during it. Stanyan's worthy reform scheme was alien to the nature of early eighteenth-century administration. Before passing judgement on the Secretaryships and the diplomats, it is worth noting that the system was little better elsewhere. Most diplomats owed their appointment to patronage; pay was often in arrears and rank at a premium; aristocratic amateurs were not always a success. States might possess a single foreign ministry, but many ministers corresponded in secret with envoys and conducted what was in effect a personal foreign policy. This was true of Prussia's Grumbkow, France's Chauvelin, various Saxon ministers, and Austria's Eugene and Sinzendorf. The British system was not notably worse than that of any other major European power. Indeed, whatever the impact of Parliament and public opinion upon the formulation of foreign policy, the conduct of diplomacy was not noticeably different to that of other European powers.

NOTES

1. Sir James Harris, Envoy Extraordinary at The Hague, to Joseph Ewart, in charge of affairs at Berlin, 15 Mar. (ns) 1785, 3rd Earl of Malmesbury (ed.) *Diaries and Correspondence of James Harris, First Earl of Malmesbury* (4 vols., 1844), II, 112-13.

2. Anon. to Waldegrave, undated [1734-5?], Chewton, The writing could be that of John Couraud, Undersecretary in the Southern Department, and could refer to the attempt to arrange a negotiated settlement of the War of the Polish Succession.

3. D. B. Horn, *The British Diplomatic Service, 1689-1789* (Oxford, 1961); M. A. Thomson, *The Secretaries of State, 1681-1782* (1932).

4. Anon., *An explanatory account of the nature; and business of the several offices in England* (1727), p. 59.

5. Whitworth to Tilson, 26 Mar. (ns) 1720, 22 Mar. (ns) 1721, PRO. 90/12-13; Pulteney to Lord Grange, 25 Aug. 1735, HMC., *Mar and Kellie*, p. 539; anon. French memorandum, 5 July (ns) 1736, AE. MD. Ang. 6 f. 108; Hervey to Ilchester, 22 June 1728, BL. Add. 51345; B. Williams, *Stanhope*, p. 445.

6. Gibson to Nicolson, 12 Ap. 1724, Bodl. Ms. A. 269; Newcastle to Townshend, 5 July 1723, BL. Add. 32686; Destouches to Dubois, 8 Ap. (ns), 17 May (ns), Chammorel to Dubois, 10 June (ns), Chavigny to Morville, 5 Sept. (ns), 21 Oct. (ns), 17 Nov. (ns), Morville to Chavigny, 18 Oct. (ns) 1723, Broglie to Morville, 20 July (ns) 1724, AE. CP. Ang. 344-6, 348.

7. On Townshend's superiority to Newcastle as a minister, anon. French memorandum, 31 Dec. (ns) 1728, AE. CP. Ang. 364.

8. Waldegrave journal, 8 Dec. (ns) 1727, Chewton; Le Connu to [Tilson] 8 Oct. (ns) 1728, PRO. 107/10; Chammorel to Chauvelin, 7 May (ns) 1730, AE. CP. Ang. 370.

9. Sauveterre, French envoy in Berlin, to Chauvelin, 30 Mar. (ns) 1728, AE. CP. Prusse, 87; Townshend to Waldegrave, 9 July 1728, 31 Oct. 1729 (quote), PRO. 80/61, 65. Townshend had a confidential correspondence with Slingelandt, Chavigny to Chauvelin, 21 Oct. (ns) 1723, AE. CP. Ang. 346; Townshend to Slingelandt, 9 Jan. 1730, PRO. 84/581.

10. Destouches to Dubois, 30 Ap. (ns) 1722, Chavigny to Morville, 5 Sept. (ns), 15 Oct. (ns) 1723, AE. CP. Ang. 341, 346; Townshend to St. Saphorin, 8 Feb. 1723, 30 June 1724, PRO. 80/48; Townshend to William Finch, 18 Mar. 1726, PRO. 84/289; Townshend to Horace Walpole, 23 June 1728, Bradfer Lawrence.

11. Townshend to Horace Walpole, 21 Aug. 1727, BL. Add. 48982; Lodge review of Vaucher, *EHR* 40 (1925), p. 440.

12. Townshend to Chesterfield, 6 Sept. 1728, PRO. 84/301.

13. Chammorel to Morville, 11 Mar. (ns) 1726, AE. CP. Ang. 354; Townshend to St. Saphorin, 14 Jan. 1726. Townshend to Chesterfield, 29 Ap. 1729, PRO. 80/57, 84/304; Townshend to Horace Walpole, 22 Aug. 1728, BL. Add. 32757.

14. D'Aix to Victor Amadeus II, 21 Ap. (ns), 9 May (ns) 1728, AST. LM. Ing. 35.

15. Townshend to Waldegrave, 16 Feb. 1729, PRO. 80/64.

16. Gibson to Hare, Bishop of Chichester, 10 Aug. 1736, N. Sykes, *Edmund Gibson, Bishop of London* (Oxford, 1926), p. 407.

17. Townshend to George II, undated, BL. Add. 38507 f. 230.

18. Newcastle to Horace Walpole, 2 Ap., 19 June 1724, Newcastle to Townshend, 21 July 1725, BL. Add. 32738, 32739, 32687; Newcastle to Hardwicke, 14 Oct. 1739, BL. Add. 35046.

19. Coxe, I, 335.

20. Cortanze, Sardinian envoy in London, reporting Carteret's low opinion of Stanhope, to Victor Amadeus, 13 Ap. (ns) 1722, AST. LM. Ing. 31.

21. Le Coq to Augustus II, 28 July (ns), 11 Aug. (ns) 1728, Dresden, 2733.

22. Tilson to Waldegrave, 19 Sept. 1729, Chewton; Stephen Kinsky and Fonseca to Charles VI, 5 Mar. (ns) 1730, C. Höfler, *Der Congress von Soissons* (2 vols., Vienna, 1871, 1876), II, 108; Stanhope to Newcastle, 1 July (ns) 1728, BL. Add. 32756.

23. Stephen Kinsky and Fonseca to Charles VI, 28 Nov. (ns) 1729, 9 Jan. (ns) 1730, Charles VI to Stephen Kinsky, Fonseca and Königsegg, 27 Aug. (ns) 1730, Höfler, *Congress* I, 361, II, 28, 260; Zamboni to Saxon minister Count Manteuffel, 18 Jan. (ns) 1729, Bodl. Rawl. 120; Chauvelin to Chammorel, 27 Nov. (ns) 1730, AE. CP. Ang. sup. 8; Stanhope to Newcastle, 9 Dec. (ns) 1728, Harrington and Poyntz to Newcastle, 2 June (ns) 1730, BL. Add. 32759, 32767; Philip Kinsky to Eugene, 25 Feb. (ns), 16 Ap. (ns) 1729, HHStA. GK. 94(b).

24. Newcastle to Horace Walpole, 2 June 1727, BL. Add. 32750; Zamboni to Landgrave of Hesse-Darmstadt, 16 Dec. (ns) 1727, Bodl. Rawl. 119; H. Duff, *Culloden Papers* (1815), p. 356; Earl of Ailesbury to his brother, 10 Dec. (ns) 1727, Trowbridge, Wiltshire R. O., Savernake Mss, 1300 X 691.

25. Newcastle to Stanhope, 3 June, Stanhope to Newcastle, 8 June (ns) 1728, Coxe, II, 629, 626-7.

26. Harrington to Newcastle, 19 May (ns) 1730, BL. Add. 32767; Reichenbach to Grumbkow, 19 May (ns) 1730, Hotham DDHO 3/3.

27. Henry Davenant, former British diplomat, correspondent of Prince Eugene, to Eugene, 24 Ap. (ns) 1733, HHStA. GK. 75(b); Degenfeld to Grumbkow, 28 Ap. (ns) 1733, PRO. 107/11; Gansinot to Törring, 22 Jan. (ns) 1734, Munich, KS 17326; Philip Kinsky to Austrian minister Count Sinzendorf, 27 Ap. (ns) 1736, PRO. 100/11.

28. Hervey, pp. 174, 345-6; Thomson, *Secretaries of State*, pp. 18, 159.

29. D'Aubenton, French commercial agent in Spain, to Maurepas, French Minister of the Marine, 3 Nov. (ns) 1729, AN.B⁷299; Dowager Countess of Portland to Count Bentinck, 24 Feb. 1730, BL. Eg. 1715; Watsdorf to Augustus II, 23 Oct. (ns) 1731, Dresden, 2676 II; Gansinot, Wittelsbach agent at The Hague, to Törring, 15 July (ns) 1732, Munich, KB 17321.

30. John to Danish minister Rosencrantz, 5 May (ns), Hop, Dutch envoy in London, to Dutch minister Fagel, 25 Aug. (ns) 1733, PRO. 107/12, 15.

31. Rantzau, Danish envoy, to Rosencranz, 18 Mar. (ns) 1732, PRO. 107/5; Tilson to Titley, 4 May 1736, BL. Eg. 2683; Ossorio to Charles Emmanuel, 11 Nov. (ns) 1737, AST. LM. Ing. 44.

32. Newcastle to Robert Walpole, 13 Nov. 1734, Coxe, III, 209.

33. Horace Walpole to the Queen, undated [early 1735], CUL. CH. corresp. 2398; Ossorio to Charles Emmanuel, 9 Mar. (ns) 1733, AST. LM Ing. 40.

34. Whitworth, Minister Plenipotentiary at The Hague, to Bothmer, 18 Feb. (ns), Whitworth to Cadogan, 5 Ap. (ns) 1718, BL. Add. 37367; Whitworth to Tilson, 9 Jan. (ns),

16 May (ns) 1720, 2 Nov. (ns) 1721, Whitworth to Townshend, 18 Mar. (ns), 3 May (ns) 1721, PRO. 90/11-15; Whitworth to Bothmer, 2 May (ns) 1722, BL. Add. 37388; Townshend to William Finch. 26 July 1726, PRO. 84/291; Townshend to Horace Walpole, 16 May 1728, Bradfer Lawrence; Robinson to Weston, 23 July (ns) 1733, PRO. 80/97; Delafaye to Waldegrave, 24 July 1733, Chewton.

35. Harrington to William Finch, 4 May, William Finch to Harrington, 26 May (ns) 1733, PRO. 84/323; Robinson to Harrington, 3 June (ns) 1733, PRO. 80/96.

36. Chauvelin to Chavigny, 29 Sept. (ns) 1735, AE. CP. Aug. 392; Newcastle to Horace Walpole, 3 Sept. 1734, BL. Add. 32785; Hervey, pp. 345-6.

37. Robinson to Newcastle, 20 May (ns) 1732, BL. Add. 32777.

38. Newcastle to Hardwicke, 15 Aug. 1741, BL. Add. 35406.

39. R. Browning, *The Duke of Newcastle* (New Haven, 1975).

40. Horace Walpole to Newcastle, 18 June (ns) 1727, BL. Add. 32750; Bussy to Amelot, 26 July (ns) 1737, AE. CP. Ang. 395; Horace Walpole to Trevor, 10 Jan. 1738, Trevor, 10; Ossorio to Charles Emmanuel, 12 Oct. (ns) 1742, AST. LM. Ing. 48.

41. Prince of Wales to Hervey, undated [winter 1730-1], West Suffolk CRO., Hervey papers, 941/47/1; Broglie to Chauvelin, 28 Nov. (ns) 1729, AE. CP. Ang. 367.

42. Clark, *Dynamics of Change;* Baxter, 'The conduct of the Seven Years War', *England's Rise to Greatness,* pp. 323-48; Lenman, *The Jacobite Risings in Britain, 1689-1746* (1980), p. 262.

43. Delafaye to Waldegrave, 19 Ap. 1733, Chewton; Newcastle to Essex, 27 Aug. 1733, BL. Add. 32782; Horace Walpole to Trevor, 23 Jan. 1738, Trevor, 10.

44. Thomas Pelham to Waldegrave, 8 Dec. 1733, Chewton; Essex to Henry Pelham, 21 Sept. (ns) 1733, BL. Add. 32782; Newcastle to Waldegrave, 7 May 1731, BL. Add. 32772.

45. Chammorel to Morville, 1 May (ns), Broglie to Morville, 29 June (ns) 1724, AE. CP. Ang. 347, 348; Newcastle to John Hedges, Envoy Extraordinary in Turin, 27 May 1727, PRO. 92/32. In 1723 Newcastle wrote to Robert Walpole of 'the hatred France must have to England', 25 Aug. BL. Add. 32686.

46. Newcastle to Robinson, 19 Ap. 1732, BL. Add. 32776; Chavigny to Chauvelin, 21 Ap. (ns) 1732, AE. CP. Ang. 377.

47. Degenfeld to Frederick William I, 31 July (ns) 1733, PRO. 107/14; Chavigny to Chauvelin, 30 July (ns), 24 Oct. 1733, 2 Aug. (ns) 1734, AE. CP. Ang. 381-2, 387.

48. Newcastle to Hardwicke, 25 Oct. 1740, P. Yorke, *The Life and Correspondence of Philip Yorke, Earl of Hardwicke* (3 vols., 1913), I, 251.

49. Newcastle to Hardwicke, 30 Sept. 1739, BL. Add. 35406. Horace Walpole to Newcastle, 13 Ap. 1740, BL. Add. 32693.

50. Newcastle to Hardwicke, 9 Jan. 1740, BL. Add. 35406; Newcastle to Harrington, 11 July 1740, BL. Add. 32693.

51. Newcastle to Horace Walpole, 3 Sept. 1734, BL. Add. 32785; Ossorio to Charles Emmanuel, 5 June (ns) 1744, AST. LM. Ing. 50. 'It is known here that tho' the Secretaries of State have their respective departments in England, yet there is a constant communication of counsels and opinions . . .' Robinson to Harrington, 2 May (ns) 1731, PRO. 80/73.

52. Townshend to Horace Walpole, 10 Oct. 1728, BL. Add. 9138.

53. Keene to Robert Walpole, 24 Ap. (ns) 1739, CUL. CH. corresp. 2860.

54. Delafaye to Horace Walpole, 14 May, Newcastle to Stanhope, 14 May, 3 June, 1728, Coxe, II, 623, 623-4, 629; Townshend to Horace, 21 Aug. 1727, 29 Oct. 1728, BL. Add. 48982, Bradfer Lawrence; Townshend to George II, undated, – July 1728, BL. Add. 38507 f. 230, 245.

55. Chavigny to Chauvelin, 29 Jan. (ns) 1732, AE. CP. Ang. 376; Saladin, Hanoverian envoy in Paris, to Hattorf, 13 July (ns) 1733, Hanover, Calenberg Brief Archiv 24, Nr. 2002;

Wachtendonck, Palatine envoy in London, to Karl Philipp, 17 Sept. (ns) 1733, Munich, KB. 84/40; Robinson to Horace, 7 Feb. (ns) 1730, BL. Add. 9139.

56. Horace to Robinson, 19 Nov. (ns) 1735, BL. Add. 23796; Horace to Trevor, 30 Jan. 1741, Trevor, 25; Horace to Waldegrave, 26 Mar. 1736, Chewton.

57. Horace to Newcastle, 26 Aug. (ns) 1735, BL. Add. 32788; Horace to Robert Walpole, 29 Oct. (ns) 1734, Coxe, III, 201.

58. Anon., *The True History of Dr. Robin Sublimate, and his Associates; or Bob turn'd Physician* (1729), p. 25; Anon., *Political Dialogues between the celebrated statues of Pasquin and Marsorio* (1736), p. 5; *Champion,* 3 June 1740; *Craftsman,* 6 Jan., 9 Sept. 1727, 20 July 1734.

59. Horace to Robert Walpole, 17 July (ns), 16 Aug. (ns) 1730, Robinson to Horace, 3 Feb. (ns), (quote) 1731, Coxe, III, 6, 18-21, 81; Horace to Newcastle, 10 Sept. (ns) 1730, BL. Add. 32769.

60. Horace to Newcastle, 20 Nov. (ns) 1723, BL. Add. 32686; Horace to Poyntz, 4 Nov. (ns) 1729, Coxe, II, 659, 662-3.

61. Chavigny to Chauvelin, 9 Nov. (ns) 1733, AE. CP. Ang. 382; Ossorio to Charles Emmanuel, 25 Feb. (ns) 1734, AST. LM. Ing. 41.

62. Ossorio to Charles Emmanuel, 13 Mar. (ns) 1735, AST. LM. Ing. 42; Chavigny to Chauvelin, 28 July (ns) 1734, AE. CP. Ang. 387.

63. Horace to Waldegrave, 24 Mar. 1737, Chewton; Horace to Trevor, 6 Jan. 1738, Trevor, 10.

64. Horace to Hardwicke, 10 Oct. 1740, BL. Add. 35586.

65. Horace to Trevor, 24 Oct. 1738, Trevor, 15.

66. Palm to Charles VI, 13 Dec. (ns) 1726, CUL. CH. corresp. 1379; Chavigny to Morville, 20 Ap. (ns) 1724, Chammorel to Chauvelin, 13 July (ns) 1730, AE. CP. Ang. 347, 370; anon. memorandum, 16 Nov. (ns) 1734, HHStA. Varia 8.

67. Memorandum for Cambis, 4 Mar. (ns) 1737, AE. CP. Ang. 394; Haslang to Törring, 24 Feb. (ns), 27 Mar. (ns) 1741, Munich, KS. 17211.

68. King, 24 July 1725, pp. 14-15; Walpole to Newcastle, 24 June 1730, PRO. 36/19; Walpole to Waldegrave, 1 Jan. 1736, Chewton.

69. *Craftsman,* 4 May 1728.

70. Bonet to Frederick William, 29 Mar. (ns) 1718, Merseburg, 41; Chavigny to Chauvelin, 19 Jan. (ns) 1736, AE. CP. Ang. 393.

71. Walpole to Newcastle, 25 July, 31 Aug. 1723, BL. Add. 3268b.

72. Robert Walpole to Newcastle, 3 July 1730, BL. Add. 32687.

73. Black, 'An "Ignoramus" in European Affairs?', *British Journal for Eighteenth-Century Studies* 6 (1983); Coxe, I, 445-6; Diemar to Eugene, 7 Dec. (ns) 1734, HHStA. GK. 85a; Wasner, Austrian envoy in London, to Count Harrach, Austrian Minister, 4 Oct. (ns) 1737, HHStA. EK. 72; Bussy, French envoy in London, to Amelot, 23 Feb. (ns) 1737, AE. CP. Ang. 394.

74. Geraldino to the Spanish Minister Torrenueva, 19 Dec. (ns) 1737, PRO. 94/246.

75. Mann to Horace Walpole, 1 Jan. (ns) 1743, W. Lewis (ed.), *Walpole-Mann Correspondence* II (1955), p. 126.

76. Anon., 'Mémoire sur l'état présent de la Grande Bretagne', 31 Dec. (ns) 1728, AE. CP. Ang. 364.

77. M. Jubb, 'The Cabinet in the Reign of George I', *BIHR* 55 (1982), p. 110. For France, M. Antoine, *Le Conseil du Roi sous le Regne de Louis XV* (Geneva, 1970).

78. Bonet to Frederick William, 25 Jan. (ns) 1718, Merseburg, 41; anon. memorandum, 5 July (ns) 1736, AE. MD. Ang. 6; Marquis de Vogüé (ed.), *Mémoires du Maréchal de Villars* (6 vols., Paris, 1884-1904), V. 115.

79. Robert Walpole to Newcastle, 2 Aug., Newcastle to Robert Walpole, 22 Oct. 1723, BL. Add. 32686; Newcastle to Robert Walpole, 7 Sept. 1725, PRO. 35/58.

80. 21 June 1728, PRO. 36/7; King, pp. 27, 86, 118-19; Visconti to Sinzendorf, 13 Jan. (ns) 1728, HHStA. EK. 65.

81. John to Christian VI of Denmark, 16 Oct. (ns) 1733, PRO. 107/7; Wyndham, 13 Mar. 1734, James Erskine MP., 14 Feb. 1735, Cobbett, IX, 465, 822.

82. *Craftsman*, 7 July, 15 Sept. (quote) 1739.

83. Earl of Bristol to his son, Lord Hervey, 15 Oct. 1740, Horace Walpole to Trevor, 28 Ap. 1741, Trevor, 27.

84. Harrington to Finch, 5 June 1733, PRO. 84/232; Charles VI to Kinsky, 7 Jan. (ns) 1734, PRO. 107/19.

85. Essex to Waldegrave, 4 July (ns) 1733, 18 Ap. (ns), 4 July (ns) 1734, Chewton; Newcastle to Essex, – Oct. 1734, BL. Add. 32786 ff. 61-4.

86. Waldegrave to Newcastle, 5 Feb. (ns) 1728, BL. Add. 32754; Wackerbarth, Saxon envoy in Vienna, to Augustus II, 11 June (ns) 1729, Dresden, 3331.

87. Newcastle to Kinnoull, 16 May 1735, PRO. 97/27; Harrington to Newcastle, 27 July (ns) 1735, PRO. 43/87.

88. Townshend to Du Bourgay, 19 Sept. 1727, 25 Nov. 1729, PRO. 90/22, 25; George II to Townshend, undated, Coxe, II, 534.

89. Robinson to Weston, 25 May (ns) 1741, PRO. 80/145.

90. Whitworth to Tilson, 29 Ap. (ns), 24 June (ns) 1721, PRO. 90/14; Richard Sutton, envoy in Cassel and Wolfenbüttel, 7 Oct. (ns) 1728, to Townshend, PRO. 81/122; Finch to Harrington, 20 Feb. (ns) 1739, PRO. 95/84.

91. Thomas Pelham to Robinson, 24 Dec. (ns) 1730, BL. Add. 23780; Thomas Pelham to Delafaye, 2 May (ns) 1731, PRO. 78/198; Chavigny to Chauvelin, 14 May (ns) 1733, AE. CP. Ang. 380.

92. Trevor to Robinson, 7 July (ns) 1736, BL. Add. 23798.

93. Le Coq to Augustus II, 15, 19 Aug. (ns), 31 Oct. (ns) 1727, Dresden, 2676, 18a; Delafaye to Horace Walpole, 1 Sept. 1727, PRO. 78/187; Finch to Townshend, 22 Ap. (ns), Finch to Newcastle, 10 June (ns), Finch to Harrington, 9 Sept. (ns) 1730, PRO. PRO. 95/54-6; Diemar to General Verschuer, minister of Frederick I of Sweden, 1 Sept. (ns) 1730, Marburg, 199.

94. Allen to Newcastle, 9 Aug. (ns) 1732, PRO. 92/34; Wachtendonck to Karl Philipp, 13 Feb. (ns) 1733, Munich, KB. 84/40.

95. Destouches to Dubois, 15 Dec. (ns) 1718, AE. CP. Ang. 311; Craggs to Stair, 25 Jan. 1720, SRO. GD. 135/141/24 16.

96. Tilson to Robinson, 7 July 1730, BL. Add. 23780.

97. K. Ellis, 'British Communication and Diplomacy in the Eighteenth-Century', *BIHR* 31 (1958).

98. 'Reflections upon the Management of our Foreign Affairs', PRO. 96/15.

99. M. Braubach, *Die Geheimdiplomatie des Prinzen Eugen von Savoyen* (Cologne, 1962); K. Müller, *Das Kaiserliche Gesandtschaftswesen im Jahrhundert nach dem Westfalischen Frieden, 1648-1740* (Bonn, 1976), pp. 46-8, 222-6.

CHAPTER 4

Parliament and Foreign Policy

'He said the King and his ministers were as absolute now and could manage the Parliament as easyly as the Emperor or French King can do their respective subjects'.

Austrian Chancellor Count Sinzendorf, as reported by Waldegrave[1]

'I did, at one time, propose to have laid before you, for your further satisfaction, a short abstract of the Proceedings of every session of the present Parliament; and had indeed, not without some trouble, digested and prepared the principal events for your perusal: but finding, that such recital of parliamentary proceedings could not but be attended with dryness, and perhaps an appearance of tediousness, which by all means I should wish to avoid, . . .'

Earl of Marchmont, *A Serious Exhortation to the Electors of Great Britain* (1740), p. 35.

In the early eighteenth century Britain was sometimes described by European commentators as a republic. Royal authority was seen as severely constrained both by constitutional and more general political factors. The inability of the monarch to prevent Parliament both from rejecting legislation he supported, such as the excise proposals of 1733, and ministers he still had confidence in, such as Walpole in 1742, lent substance to interpretations of the British political system that stressed monarchical weakness. Contemporary evaluations of the constitution centred on Parliament. Given the fact that Parliament sat for less than half the year, and that the Court, rather than Parliament, was often the centre of ministerial activities, this might appear surprising. Furthermore, in the field of foreign policy, the area that attracted most foreign interest, Parliament's right to intervene was constitutionally limited greatly by the royal prerogative. The King had the right of making peace and war, signing treaties without any need for prior consultation, appointing and dismissing Secretaries of State and diplomats, giving them instructions and receiving their reports. Parliament's major function in the field of foreign policy was the voting of the funds necessary for the military forces, British and foreign, and the subsidy treaties, that were expected to give substance to foreign policy. In the age of Walpole such funds were always voted as requested.

To devote so much attention to Parliament might appear surprising therefore. Furthermore, many European politicians and diplomats argued that the Walpole ministry so thoroughly controlled Parliament that it had ceased to be of any independent importance in the field of foreign policy. The standard opposition argument, that the ministry controlled both Houses through the widespread distribution of places and pensions, was repeated by many diplomats. 'Gold continues still a great majority', wrote Sarah Marlborough in 1727. Four years later Noodle (Walpole) declared in a ballad,

75

> The House shall my conduct approve,
> I have most of them under my Thumb.
>
> Whilst Pensions and Bribes do prevail,
> And a R-v-r-nd B-nch will stand by me.

These themes were repeated by diplomats, the Austrian Palm in 1726, the Sardinian D'Aix in 1728, and French envoys – Chammorel, Broglie and Chavigny – throughout the period.[2] Foreign statesmen argued often that through their control of Parliament the British ministry could obtain what they wished, however difficult or inconvenient. Several, such as the French foreign minister Dubois in 1722, condemned the British ministry for using Parliament as 'une exclusion facile' for whatever they did not wish to do. In 1728 the leading Dutch statesman Slingelandt pressed the British ministry to bring the return of Gibraltar before Parliament 'where His Majesty's influence was known to be sufficient to make it pass; . . .' Two years later the French foreign minister Chauvelin, replying to British ministry claims that they would be unable to persuade Parliament to vote a subsidy for Bavaria, agreed that it would require careful management, but noted that the ministry could obtain support for more difficult proposals when it suited them.[3]

In such an interpretation Parliament was of little significance: most parliamentarians displayed little independence. In 1729 the *Craftsman* in a list of animals for sale included 'Above two hundred fine talking Parrots . . . They all say Yes or No, as their Master bids them, upon the least Nod or Wink of the Eye'.[4] Furthermore, it has been claimed that parliamentary debates on foreign policy were of low calibre. Chesterfield thought so, and recently Jones has stated that 'Wilful misrepresentation of facts, sensationalism and pandering to popular prejudices, partisanship and appeals to xenophobia characterised most parliamentary debates'.[5] This chapter will advance a different view. It will be suggested that Parliament's independence can be underestimated, that parliamentary views on foreign policy were held to be of great importance and that the standards of debate were far from abysmal.

I

During the recent lengthy wars with France Parliament had acquired a position of considerable importance in the field of foreign policy. As two pamphleteers wrote in 1730, 'As to the right of making peace and war, the same is allowed and granted to be part of the King's high prerogative, tho' we find that the wisest of our monarchs have very rarely enter'd into any war without the approbation and consent of their parliaments: for who can give better and more wholesome advice and counsel in such arduous affairs?'

'Tho' the making of peace is acknowledged to be within the prerogative of the Crown, yet it will most certainly be brought before you for your Approbation; which ministers always esteem to be some kind of security for them . . .'[6]

In practice there were disagreements over the extent to which Parliament could and should advise and enquire into the conduct of foreign policy, and the King could ignore advice. Thus, the ministerial weekly paper, the *London Journal,* claimed, 'if 'tis Right in the King to break, vary from, or not execute a Treaty when the Parliament tells him, that 'tis against the Interest of the Nation; 'tis certainly equally Right for him to break, vary from, or not execute the Treaty, when he perceives it to be against the Good of the Nation, whether the Parliament tells him so or not. For 'tis the Duty of the Father of his People, to act always for the Good of his People'.[7] On the whole the ministry sought to defeat suggestions that Parliament's scope should be extended. In 1731 there was anger at Chauvelin's suggestion 'that he would not engage with England unless the Parliament was bound for the execution of the agreements . . .'; four years later Horace Walpole criticised Parliament for exposing the military weakness of the British West Indies; and in 1739, Newcastle was at pains to avoid letting it appear that Parliament was instructing envoys.[8] The ministry did not deny Parliament's right to call for diplomatic papers, but claimed, correctly, that it was troublesome, exposed foreign sources and angered foreign powers.[9] They also resisted opposition suggestions, such as that of the Tory leader Sir William Wyndham in 1739: 'We have long tried what can be done by ministers; let us now try what can be done by Parliament'.[10]

However, it would be mistaken to suggest that ministers sought to deny Parliament opportunities to express views on foreign policy. Ministers were well aware that parliamentary approval could bolster their hand, both at home and abroad. In 1740 a ministerial paper setting out options on policy, in a difficult international situation, included 'to lay the whole before the Parliament, and take their opinion thereupon'.[11] The ministry argued that success in Parliament would help their negotiations, 'our parliamentary affairs have been opened with great success, and there never was a fairer prospect of a prosperous session than there is at present, the weight of which your Excellencys will find in all your negotiations'. Envoys were instructed to spread accounts of parliamentary successes, and the ministry used the argument of needing to impress foreign powers when seeking to win parliamentary support.[12] In his speech at the opening of the 1728 session George II, speaking of the prospect of peace, claimed, 'I am satisfied that nothing will more effectively contribute to, and secure this desirable end, than such an unanimity, zeal, and dispatch of the publick business in this Parliament, as may convince the world, that none among you are capable, out of any views or considerations whatsoever, to wish the distress of their country, or to give an occasion, from the prospect of difficulties that may arise, and be fomented here at home, to interrupt or disappoint our present promising expectations . . .'

In 1740 Lord Chancellor Hardwicke spoke in the Lords of 'the weight His Majesty's councils may have at present with the several courts of Europe: and can anything add to this weight so much as a prevailing opinion abroad, that there subsists an entire harmony between His Majesty and his Parliament; that his people place an entire confidence in his wisdom and conduct; and that the whole power of the British nation will be applied as he shall think fit to direct it?'

These ministerial statements, and those that appeared in press and pamphlets,[13] were not simply attempts to create parliamentary quiescence. The ministry was well aware both from intercepts and from conversations that foreign envoys devoted great attention to Parliament. In addition British envoys reported regularly upon the attention displayed by foreign governments. In 1728 Keene reported the Queen of Spain reading the addresses of both Houses with great attention. Two years later Waldegrave, envoy in Paris, recorded a conversation with the Dutch envoy: 'Mr. Van Hoey told me in confidence that he was sure that the French ministers would not come to any resolution or expence about war, till they saw how our sessions of Parliament did begin and was likely to go on. He said that this was the true reason of France's backwardness in the late discussions on that head, that the French ministers are informed from England that the present ministry cannot subsist, and that the subsequent will destroy whatever this has begun'.

In 1741 the envoy in Paris recorded a trip to Versailles in which his conversations with Fleury and Amelot, the foreign minister, were 'chiefly about the late attack made upon Sir Robert Walpole, in the two Houses of Parliament, for which they had received very particular accounts'.[14]

An examination of European diplomatic archives reveals great attention being devoted to British parliamentary events, not only by diplomats posted in London, but also by others throughout Europe.[15] A close relationship was felt to exist between the ministry's success in Parliament and their ability to implement their foreign policy. In February 1730 Stephen Poyntz reported from Paris that the leading members of the French ministry lamented 'the ill impression which our showing ourselves susceptible of such jealousys against France will make in the present situation of affairs at Vienna and elsewhere'. Debates on domestic matters were of equal significance. That same session the ministry's defeat on a place bill in the Commons caused great excitement in Europe, the Austrian Chancellor hoping that it would lead George II to 'discard his old ministers and employ none but Imperialists'.[16] The defeat of the Excise bill in 1733 led to predictions of Walpole's fall and claims that the ministry would be too weak to participate in European affairs.[17] In addition, the ministry believed that there were close links between domestic opponents and unfriendly foreign states, that the former deliberately resisted policies in order to encourage the latter to oppose Britain and thus create difficulties for the British government that could benefit the domestic opposition.[18]

There is considerable evidence for links between foreign powers and British domestic opposition. Many of these links were inspired by Jacobitism. The Jacobites sought to embarrass the ministry in Parliament in order to encourage foreign support, attempted to raise issues that would harm British relations with European powers, and tried to persuade these powers that the British ministry was weak. The Anglo-Austrian split in 1725 led the Jacobites to regularly forward favourable parliamentary information to their envoy in Vienna. Accounts of parliamentary opposition were presented to the Austrians as evidence of ministerial weakness. Diplomatic moves that would influence Parliament were sought. In 1726 the Jacobite Secretary of State wrote, 'Upon the first meeting of next sessions of Parliament, it would contribute very much to disconcert the present government, did the Emperor and King of Spain, raise their voice and make strong demands of Gibraltar and Port Mahon and show the people of England by some publick act, that the great expence the Government has made this year, has not served to remove the apprehensions of a war, and has not frightened those who are at present in no friendship with England'.[19]

European states were sceptical about Jacobite claims. Sinzendorf greeted one account of parliamentary proceedings with the reflection, 'the court . . . carry'd all before them'.[20] However, many governments were willing to meddle in British politics, to encourage opposition to the ministry and to supply information and documents accordingly. Thanks to their interception system the British ministry were well aware of intrigues by envoys such as the Swedes Gyllenborg (1716-17) and Sparre (mid-1730s), the Spaniards Monteleon (1718), Pozobueno (1726) and Montijo (1733-5), the Prussian Reichenbach (late 1720s), the Austrians Stahremberg (1725), Palm (1726-7), Kinsky (1729-30) and Strickland (1734-5), and the French Broglie (1730-1) and Chavigny (1732-6).[21] The ministry bitterly attacked the opposition for such intrigues. In 1734 Horace Walpole accused the opposition of links with foreign powers, and his brother attacked 'those gentlemen, who may perhaps have hearkened to every little whisper of some of the foreign ministers at this court, which is, I believe, the only foundation they have for what they have asserted'. The ministerial London newspaper the *Daily Courant* condemned the opposition: 'Has Britain ever had a foe, or a suspected foe, whom they have not caressed as a friend? Have they not trucked with foreign ministers and foreign courts, to promote the cause of their faction here at home?'[22] Many of the intercepts upheld these claims. It was clearly common for British oppositions to maintain links with foreign envoys. The Whigs had done so during the 1710-14 Tory ministry, and in 1718, during the Whig Split, Spencer Compton had a secret meeting with the Spanish envoy Monteleon and assured him that Spanish measures against British commerce would cause grave problems for the British ministry. Such activities were politically dangerous, however, if discovered. The Earl of Strafford was playing with fire in his intrigues with Reichenbach, for George II was probably more concerned about relations with Prussia than with any other power. Claims that the Tories were a loyal opposition seeking royal favour accord ill with Strafford's activities and with Wyndham and Bolingbroke's close relations with Chavigny. In 1730 the ministry intercepted letters from Reichenbach seeking information from Berlin about the Hotham mission, information which he claimed the opposition had asked him for, and he sent Berlin supposed opposition advice to reject Hotham's terms and thus gain concessions.[23]

Foreign envoys were in a difficult position. To seek to influence British opinion was natural, and by no means necessarily indiscreet. Cantemir the Russian envoy in the mid-1730s planted pro-Russian pieces in the press, a common activity, whilst Haslang, the Bavarian envoy, was asked by MPs in 1741 for Bavarian declarations.[24]

However, similar activities by diplomatic representatives of powers with unfriendly relations with Britain were not viewed favourably. An attempt to insert pro-Spanish material in the press in 1726 led to government action. It was a major problem for envoys, such as the Swede Sparre in 1733, to decide how far they could approach the opposition when ministerial policies were unfavourable to their country. Discussing matters with MPs appears to have been perfectly normal for envoys of friendly powers, such as the Brunswick-Wolfenbüttel Thom and the Hesse-Cassel Diemar who sought to protect subsidy treaties. Similar conduct in other circumstances led to complaints, though British envoys, often in response to orders from London, were quite prepared to intervene in the internal politics of other countries, in order to influence their foreign policy.[25]

It is questionable how effective lobbying by foreign envoys was. Destouches, the French envoy, pressed MPs and Peers against anti-Catholic legislation in 1723; Chammorel, a diplomatic colleague, was ordered in 1729 to defend French conduct against those who attacked it.[26] Neither appears to have had much success. Intriguing with the opposition appears also to have been generally unsuccessful in that, although the ministry could be embarrassed, it was not as easy to overthrow as several envoys believed. The most successful opposition over an issue of foreign policy, that of 1737-9 over Spanish depredation, which gravely limited the ministry's freedom of manoeuvre, owed nothing to the activities of foreign envoys. It is questionable whether the powerful displays of dissatisfaction in the sessions of 1729-30 with the anti-Austrian, pro-French policy of the ministry owed anything to Kinsky. Foreign envoys tended to exaggerate their influence – Chavigny was a particularly serious offender – and great care is required in using their accounts of British politics.

II

Besides the interpretation of Parliament as easily manipulated by the ministry, there was therefore also a belief that it was an unpredictable element in the political system that could overthrow ministry and measures. During the 1720s and 1730s the ministry did not lose divisions on foreign policy issues, and yet these divisions were watched with great attention. These clear contrasts make it important to examine the impact of Parliament on foreign policy.

The issue of divisions is an interesting one, for winning a division was not considered sufficient. For a ministry to command respect and enjoy confidence it needed a large majority.[27] Failing this, an atmosphere of crisis was engendered, as in 1730 and 1733. It was this atmosphere that was of crucial significance. The suggestion that the ministry might fall, alter or change their policies was sufficient to create unease among allies and give opponents confidence,[28] and this, in turn, would engender difficulties for British foreign policy, and might make the monarch feel that it was best to alter the ministry. The political situation, both in Britain and Europe, was unpredictable – the natural result of the great importance of the personal views of the monarch – and devoid of sure channels of political information. Rumour flourished in a political situation dominated by courts, and these rumours in turn shaped political developments. It was the belief that George II might dismiss Walpole in 1727 and 1733 that played such a major role in the political difficulties he faced in these years.

In such a context the suggestion that the ministry was not in secure control of Parliament was of major importance. It led in 1730 to French hesitation about the value of the British alliance and probably played a role in influencing the Austrians and Spaniards in their opposition to Britain in the late 1720s.[29] Whether Walpole would be able to retain control of Parliament during the 1734 session was of considerable interest to other European powers.[30] Thus, precisely because parliamentary events were believed to indicate the stability of the ministry, they acquired an importance that appears disproportionate. Any fall in the ministerial majority might be regarded as serious by diplomats and commentators predisposed to regard the British political system as unstable. For the ministry to win a majority would not suffice. It was necessary to win, and maintain, large majorities, to avoid divisions on key issues if possible, and to prevent speeches or protests that might be commented on abroad. In turn the ministry would seek to benefit from success in the session to achieve concessions abroad. In 1726 the envoy in Berlin was instructed to inform the Prussian ministers that 'His Majesty is so secure of the powerful support of his Parliament, and sees that what he has done is so much to the general taste of the nation, that he will not lie under the least necessity of making his court at Berlin by constraint, and ill treatment'.[31]

Any failure to achieve such support was serious, and, in order to persuade foreign powers that policies were supported, it was necessary to ensure parliamentary support, in circumstances where there was no constitutional or domestic political necessity. Thus, in 1723-4, St. Saphorin pressed for parliamentary action against the Austrian East India trading venture, the Ostend Company. This was necessary because the British ministry needed to convince the Austrians of the strength of British domestic opposition to the Company. In early 1723 Townshend told the Austrian Ambassador Count Stahremberg that an Anglo-Austrian treaty that would accept the position of the Company was impossible due to the opposition of the nation, and he referred directly to the role of Parliament: 'il savoit bien comment les choses alloient icy, ou au lieu de dépendre de la volonté d'un seul, on s'accommodoit aux avis de sept à huit cens'.

Having taken this stance, the standard ministerial line on contentious foreign policy issues, it was therefore necessary to ensure parliamentary support for specific policies. In 1724 St. Saphorin felt that his negotiating position in Vienna was dependent on parliamentary agitation over the Ostend Company, and he suggested that the British East India Company present a petition to Parliament on the issue, in which they demand the right to seize Ostend vessels in Indian waters. Parliament was to be manipulated to create the image the ministry needed; parliamentary debate of foreign policy was to be extended for diplomatic reasons.[32]

Aside from the diplomatic motives for encouraging parliamentary discussion of foreign policy issues, the opposition also had reasons for raising them. Foreign policy was regarded as a prime concern of government; it was also one of the areas in which the ministry were most vulnerable to attack. The Nine Years and Spanish Succession Wars had not only established foreign policy as a major subject of political debate, in Parliament, as in the press; they had also encouraged false expectations of national capability in the field of foreign policy, established defined party stances on the subject, and fostered the habit of judging achievement by high, indeed often unrealistic, standards. Thus, a government would be expected to ensure national interests and influence, if not determine, European affairs in desirable directions. This false perception of national capability, and arguably of national interest, had been further encouraged by the foreign interventionist policy associated with George I and Stanhope. This policy invited attack, and its failures encouraged further assault, as did ministerial determination to ensure parliamentary support. Tories had an additional motive for challenging foreign policy. They could defend themselves from charges of Jacobitism by drawing attention to the supposed manner in which the Whig ministry surrendered national interests to a foreign ruler, the Elector of Hanover.

The major role of foreign affairs in the political struggles of the late 1710s further ensured their importance as a subject of political, including parliamentary, debate. It followed that in the peaceful years of the early 1720s foreign policy was still actively debated, even though it was no longer so controversial. The revival of international tension in 1725, coupled with the attempt by Lord Bolingbroke and William Pulteney to create a new 'Country' opposition composed of Tories and disaffected Whigs, ensured that the sessions of 1726-31 were dominated by discussion of foreign policy. The ministry needed parliamentary support to influence allies and gain approval for the fiscal measures necessary to support heavier armaments and subsidy treaties. They were perceived as needing this support: 'The King of Sardinia refused to declare which of the Treaties he would accede to, till he saw how the Treaty of Hanover would be received by the Parliament of Great Britain and the States' General'.[33]

The new opposition benefited from this situation, from the economic strains created by the international situation and from the lack of widespread support for the French alliance, by concentrating their attacks on foreign policy issues. In 1728 they 'let themselves into the whole state of publick affairs from north to south'. The 1729 Commons debate upon the address was 'chiefly upon the occasion of the delays of the negotiations at Soissons'.[34] The largest recorded divisions were for debates on foreign policy,[35] which also witnessed the principal parliamentary challenges faced by the ministry. Their impact is difficult to evaluate. 'Il y aura des débats et des harangues violent du parti contraire, mais la cour s'en mocquera comme des cris en l'air, sans force et sans effet', claimed one anonymous writer in 1728.[36] It is unclear how far the opposition campaign played a role in the increasing British ministerial dissatisfaction with the French alliance that led to the unilateral approaches to Austria in 1729 and 1730. There is no British series of memoranda on policy options comparable to the French *Mémoires et Documents* series, no series of Council records giving detailed opinions similar to those of the Austrian *Konferenz* of ministers.

Whatever the significance of the opposition parliamentary attacks upon foreign policy in 1726-31, they further established foreign policy issues as prime subjects for parliamentary discussion. Their failure to dominate the next few sessions reflected a variety of factors. The replacement of a French by an Austrian alliance and of an interventionist by a more cautious style of policy conformed to opposition demands in the period 1726-31. Indeed the opposition claimed that the ministry had simply borrowed their policy.[37] This made it more difficult to challenge the new policy. The British envoy in the Hansa Towns, Sir Cyril Wych, observed in 1732, 'I suppose we may expect a pretty quiet session, for as the opposers always declared for friendship with the Emperor there is reason to hope the House of Commons will be unanimous in their address, and in their opinion that the Guaranty of the Pragmatick Sanction is necessary to preserve the Balance of Power in Europe'.[38]

In fact the opposition did challenge aspects of foreign policy in the sessions of 1732-3. However, the relatively peaceful international situation during this period, the cuts in taxation and the contentious fiscal legislation advanced by the ministry in each session ensured a concentration of effort elsewhere. There was more discussion of foreign policy during the sessions of 1734-5, understandably so, as Europe was convulsed by war, but far less than in 1726-31. There are several probable reasons: the after-effects of the Excise Crisis and of the 1734 general election provided many topics for debate, permitting opposition attacks on supposed instances of conspicuous tyranny and corruption. The ambivalent, indeed divided and changing, ministerial, response to the War of the Polish Succession made it difficult to define government policy, and to select an aspect of it, such as the French alliance in the late 1720s and supposed weakness in the face of Spanish depredations in 1737-9, on which a popular and effective attack could be mounted. The opposition were also divided in their attitudes to the war: Wyndham, Bolingbroke and the Tories enjoyed close links with Chavigny, and did not share the anxieties about the Austrian cause and the supposed threat to the balance of power voiced by such opposition Whigs as Chesterfield, Stair, Pulteney and Cobham.[39] Furthermore, neither session was conducive to a full-scale attack on current ministerial foreign policy. The 1734 session was not only the last before a dissolution; it was also one of the shortest in the period 1715-54, and dominated by the forthcoming elections. Delafaye sardonically remarked, 'The King of Poland did not time his death right; he should have lived a twelvemonth longer, that we might have had a new Parliament sitting'.[40] In addition, British policy was far from clear. The king's speech was a masterpiece of obfuscation, whilst the British ministry told all and sundry that policy would not be decided until they were informed of the views of the combatants, and encouraged all to assume that policy initiatives would be delayed until after the election.[41] The 1735 session took place against the diplomatic background of negotiations that might produce a European peace. It was therefore understandable that the opposition were disinclined to attack a policy that might soon be revealed as a major success. Instead opposition speakers blamed the ministry for causing the war. James Erskine, better known as the kidnapper of his wife and a parliamentary expert on witchcraft than for his expertise on foreign policy, held the ministry responsible for the rise of the Bourbons, 'since all flowed from the introduction of Don Carlos in Italy, which was done by our own fleet'.[42] In taking this line opposition speakers were betraying a characteristic of parliamentary debates on foreign policy in this period: a marked preference for discussing past policy and treaties, such as those of Utrecht, Seville and the Quadruple Alliance. This was understandable, given the difficulty of obtaining reliable information on current policy, about which the opposition complained often, but it also reflected an obsession with past conduct of foreign policy that did not always illuminate current problems.

The 1736 session did not see a major parliamentary discussion of the recent European war. Ministerial claims that the peace settlement reflected the terms of British proposals were difficult to challenge, whilst the Franco-Austrian pact was both unprecedented and possibly ephemeral, which made discussion of it difficult. Contentious ecclesiastical legislation, election petitions and the Gin Act were more attractive issues for debate than the fate of Parma and Piacenza. The following session, with its debates on the national debt, the Porteous Riot, and the allowance for the Prince of Wales, saw a general lack of interest in foreign policy. Robert Walpole wrote to Waldegrave, 'Your Lordship will not very much wonder that we have been behindhand of late in our foreign correspondencies, considering how fully we have been imployed in our domestic broils and contests, the most troublesome I ever knew, and from the great objects of division, the most dangerous that could have been attempted . . .[43]

The revival of foreign policy as one of the most contentious issues of parliamentary debate in the last sessions of Walpole's ministry reflects the opposition's success in finding an issue – Spanish depredations – that could be exploited in all spheres of political debate, and where the ministry's room for political manoeuvre was very limited. The emotional nature of the issue, in particular the idea of sullied national honour, outweighed the ministry's possession of a reasonable case, which they expounded fairly well in Parliament. The exuberant jingoism of the opposition ignored the European situation. Trevor, commenting on the size of the opposition vote in the Lords, wrote of his 'surprise at there being found 79 such vigorous sparks amongst their Lordships, as can not be contented with obtaining all they can naturally desire of a poor Girl, without forcibly ravishing her, and drawing the whole family upon their backs'.[44]

The decision to fight Spain had an impact similar to that of the Second Treaty of Vienna: the ministry, by adopting the policy advocated by the opposition, made it more difficult for the latter to mount a plausible attack on foreign policy issues. Furthermore, the decision to assist Maria Theresa with money led to a degree of agreement in the 1741 session over foreign policy that surprised commentators such as the Bavarian envoy Count Haslang.[45]

III

The ministry sought to settle contentious issues before Parliament met,[46] Horace Walpole becoming frantic as a result of pressure to settle Anglo-Spanish differences before the session of 1728, though two years later he despised similar ministerial anxieties over Dunkirk.[47] Had the ministry taken intimations of forthcoming trouble over Dunkirk more seriously, they might have avoided the most serious parliamentary storm of the 1730 session;[48] their determination to avoid a repetition of this mistake led to diplomatic pressure before the 1731 session. There is no suggestion in private ministerial correspondence of a pliant parliamentary majority willing to accept anything. Instead, ministerial attitudes were similar to those conveyed to foreign powers. In February 1729 Townshend, writing in order to persuade Fleury to act 'a friendly part towards the king', claimed that he was 'mistaken, if he thinks that the Parliament is influenced by money, to be thus unanimous in the supporting His Majesty in all he has done. This zeal proceeds from the chief men in both houses being convinced, that the measures His Majesty has hitherto taken are right; but these persons, tho' they have heartily concurred in what has been done hitherto, are under the greatest anxiety, at the uncertain state of our affairs; and will not be kept much longer in suspence'.

The following year Townshend wrote to explain the impossibility of persuading Parliament to grant peacetime subsidies to Sweden, and drew the attention of the Swedish ministry to their own experience: 'Count Horn cannot be ignorant how cautiously and tenderly such assemblys are to be managed in affairs of this nature'.[49]

Just as the majority of British commentators misunderstood the nature of the governments of most European countries, endowing them with a despotic power they lacked, so many misunderstood the nature of British parliamentary government. It was far from anarchic; a number of developments, including the Septennial Act and the exclusion of the Tories from any serious chance of royal favour, had created a degree of political stability.[50] Equally, it was not a parliamentary absolutism, a state where a dependable parliamentary majority produced an effective despotism. Instead, the difficulty of ensuring a secure majority helped to produce one of the characteristic features of the Walpole period: the relative absence of major legislative programmes (other than in fiscal matters). This contrasted with the position in the 1710s, when first the Tories, and then the Whigs under Sunderland, had sought to use their parliamentary majorities in order to enact very controversial and wide-ranging legislation. Walpole's parliamentary management was a reaction against the moves that had split the Whigs in 1717. Just as he opposed any interventionist foreign policy, so he sought to avoid contentious legislation – his most contentious step, the Excise Bill, was conceived in the belief that it would be popular – and to follow a more subtle managerial technique than that of the peremptory Sunderland ministry.

IV

'Though the House sat till eleven at night, I neither heard one argument above the style of a Coffee House, or one joke above the mirth of an Ale House'.[51] Lord Hervey's caustic comment on the 1730 Lords debate on the Address can be matched elsewhere. It is difficult to evaluate the quality of debates in early eighteenth-century European representative institutions. Conventions of behaviour and speech, standards of argument and proof were different from those of today, and it would be as anachronistic to condemn those of the early eighteenth century as it would be to make unfair comparisons about the nature of operatic and theatrical productions. Foreign visitors tended to be very impressed by the quality of parliamentary debates, and compared them favourably with those of European institutions. Dubois attended the debate on the capital penalty clause of the Mutiny Bill by a Committee of the Commons in February 1718. He wrote it, 'Je n'ai jamais entendu de discours plus précis et plus forts; ils ne sont point estudiés et recités de mémoire . . .'[52] A major problem in judging the quality of parliamentary debates on foreign policy is the nature of the evidence. There is no reliable account of debates giving speeches in full, and the surviving accounts are very patchy. Parliament took steps to restrict spectators and to prevent press coverage.

In 1728 and 1729 the Commons attacked the coverage of parliamentary activities printed in Robert Raikes' *Gloucester Journal* and on 8 March 1729 passed a resolution 'that it is an indignity to and breach of the privilege of this House for any person to presume to give in written or printed proceedings of this House or of any committee thereof', as a result of which press reporting greatly diminished. Moves to restrict entry also had their effect. In 1740 Dr. John Savage, who had sent reports on Parliament to the second Earl Cowper, wrote to him, 'you have shut us curious people out of the House of Lords'. The records for many debates, particularly those in the 1730s, do not distinguish between speakers, but simply group together all opposition and ministerial arguments. Debates that are known to have lasted several hours leave recorded speeches that would have taken little time to deliver.[53]

Aside from the scanty nature of the sources, there is also the problem of bias in those that survive. First, it is likely that many sources, particularly the press, simplified the arguments in order to present two clear-cut positions, and deliberately stressed rhetorical stances (the 'sensationalism' noted by Jones) at the expense of cautious discussion and the use of evidence. Secondly, the principal surviving sources are those of MPs who had no particular interest in, or knowledge of, foreign policy: this is particularly true of the records left by Sir Edward Knatchbull and Viscount Perceval. It is possible that a wider search for parliamentary accounts would yield a different picture. There are quite a few unprinted accounts, some of which yield valuable additional material. Good examples are Winnington's letters describing the 1729 session and Hay's describing those from 1734.[54] Foreign sources are also of particular value, as the accounts sent abroad stressed issues of foreign policy. In 1906 Mantoux suggested that the French archives constituted a significant source for the history of Parliament. In the *Correspondance Politique Angleterre* there are many reports of parliamentary debates, as indeed there are in many European diplomatic archives. It has been suggested that these reports were produced in London by a group of newswriters. Some reports were, however, despatched by foreign diplomats, who occasionally visited Parliament. Records of such visits are difficult to find, as diplomats were in no way obliged to seek permission for them, and as there are no registers of important visitors to Parliament. Major debates, such as those over the Excise Bill in 1733, and the voting of increased funds for the Prince of Wales in 1737, were certainly attended by several diplomats. Attendance at other debates clearly depended on the diplomat's knowledge of English, but this was possessed by a surprising number of, particularly, second-rank diplomats, doubtless reflecting the long duration of most of their postings. Reichenbach the Prussian Resident had a good command of English and definitely attended debates, as did Diemar, the Hesse-Cassel Envoy Extraordinary.[55] In 1733 the anglophile Prussian diplomat Count Degenfeld, attended the Commons debate on the army estimates. His account of the debate contains much that is missing from other sources, and, in particular, an important discussion of foreign policy issues. The

Degenfeld dispatch suggests that parliamentary knowledge of European affairs and British foreign policy was widespread. Sir William Yonge, a Lord of the Treasury, is recorded as stating that though Frederick William I was not named, 'yet he was satisfied that everybody judged as he did who was meant,' and the speeches of both Yonge and the Jacobite William Shippen rested upon the assumption that the already restless Commons would be able and interested enough to follow an exchange upon Anglo-Prussian relations.[56]

Expert opinion could be presented in Parliament. Both chambers contained several diplomats or former diplomats, and some of these contributed their knowledge to the debates. Though some envoys, such a William Finch, rarely attended Parliament, and are not recorded as having spoken in this period, others spoke frequently. In the Commons the pool of talent included such former envoys as Sir Robert Sutton, Methuen, Hedges and Dodington; in the Lords the opposition case in the 1730s was argued by well-informed experienced ex-diplomats, Chesterfield and Carteret. The debates that are recorded reveal a high standard of argument, and suggest that additional information was presented. In 1729 Horatio Walpole began his Commons speech in defence of the continuation of the same number of land forces, in the same manner as in the preceding year, by 'an account of the proceedings of several courts of Europe and the Ministers employed at them'. Edward Finch in the Commons debate on the Address in November 1742 gave 'an account of all his negotiations, and the interest as well as the views of every court in Europe'. Clearly not all parliamentarians shared this expert knowledge or participated in debates on foreign policy.[57] This was only to be expected. Equally clearly debates on highly charged issues such as Spanish depredations witnessed some extraordinary displays of rhetorical stupidity, whilst the opposition in its attacks on ministerial policy were often unfair in their criticisms and unrealistic in their demands. Such was, and is, the normal stuff of parliamentary debate. To use it to stigmatise all debates is unreasonable. Parliament, like the press of the period, should be given credit for an ability to discuss sensibly a rapidly altering and unpredictable European system. If sometimes outdated concepts were expressed and ludicrous simplifications employed, that is no different to the position today.

NOTES

1. Waldegrave to Horace Walpole, 8 Jan. (ns) 1729, Chewton.
2. Marlborough to Captain Fish, 'Bearleader' of her grandsons, 13 Mar. 1727, BL. Add. 61444; Anon., *A New Norfolk Ballard, concerning the late Vienna Treaty* (1731), pp. 7-8; Chammorel to Morville, 30 Ap. 1725, Broglie to Chauvelin, 9 Feb. (ns) 1730, AE. CP. Ang.

350, 369; Palm to Charles VI, 13 Dec. (ns) 1726, CUL. CH. corresp. 1379; Austrian diplomat Pentenriedter to Fonseca, 22 Mar. (ns) 1727, HHStA. Fonseca, 21; D'Aix to Victor Amadeus, 30 July (ns) 1727, 15 Nov (ns) 1728, AST. LM. Ing. 35; Anon., 'Situation de L'Angleterre' 27 June (ns) 1739, AE. MD. Ang. 8 f. 199.

3. Dubois to Destouches, 21 Ap. (ns) 1722, AE. CP. Ang. sup. 7; Chesterfield to Townshend, 3 Aug. (ns) 1728, PRO. 84/301; Chauvelin to Chammorel, 29 Jan. (ns) 1730, AE. CP. Ang. sup. 8; Robinson to Harrington, 10 Mar. (ns) 1732, 2 Feb. (ns) 1733, PRO. 80/86, 93.

4. *Craftsman,* 13 Sept. 1729; William Pulteney, leader of opposition Whigs in Commons, 11 Feb. 1729, Egmont, III, 341.

5. J. R. Jones, *Britain and the World, 1649-1815* (1980), pp. 13, 185.

6. M. Gordon, *The True Crisis,* p. 7; Anon., *The Remembrancer: Caleb's Sensible Exhortation,* p. 4.

7. *London Journal,* 19 Dec. 1730.

8. Waldegrave to Newcastle, 13 Jan. (ns) 1731, Horace Walpole to Newcastle, 3 May (ns) 1735, Newcastle to Hardwicke, 24 Feb. 1739, BL. Add. 32771, 32787, 35406.

9 *London Journal,* 27 Oct. 1722; Anon., Robert Walpole, 29 Nov. 1739, Newcastle, 1 Dec. 1740, Cobbett, XI, 270-1, 293-4, 714; Diemar to Eugene, 5 Feb. (ns) 1734, HHStA. GK. 85a.

10. Wyndham, 21 Nov. 1739, Cobbett XI, 221-2.

11. Anon. memorandum, 7 Oct. 1740, BL. Add. 32993 f. 107, PRO. 36/53.

12. Carteret to Polwarth and Whitworth, 22 Oct. 1722, BL. Add. 37390; Harrington to Robinson, 28 Jan. 1731, PRO. 80/71; Townshend to William Finch, 30 Jan. 1728, PRO. 84/299; O'Rourke to James III, 19 Feb. (ns) 1735, RA. 177/176.

13. George's speech, 27 Jan. 1728 (1728), p. 4; Hardwicke, 18 Nov. 1740, Cobbett XI, 675-6; *British Journal* 29 July 1727.

14. Keene to Newcastle, 22 Mar. (ns) 1728, BL. Add. 32754; Waldegrave Journal, 21 Aug. (ns) 1730, Chewton; Thompson to Couraud, Undersecretary of State in Southern Department, 8 Mar. (ns) 1741, PRO. 78/225; Edward Finch to Townshend, 26 Jan. (ns) 1726, PRO. 88/32.

15. Albert to Törring, 6 Oct. (ns) 1726, Munich, KS. 17091; Stainville, Lorraine envoy in Paris, to Francis of Lorraine, 29 Jan. (ns) 1735, Nancy, 88 no. 16; Canale, Sardinian envoy at The Hague, to Charles Emmanuel, 28 Jan. (ns) 1735, AST. LM. Olanda 31; Elsacker, Bavarian envoy in The Hague, to Haslang, 12 Dec. (ns) 1741, Munich, Bayr. Gesandtschaft, London, 360.

16. Poyntz to Delafaye, 28 Feb. (ns) 1730, PRO. 78/194; Horace Walpole to Harrington and Poyntz, 2 Mar. 1730, Coxe, II, 668-9; Waldegrave to Tilson, 15, 18 Mar. (ns) 1730, PRO. 80/67; Horace Walpole to Waldegrave, 24 Mar. 1730, Chewton.

17. Wachtendonck to Karl Philipp, 18 Aug. (ns) 1733, Munich, KB. 84/40; Chavigny to Chauvelin, 4 Sept. (ns) 1733, AE. CP. Ang. 381; Maurepas, French minister of the marine, to Mandel, ministry agent in London, 5 Sept. (ns) 1733, AN. AM. B⁷ 145; Villettes to Delafaye, 6 May (ns) 1733, 16 Jan. (ns) 1734, Essex to Newcastle, 13 Sept. (ns) 1733, 24 Ap. (ns) 1734, PRO. 92/35, 92/37; Charles VI to Kinsky, 7 Jan. (ns) 1934, PRO. 107/19; G. Quazza, 'Un Conflitto tra governo e paese in Inghilterra', *Nuova Rivista Storico* 30 (1946); Gastaldi, Genoese Chargé d'affaires in London, to Senate of Genoa, 25 (ns) 1733, ASG. LM. Ing. 11.

18. Newcastle to Waldegrave, 15 Ap. 1731, BL. Add. 32772.

19. Hay to Graham, Jacobite agent in Vienna, 12 Oct. (ns), Graham to Hay 19 Oct. (ns), 23 Nov. (ns), Hay to Hamilton, 6 Nov. (ns) 1726, RA. 98/7, 98/46. 99/71, 98/156.

20. Graham to Hay, 6 Ap. (ns) 1726, RA. 92/110.

21. Newcastle to Townshend, 30 June 1725, BL. Add. 32687; Sinzendorf to Palm, 23 Mar. (ns), CUL. CH. corresp. 1290; Newcastle to Waldegrave, 15 Ap. 1731, BL. Add. 32772; Kinsky to Eugene, 8 Feb. (ns) 1729, HHStA. GK. 94(b); Zamboni to Landgrave of Hesse-Darmstadt, 18 Sept. (ns) 1733, Darmstadt, E1 M10/6.

22. Horace Walpole, Robert Walpole, 25 Jan. 1734, Cobbett, IX 222, 229; *Daily Courant* 13 July 1734; *London Journal* 2 Mar. 1734. Zamboni and De Löss accepted these charges, Zamboni to Saxon minister Bunau, 19 Feb. (ns) 1734, Bodl. Rawl. 120, De Löss to Augustus III, 9 Feb. (ns) 1734, Dresden, 638 IIa. Count Albert urged such action, Albert to Törring, 5 Feb. (ns) 1734, Munih, KS 17132.

23. Black, 'Crisis of 1717-18', *Parliamentary History Yearbook;* Reichenbach to General Grumbkow, 14, 18 Ap. (ns) 1730, Hull, DD HO 3/3.

24. Haslang to Törring, 21 Mar. (ns) 1741, Munich, KS. 17211. Providing public hospitality to celebrate the victory of Austria over the Turks in 1717 was acceptable, the Spanish Ambassador's hospitality to the Excise rioters was not.

25. Sparre to Swedish minister Count Horn, 21 Aug (ns), 16, 30 Oct. (ns), Horn to Sparre, 12 Sept. (ns) 1733, PRO. 107/15-17; Diemar to Eugene, 17 Dec. (ns) 1734, HHStA. GK. 85(a); Visconti, Austrian agent in London, to Sinzendorf, 13 Ap. (ns) 1728, HHStA. Ek. 65.

26. Destouches to Dubois, 17 May (ns) 1723, Chauvelin to Chammorel, 13, 21 Jan. (ns) 1729, AE. CP. Ang. 341, sup. 8.

27. Zamboni to Manteuffel, 29 Mar. (ns) 1729, Bodl. Rawl. 120; 23 Feb. 1739, Egmont, III, 27; Cambis, French Ambassador in London, to Amelot, French foreign minister, 12 Mar. (ns) 1739, AE. CP. Ang. 404; Chavigny to Ossorio, 11 Ap. (ns) 1739, PRO. 107/26; Le Coq to Saxon envoy in Vienna, Marquis de Fleury, 12 Ap. (ns) 1726, Dresden, 2674; De Büy, Saxon envoy in Spain, to Manteuffel, 29 Feb. (ns) 1729, Dresden, 3105 II; Wackerbarth, Saxon envoy in Vienna, to Augustus II, 12 Mar. (ns) 1729, Dresden, 3331 I; Chauvelin to Chammorel, 16 Feb. (ns) 1730, AE. CP. Ang. sup. 8.

28. Bothmer to Whitworth, 20 Mar. (ns) 1722, BL. Add. 37388; E. Phillips, *The State of the Nation in respect of her Commerce, Debts and Money* (2nd ed., 1726), p. 3; Graham to Atterbury, 5 Sept. (ns) 1727, RA. 110/8; Waldegrave Journal, 28 Sept. (ns) 1727, Chewton; *British Journal,* 9 Dec. 1727; *London Journal,* 3 Aug. 1728.

29. Waldegrave to Horace Walpole, 8 Jan (ns) 1729, Chewton; Chesterfield to Townshend, 1 Oct. (ns) 1728, PRO. 84/302; William Finch to Townshend, 16 Jan. (ns) 1728, PRO. 84/299. For a similar effect upon Spain in 1739, Horace Walpole, undated, 'Mr Walpole's Apology', BL. Add. 9132 f.99.

30. Robinson to Harrington, 31 Oct. (ns) 1733, PRO. 80/100.

31. Townshend to Du Bourgay, 22 Feb. 1726, PRO. 90/22; St. Saphorin to Tilson, 18 Nov. (ns) 1722, PRO. 80/47; Harrington to Robinson, 28 Jan. 1731, PRO. 80/71.

32. Townshend to St. Saphorin, 8 Feb. 1723, St. Saphorin to Townshend, 20, 26 Feb. (ns), 12 Ap. (ns), 6 May (ns) 1724, PRO. 80/48, 80/52. Dodington recommended similar action with Spain, Dodington to Stair, 22 July (ns) 1716, SRO. GD. 135/141/3A.

33. *London Journal,* 19 Feb. 1726; *Whitehall Evening Post,* 15 Nov. 1718.

34. *Wye's Letter,* 23 Jan. 1729.

35. R. R. Sedgwick (ed.), *The House of Commons, 1715-54* (2 vols., 1970), I, 13.

36. 'Mémoire sur L'Etat présent de la Grande Bretagne', 31 Dec. (ns) 1728, Amelot to Cambis, 3 Mar. (ns) 1739, AE. CP. Ang. 364 f. 395, 404.

37. *Craftsman,* 24 Ap. 1731.

38. Wych to Tilson, 1 Feb. (ns) 1732, PRO. 82/49; Watsdorf to Augustus II, 29 Jan. (ns) 1732, Dresden, 2676 III.

39. The Austrians considering using Davenant to lobby M.P.s, Eugene to Kinsky, 2 Jan. (ns) 1734, Kinsky palais, papers of Count Philip Kinsky 2 (d).

40. Delafaye to Waldegrave, 5 Feb. 1734, Chewton.

41. De Löss to Augustus III, 13, 16, 23 Oct. (ns) 27 Nov. (ns) 1733, 1 Feb. (ns) 1734, Dresden, 638, I, IIa.

42. Wyndham, 25 Jan. 1734, Erskine, 14 Feb. 1735, anon., 6 Mar. 1735, Cobbett, XI, 225, 822, 869.

43. Walpole to Waldegrave, 7 Mar. 1737, Chewton.

44. Trevor to Couraud, 17 Mar. (ns) 1739, Chewton.

45. Hasland to Törring, 25 Ap. (ns) 1741, Munich, KS. 17211.

46. Mrs Caesar, BL. Add. 62558 f. 45; Duc. d'Antin, memorandum [1735-6], AE. MD. 504 f. 6.

47. Newcastle to Horace Walpole, 5, 14, 21 Dec., Horace to Newcastle, 21, 27 Dec., 1727, BL. Add. 32753; Townshend to Horace, 13 Dec. 1727, BL. Add. 48982; Waldegrave Journal, 2 Dec. (ns) 1727, 15 Jan. 1728, Chewton; Horace to Delafaye, 14 Dec. (ns) 1729, PRO. 78/192; Townshend to Newcastle, 1 July (ns) 1729, PRO. 43/77.

48. Delafaye to Waldegrave, 7 Jan. 1730, Chewton; Wager to Delafaye, 8 Jan. 1730, PRO. 42/20.

49. Townshend to Poyntz, 21 Feb. 1729, BL. Add. 48982; Townshend to Edward Finch, 3 Feb. 1730, PRO. 95/54; Cadogan to Stair, 4 Dec. (ns) 1716, Craggs to Stair, 31 Mar. (ns) 1719, SRO. GD. 135/141/6, 19A.

50. Tilson to Whitworth, 9 Mar. 1722, BL. Add. 37388.

51. Hervey to Henry Fox MP, 15 Jan. (quote), 4 Feb. 1730, Ilchester, pp. 44, 47.

52. Dubois to Orléans, 17 Feb. (ns) 1718, AE. CP. Ang. 312.

53. M. Ransome, 'The Reliability of Contemporary Reporting of the Debates of the House of Commons, 1727-41', *BIHR* 19 (1942-3); *Original Mercury, York Journal: or Weekly Courant*, 2 Ap. 1728; Savage to Cowper, 29 Jan. 1740, Hertford, Hertfordshire CRO., Panshanger Mss. D/EP F250; George Drummond to Duncan Forbes, 4 June 1717, D. Warrand (ed.), *More Culloden Papers* II (Inverness, 1925), p. 173: *Worcester Post-Man*, 16 Jan. 1719, 25 Mar. 1720. For misreporting, Horace Walpole the younger, 'Short Notes of my Life', *The Letters of Horace Walpole*, edited by P. Cunningham (Edinburgh, 1906), I, lxix.

54. Winnington to Hervey, 24 Mar. 1729, Winnington to Stephen Fox, 9 Ap. 1729, Dorchester, Dorset CRO. D124/box 240; notebook of William Hay, MP Seaford, Northampton, Northamptonshire CRO. L(c) 1732-3.

55. Diemar to Landgrave Karl of Hesse-Cassel, 18 Feb. (ns) 1729, Marburg, 197; Reichenbach to Grumbkow, 21 Mar. (ns) 1730, Hull, DDHO 3/3; P. J. Mantoux, *Comptes rendus des Séances du Parlement Anglais* (Paris, 1906); Mantoux, 'French Reports of British Parliamentary Debates in the Eighteenth Century', *American Historical Review* 12 (1907); *Newcastle Courant*, 13 Feb. 1731, *Grub Street Journal*, 22 Mar. 1733, *London Farthing Post*, 3 Mar. 1739, *Wye's Letter*, 17 Nov. 1739, for envoys attending debates.

56. Degenfeld to Frederick William, 20 Feb. (ns) 1733, PRO. 107/9.

57. Egmont, III, 338; Duncan Forbes MP to John Forbes, 1 Feb. 1729, H. Duff (ed.), *Culloden Papers* (1815), p. 104; Henry Finch to Lord Malton, 18 Nov. 1742, Sheffield, Public Library, Wentworth Woodhouse papers, M3-122.

Trade and Foreign Policy

'It is part of the indispensable duty of those who are at the helm, to turn their thoughts
upon the improvement of what appears to be the peculiar blessing of this island. And it is
very well it is so; because they must be supposed to be much more disinterested in this
affair, than private persons can often be. And therefore, whilst men, who are themselves
concerned in the particular branches of our trade, are every one of them naturally biassed
and drawn into one particular set of maxims by that particular interest which lies always
before their eyes, those who are to frame and amend the laws relating to this great good
can compare all the private opinions of interested men together; can have recourse to the
true and genuine foundations of trade . . . For this is properly the work of government, –
to consider the whole, and not a part only.'

Bishop Hoadly, *London Journal*, 16 May 1724

All politicians could agree in praising the virtues of trade, and all could see
the advantage of expounding foreign policy in the light of commercial
considerations. 'Commerce, upon which the riches and grandeur of this
nation chiefly depend', claimed the royal speech to Parliament in October
1721, and such themes can be found in the parliamentary speeches,
diplomatic correspondence and press and pamphlet literature of this period.
Foreign trade served to increase the wealth of the nation, and fulfilled the
important social function of providing employment to the poor by
encouraging export industries, particularly that of woollen cloth. It was also
claimed that, far from there being any difference between the landed and
the mercantile sections of society, they shared common interests. The value
of land and the state of the rural economy, both depressed in the Walpolean
period, were held to depend on the ability of the manufacturing and
mercantile sector to process and export rural products, principally wool and
grain.[1]

Several historians have argued that British foreign policy in the
eighteenth century was dominated by commercial considerations,
principally a search for markets, colonial and European, and a firm
opposition to competitors. Symcox has claimed recently that there was a
'close relationship between the two fundamental elements in British foreign
policy, so often treated as separate and unrelated: the pursuit of a strategic
and political balance of power in Europe, and the thrust toward commercial
expansion. I would argue that successive British governments in this period
saw war as a means of promoting commercial growth and sought to achieve
a military and diplomatic equilibrium as the essential condition for
maintaining and extending trade'.[2]

From its public pronouncements and private writings there is no doubt of
the Walpole ministry's support for trade and concern for commercial
considerations. And yet the ministry were attacked for being opposed to

trade and to merchants, blamed for the poor economic conditions of the period and hounded for their supposed failure to defend British interests in the trade that received most public attention: that to Spain and the Spanish Empire.[3] The opposition press could portray a ministerial gang shouting 'No Merchants' and, claiming that Walpole had said 'that he hoped to make all the merchants of England, as poor as so many German princes', concluded, 'Things seem to be come to a kind of crisis betwixt him and the merchants . . . either he or they must fall'.[4]

The available literature is good. There is extensive work on Anglo-Spanish relations, there are major studies of British trade with Portugal, Russia, Scandinavia and the United Provinces, and there is an important thesis on Walpole's fiscal policy. However, there is no major study of commercial policy as a whole nor of its relationship with other diplomatic concerns. Furthermore, although the links between some mercantile groups, particularly the East India, Russia and South Sea companies, and the ministry have been studied, there is no comprehensive work either on the role of mercantile lobbying or on ministerial-mercantile relations.[5] There is much work still to be done on the subject. In this chapter it is only possible to trace a few themes, and the relationship between commercial factors and foreign policy will receive most attention. It will be suggested that the ministerial response to commercial needs was more ambiguous, and more constrained by political factors, than some historians have suggested.

Willing to support trade, the ministry were confronted by complex issues, disparate interests and contrary lobbying. Much parliamentary time was spent in discussing commercial matters, but Parliament and the ministry were not confronted by a united commercial lobby. Instead, the disparate views of the various interests detracted from the general effectiveness of commercial lobbying. Defending the Board of Trade against opposition attacks, the London ministerial newspaper the *Daily Gazetteer* claimed in 1740, 'such as are acquainted with these affairs know very well that merchants are seldom unanimous in prospects for promoting trade; that it too often happens what would benefit one would prejudice another set of men which occasions eager contentions . . . As to the disappointment of a Bill for prohibiting foreign linnens, that sprang from an opposition made to it by traders'.

Five years earlier the same paper had commented on 'how little hitherto we have been agreed in matters of trade . . .'[6] An examination of press and pamphlet material reveals that such claims were correct. Protection and support were demanded by all, and projected legislation was rarely free from contention. The great trading companies pressed for assistance against rivals, both British and foreign. In 1724 the Royal Africa Company, a frequent demander of support, pressed the ministry for assistance against the South Sea Company. Schemes for overland trade with Persia via Russia set the Russia against the Levant and East India companies. The companies were jealous of interlopers and expected ministerial support in maintaining their monopoly positions, which posed major problems for the Walpole ministry as it was a contentious political issue.

Quarrels between British merchants were matched by conflicts of interest between British and colonial merchants and between merchants and manufacturers.[7] In 1739 traders supported agitation for the export of sugar from British West Indian colonies direct to European markets, a move resisted by the British sugar refiners. Traders handling Swedish iron imports were opposed to moves to substitute the North American colonies as a source of iron. The British mining interest campaigned successfully to prevent the payment of a drawback when Barbary copper refined in Britain was re-exported, which copper importers campaigned for from 1727 to 1734. The cloth manufacturing lobby, supported by parliamentary legislation, sought to keep British wool prices low and foreign cloth manufacturers weak by preventing the export of wool. Irish and British wool producers, unsuccessful, on the whole, in Parliament, indicated their views by smuggling vigorously. In the War of the Austrian Succession there was to be a fierce debate over grain exports to France.

Thus, commercial interests were bitterly divided, irrespective of ministerial intervention. This placed the ministry in a difficult position, particularly since mercantile interests were well represented in Parliament. The ministry were expected to protect commerce, they were vulnerable to political attacks on the issue, and yet the divergence of commercial interests meant that internal pressure was divided, and therefore both more strident and harder to satisfy. Ministerial defence of British commercial interests therefore took place against a difficult domestic background. The European situation was even harsher. Two major problems confronted the British ministry: European resentment at Britain's position after the Peace of Utrecht, and the rise of European competition. By the Utrecht settlement British possession of Gibraltar and Minorca, both important for the protection of Mediterranean commerce, had been recognised, and Britain had been granted both the *Asiento,* the contract to supply African slaves to the Spanish colonies in America, and the right to send an annual ship of 500 tons to the fair at Portobello in Central America. These concessions reflected the position of maritime supremacy Britain enjoyed at the end of the War of the Spanish Succession. They were important both in their own right and because they symbolised British maritime dominance.

The British position was widely resented in Europe. France and the United Provinces were envious, and Spain was determined to limit British commercial penetration of her American empire. An English pamphlet of 1727 noted, 'how envious an eye the Dutch beheld the separate privileges in trade, and the sole possession of G[ibraltar], and of the Island of Minorca, which we obtained at the last peace'.[8] In 1727 the British ministry were concerned about the amount of Dutch diplomatic assistance they could expect in pressing Spain to satisfy British demands over Caribbean trading conditions. There was no doubt that the Dutch mercantile community were envious of the British position both in Europe and elsewhere. Diplomatic reports noted Dutch envy of the British position in Portugal and Spain; the Dutch resented the British dominance of Russia's Baltic trade in the late 1730s and the Anglo-Russian Commercial Treaty of 1734. During the diplomatic negotiations of the 1720s and, in particular, at the Congress of Soissons in 1728, the Dutch ministry proved hesitant in supporting British commercial interests. Although some British ministers privately supported the return of Gibraltar, the British ministry responded harshly to the 1728 suggestion of Slingelandt, the leading Dutch minister, that Gibraltar be returned. In the War of the Polish Succession British diplomats and ministers replied to Austrian demands for intervention by stating that Britain would not intervene if the Dutch were to be neutral, as this would entail the loss of British trade. This argument was a convenient one for a ministry disinclined anyway to intervene, but it also reflected a genuine anxiety about Dutch competition and an awareness of the political dangers it represented. There was no suggestion that world trade was anything other than finite and limited: Dutch gains would be at Britain's expense.[9]

The reality of commercial rivalry, as well as the weakness of the traditional Anglo-Dutch alliance, was revealed in the late 1730s. Britain and the United Provinces did not cooperate in commercial negotiations with Spain, though both powers suffered from Spanish depredations; the Convention of the Pardo was negotiated by Britain alone, and British diplomats gleefully hoped that it would damage the Dutch position. When war broke out between Britain and Spain in late 1739, the Dutch resisted strong British pressure to provide assistance, just as they had refused, in 1735, to participate in the British despatch of a fleet to the Tagus to protect Portugal, and Portuguese trade, from Spanish attack.

Anglo-Dutch commercial animosity was therefore an important factor.[10] The two countries could usually cooperate only in preventing other powers, such as the Austrian Ostend Company, from intruding into their preserves. Otherwise the position was one of conflict, sometimes open, as on the coast of West Africa, but more usually a background source of tension.

France was similarly envious of the British position. French oceanic and European trade, and the French navy and mercantile marine, were in a poor state at the end of the War of the Spanish Succession. Thereafter they recovered, albeit unevenly, and the recovery implicitly challenged the British colonial, maritime and commercial position. This became increasingly the case in the 1720s. The French Secretary of State for the Marine, Maurepas, launched an ambitious programme of naval construction, and actively sponsored projects for colonial and mercantile growth. During the Orléans Regency (1715-23) there had been Anglo-French rivalry, particularly in relation to the financial, colonial and commercial schemes of Orléans' fiscal adviser, the Scot John Law. However, neither Britain nor France had sought to push these issues of rivalry, and a major reason for the recall in 1720 of the Ambassador in Paris, the Earl of Stair, was his inability to accept that Law's position harmed relations.

There were increasing signs of commercial and colonial rivalry straining relations in the 1720s. In particular, the British felt that France was seeking to supplant them in Spanish, Spanish American and the Mediterranean trade. These opinions, expressed frequently in press and pamphlet literature, were matched by increasing ministerial unease, particularly in late 1727 when France negotiated a temporary settlement of Anglo-Spanish differences unacceptable to the British ministry, and in 1728 at Soissons. The British ministry resented French failure to provide adequate diplomatic support over Gibraltar and over the British commercial privileges in the Spanish empire; French ministers argued that Britain was selfishly jeopardising the interests of the Anglo-French alliance.[11] Spanish resentment at humiliating peace terms was understandable. Relations were improved by the 1715 commercial treaty negotiated on the British side by George Bubb (better known by his later name, Dodington). However, political differences superseded mercantile considerations. In 1718-20 and 1725-9 confrontation and conflict interrupted trade. In addition, the Spanish determination to protect and increase the profitability of their American empire conflicted with the interests of British merchants determined to exploit these markets and to secure Spanish bullion. The resultant contraband trade and Spanish moves to prevent it exacerbated relations.

Thus, relations that were naturally bad as a result of Spanish anger over the Utrecht settlement were further harmed by the issue of Caribbean trade. Spanish resentment at continual diplomatic pressure, supported at times by naval armaments, was clear. In 1727 the Queen of Spain, Elisabeth Farnese, attacked the British who 'pretended to lord it over everybody'. The importance and political sensitivity of Anglo-Spanish trade made this a very difficult issue for the British ministry.[12]

Further problems were posed, both for British trade and for the ministry, by the adoption by many European states of policies that have been termed 'mercantilist'. Attempting to improve their economy, many European states sought to further trade and industry by making the import of manufactured products more difficult and by establishing oceanic trading companies. These state-sponsored and directed economic initiatives presented major problems for British trade.[13] Several European states with which Britain had important commercial relations established or increased import tariffs. This was particularly so with Sweden, Denmark, Sardinia and the Austrian lands, and threatened British cloth exports in particular. In 1732 Edmund Allen, Secretary in Turin, wrote to the Undersecretary of State in the Southern Department of 'our Trade, which as you justly observe, may be considered as the very Blood and Vitals of our country, and which at this time lies here expiring, and at its last Gasp, except some proper Remedy and that soon be found out, and applied in order to restore it to its usual strength and vigour'.[14]

A variety of methods were used by European states to aid their commerce and industry: outright prohibitions on imports, moves against trade in foreign shipping (many very similar to the British Navigation Acts), high tariffs or, as in Sardinia in the mid-1720s, pressure on merchants to handle local produce. The British ministry attempted to protect Britain's trade and industry, and thus appear to have vindicated to some extent historians who see this as a major element of British foreign policy. Foreign envoys, such as the Sardinian Ossorio, were pressed by the ministry, British envoys were instructed to remonstrate. In 1734 the Earl of Essex, Ambassador in Turin, wrote that he 'ever looked upon it as one of the most essential parts of my duty to protect as much as possible, His Majesty's trading subjects'.[15] Particular efforts were devoted to attempting to limit the oceanic trading aspirations of other states. In this period a host of countries, including Sweden, Denmark, Prussia, Tuscany and Russia, founded, revived or considered founding companies trading to the East Indies. These threatened the existing effective monopoly enjoyed by Britain, France and the United Provinces, and were blamed when the East India companies of these latter countries suffered diminished profits.[16] This was serious in Britain where the East India Company enjoyed great political influence, partly because of its important position in the state's fiscal machinery.

Limiting the activities of these new companies posed diplomatic problems. Edward Finch, pressing Frederick I of Sweden over the Swedish East India Company, which had received its charter in 1731, 'told him that nobody pretended to dispute his right, as an independent sovereign Prince, not tied up by any previous treaty, to trade where he pleased'. With most companies it was only possible to attempt to prevent their using British capital and British seamen and officers, which was the method followed with the Swedish company. For in international law Britain could not seek to prevent these new companies trading, just as she had little legal reason to complain when European states enacted commercial protectionist legislation that emulated that of Britain herself. There was no comparison between the position over trade with Spain's American possessions, and that over trade with the East Indies.[17]

One foreign company the British made major efforts to hinder was that founded in order to trade to the Indies, at Ostend, by the Emperor Charles VI. It was founded in December 1722, was initially very successful, and led to major Dutch and British diplomatic efforts to suppress it, efforts that led to its suspension in 1727, and suppression four years later, as part of the price the two powers demanded in their negotiation of an alliance with Austria.[18]

Thus, instances can readily be found of diplomatic pressure being exerted for commercial ends. It is difficult to contend, however, that these constituted a policy aimed at using foreign policy in order to improve Britain's commercial and industrial position. Firstly it is unclear how far British diplomatic moves reflected more than occasional responses to mercantile pressure. Secondly it is clear that these diplomatic moves were usually subordinated to political considerations, and often suppressed in their favour. Thirdly it is clear that antipathy towards mercantile pretensions was fairly common in the British diplomatic service. The last is very clear from the official and private correspondence of many diplomats, particularly in the case of successive envoys in Spain who drew attention to the detrimental consequences for Anglo-Spanish relations that support for mercantile claims would produce. Benjamin Keene, whose supposed failure to protect mercantile interests led to domestic criticism and to his being nicknamed Don Benjamino, was particularly clear on this point, and in 1736 wrote, 'if ever I have another commission in my days it shall be in a country where there are no sea ports'.[19] Lord Tyrawly was biting in his comments from Lisbon. In 1728 he complained that the factory (the British mercantile community) claimed excessive privileges, and in 1729 wrote of them: 'excepting Mr Stert, and some 4, or 5 more, they are a parcel of the greatest jackanapes I ever met with, fops, beaux, drunkards, gamesters, and prodigiously ignorant ever in their own business'. Similar views were expressed, albeit less pungently, by other diplomats.[20] Their consequences are difficult to assess. Possibly they led some merchants to feel that it was only through political pressure in London that they could obtain support.

Mercantile pressure in London was fairly continuous. This was a period of great political and parliamentary lobbying, and mercantile groups were well organised and wealthy enough to take advantage of the accessibility of the system to lobbying. The ministry and Parliament expected to be lobbied, and professional lobbyists existed.[21] Pamphlets and newspaper articles were produced in order to influence decisions. The anonymous pamphlet *The Interest of Great Britain in supplying herself with iron impartially consider'd* was produced whilst a relevant bill was being considered in the Commons.[22] To a certain extent this situation was welcome to the ministry. Seeking to aid commerce, they relied, to a great extent, for information and suggestions on advice from mercantile circles. Hunt has indicated the crucial role of such advice from the Russia Company in the negotiation of the Anglo-Russian Commercial Treaty of 1734.[23] Similar evidence, though not to the same extent, can be found elsewhere. In 1732 the Duke of Newcastle, Secretary of State for the Southern Department, instructed Essex to seek information on Sardinian moves against British trade 'from some of the Merchants of the best credit residing at Turin'.[24] Commenting in 1730 on the adverse effects of wool and yarn exports to France, a press report noted, 'several of the most eminent traders in our manufactures have been sent for by Sir Robert Walpole to give their opinion in this matter, in order to lay the whole before the Parliament, which will be done by petition early in the ensuing session'.[25] In 1725 Spain's response to the South Sea Company's *Asiento* pretensions was sent to the company for their comment.[26]

Mercantile advice and participation were an integral part of the procedure by which commercial policies were evolved and legislated. Given the often contrary interests of varied groups, this produced political conflict. More serious for the ministry were situations in which views advanced by influential sections of the mercantile community were challenged, not by other sections but by the ministerial wish to further good diplomatic relations with other states. With weak states the ministry could afford to adopt a high, almost bullying, tone. Venice is a good instance. The state enforced and sought to extend protectionist legislation. The British ministry attempted to protect British trade. In 1731, the Duke of Newcastle responded to reports of a new Venetian duty on British fish exports by instructing the British Resident, Colonel Elizeus Burges, to have it removed. Burges was told, in no uncertain terms, to protect British trade and to send reports on his progress in the matter. Three years later merchants and sugar refiners in Bristol and London petitioned George II to have revoked a new duty of 25% ('amounting to a prohibition') on British refined sugars imported into Venice. Orders accordingly were sent to Burges. The Venetian envoy Imberto was bullied, and Britain threatened reprisals on Venetian imports.[27]

Such an approach could not be adopted with most of Britain's trading partners. Reprisals could be threatened but they were not easy to implement. In 1739 Finch suggested that the Swedish government needed to have its eyes opened by parliamentary legislation affecting Anglo-Swedish trade. Sweden was threatened with the substitution of American for Swedish iron imports. However, no steps were taken to limit these Swedish imports, and their size seemed to produce British dependence on Sweden rather than vice versa.[28] Threats rang hollow when Britain needed diplomatic support, and it was difficult to pursue commercial disputes with Sweden, Denmark and Sardinia when Britain was seeking to prevent them from siding with diplomatic rivals, Austria in 1725-30, France thereafter. It was simpler to claim that new industries and trades in these countries would collapse for socio-economic reasons. Sir Cyril Wych, Envoy Extraordinary in Hamburg, wrote in 1737 concerning new manufacturing industries in Denmark: 'I believe we shall find in a little time, that all will come to nothing; it being a very sure rule, that trade will not be forced, nor can it flourish in a country, where property is not secured, and where the credit of the subject is as slender, as his riches are uncertain'.

There was a certain degree of truth in these reassuring Whig views. Many of the feared European industrial and commercial schemes collapsed or were less competitive than anticipated.[29] This was true of the projects for Tuscan trade to the Indies, a Russian colony in South America, the Spanish Philippines Company and many of the Danish schemes. However, letting sleeping dogs lie could not be the ministry's policy, and efforts were made to protect trade. Their relationship with other foreign policy goals was a complex one, and usually commercial interests were not pushed hard. This can be seen by considering relations with Austria, France and Spain.

Charles VI of Austria was a keen supporter of industrial and commercial enterprises. He sought to encourage industrial production in the *Erblande*, the Habsburg hereditary dominions in east-central Europe, and to develop trade, both from Ostend and from Trieste on the Adriatic. In 1725 part of the Austro-Spanish alliance known as the First Treaty of Vienna included a commercial treaty by which Spain promised to allow the Ostend Company to trade in some of her possessions and to give the Emperor's subjects the same privileges as those enjoyed by the British and the Dutch. This treaty led not only to confrontation with Britain but also to moves against British trade with Austrian possessions, such as Sicily. Moves against British imports were made in 1726. In July 1728 imports of products manufactured from wool and silk were prohibited. The British Ambassador Lord Waldegrave argued that this measure was chiefly aimed at Britain and suggested that the British might retaliate by prohibiting imports of lace and linen from Austrian lands.[30]

These Austrian moves aroused British anger, and the ministry were willing to support dramatic action against the Ostend Company, the forcible seizure of whose ships in European waters was considered. Austrian commercial schemes were widely criticised, and in 1730 one pamphlet noted, 'We have all seen the irresistible propensions of the Imperial Court

H

to promote a commerce, as by way of emulation, to the great prejudice of
the Mercantile Interest of this Nation and the Diminution of the Royal
Revenue'. Ministerial speakers in Parliament, pamphlets and newspapers
all used Austrian commercial policies in the late 1720s in order to claim
support for ministerial anti-Austrian policy. Edward Finch, then at
Warsaw, could describe 'the Ostend Company as the source of the present
misunderstanding'. Aside from arousing domestic support, stress on the
Ostend Company helped to produce Anglo-Dutch cooperation against
Austria. The British ministry demanded and eventually achieved its
suppression. [31]

However, an examination of Anglo-Austrian relations in the period
1718-31 suggests ambivalence in the British position. The Ostend
Company played only a small role in the secret Anglo-Austrian negotiations
in the spring and summer of 1729. Prior to 1725 it had been possible for the
opposition to suggest that the ministry were failing to take sufficient steps
against the Company. Ministerial connivance was suggested in 1718 and in
the early 1720s. The ministry not only failed in 1731 to obtain revocation of
Austrian protectionist legislation; they made no real effort in this
direction. [32]

A similar policy characterised the British stance for the rest of the
Walpole ministry. Major efforts were made in 1731-3 to prevent Ostend
trade, directly or via Hamburg, but less effort was made in non-colonial
trade. Angry over supposed Austrian connivance in trade to the Indies from
Hamburg, the ministry threatened that it would harm relations, Lord
Harrington writing in 1732 that it 'would extremely alienate people here
from an alliance with the Emperor, and consequently make it much less
practicable for the King to support upon occasion the interests of that
Prince and his family so powerfully as he himself would be desirous to do'. [33]
In fact, the state of Anglo-Austrian trade played no role in the decisions not
to aid Austria in 1733, and to aid her in 1741.

In the late 1730s Anglo-Austrian commercial relations were marked by
both hope and disappointment, the latter owing to clearly differing
positions in negotiations that began in late 1737 on the tariffs in the
Austrian Netherlands. Britain and the United Provinces were determined to
preserve the latter as an economic colony, and rejected Austrian attempts to
improve their position. It is far from clear that the British ministry put
much effort into the negotiations. The principal British negotiator, Colonel
Bladen, wrote from Antwerp in 1737, 'It is a vanity, incident to human
nature, to imagine whatever we are doing, attracts the attention even of our
superiors'. [34] Indeed righteous indignation was the principal British
response, Horace Walpole writing of Charles VI in September 1738: 'does
he expect that the Maritime Powers should hasten to his aid, and he still

keep up his pretensions of not executing the Barrier Treaty, or of insisting upon unreasonable terms of trade in the low countries, which they conquered at the expense of so much blood and treasure?'[35]

Angry at the Austrian position over trade with the Austrian Netherlands, the British were more optimistic about the possibility of trade with the *Erblande* via Trieste, and scheme to develop such trade was pushed from 1738, the initiative apparently having come from merchants active in Anglo-German trade, such as the Gore family, several of whom were MPs. It was hoped to replace the disparate tariffs of the *Erblande* by one duty, payable at Trieste, and to develop the area both as a market for British colonial re-exports such as sugar and for British manufactures, particularly woollen cloth, and as a source of raw materials, particularly minerals. Negotiations in Vienna in 1739-40 revealed an Austrian determination to protect their woollen industry, and initial British enthusiasm had waned by early 1740. It is very interesting to note that despite the desperate Austrian need of British diplomatic and military assistance in 1741, first against Prussia and then against Bavaria and France, the British ministry did not attempt to make assistance, including the payment of large subsidies, conditional upon the granting of commercial concessions. The need to secure Austrian agreement to territorial concessions to Prussia may have reduced the diplomatic leverage enjoyed by the British ministry, but it is interesting to note that the primacy of commercial considerations claimed by some historians cannot be substantiated by an examination of policy towards Austria in the last years of the Walpole ministry.[36]

The legacy of nearly thirty years of warfare ensured that Anglo-French commercial relations were in a poor state when the two governments signed a treaty of alliance in 1716. High tariffs had been imposed during the previous century, and an attempt by Bolingbroke in 1713 to follow the peace treaty of Utrecht by a treaty liberalising Anglo-French trade failed. The political storm that had greeted this proposal probably helps to account for the fact that during the Anglo-French alliance of 1716-31 the Whig ministry made no attempt to revive it. High tariffs remained on both sides of the Channel, and the mercantile communities of each country, supported by their governments, considered themselves in active competition. There is little sign that either government regarded this as unnatural, and there were singularly few proposals to improve trade links. Rather than following such a policy, Britain and France simply sought to avoid the worst consequences of colonial rivalry. A few proposals were made to improve direct trade links. One such is in the Stair papers, advocating the encouragement of imports of French alcohol into Britain in return for French concessions on British fish products. In 1724 it was rumoured that a commercial treaty was being considered.[37] Nothing came of such proposals and rumours, and it was widely accepted, during the period of the alliance, that both powers were in active competition. This was certainly a theme in the diplomatic instructions of the period. The French foreign minister Chauvelin wrote in 1730 that France hoped that better Anglo-Russian relations would have good consequences for the alliance, but was opposed to Britain gaining commercial concessions in the Russia trade.[38] There was particular tension over trade with Spain and with the Spanish colonies.[39] The French ministry resented British commercial concessions in these areas, and were under strong pressure from mercantile groups to improve the French position. In May 1728 the Bayonne Chamber of Commerce sent a memorandum to Chauvelin arguing that British possession of the *Asiento* limited markets for French industry. Similar representations were frequent, and the French ministry claimed, with some justice, that these affected their negotiations with Spain.[40] The British ministry, subject to domestic pressures on the issue, feared that their position was being eroded by French competition.

A major source of Anglo-French tension was colonial competition, in the West Indies, West Africa, North America and the Indian Ocean. In the Walpole period competition in the last sphere was not particularly serious, and the French East India Company, refounded in 1723, was willing to cooperate with the British in excluding new commercial rivals, Ostenders and Swedes, from Indian waters. In late 1733 governor Pitt of Madras and governor Lenoir of Pondicherry jointly seized the cargo of the Swedish East Indiaman the *Ulrica Eleonora* in the Indian roadstead of Porto Novo. There was British concern over the expansion of French commercial activities in the Indian Ocean, particularly the development of the French position in the Île de France (Mauritius) and the Île de Bourbon (Réunion) in the late 1730s, but tension did not rise to the levels it reached in the western hemisphere.[41]

West Africa, the source of slaves for the Americas, and of other valuable products such as gum, was a major area of tension involving not only Britain and France, but other European states also, particularly Portugal and the United Provinces. In the 1720s the principal rivals of the British were the two latter powers, both allies of Britain, and considerable violence characterised their competition, the British Royal Africa Company frequently complaining of attacks. In October 1723 the Portuguese destroyed its trading settlement at Cabinda, in 1725 it complained about French action on the Guinea coast, and in 1728 Dutch attacks upon its ships led to demands for naval protection, and the despatch of a British warship. As with the Dutch and Portuguese, so with the French, colonial competition was compatible with European alliance, particularly when, as in this case, the issue did not arouse much domestic interest.[42]

In the 1730s tension in West Africa centred on Anglo-French competition, but this was not noticeably different in type to the period when the two powers had been in alliance. Determined to protect their gum trade from the river Senegal, the French sought to limit the establishment of a British position on the river Gambia. In March 1733 Chauvelin complained to the British envoy that Britain was planning to invade the property of the French African Company and claimed that France would look upon such a step as an act of hostility. The British stated that French settlements on one part of the coast did not give the French a right to the trade of the whole coast, and that 'the French would engross the Gum trade because they buy that for 5 pounds a ton which sells for £100, if they can exclude others'.[43] Disagreements persisted, and diplomatic moves were made by both powers,[44] but conflict was avoided largely because neither state sought to fight and neither was under significant domestic pressure on the issue. The contrast with the fate of comparable Anglo-Spanish differences in the West Indies is an interesting one. In each case there was a contentious background of past agreements and settlements, and a dispute over the right to trade with unoccupied territory, but over West Africa the domestic pressure was weaker. The Royal Africa Company was unpopular in Britain: it suffered from a widespread dislike of the monopolistic position of chartered companies, and its frequent demands for assistance led to further criticism. The attitudes of the companies were important, but not decisive. Much depended on their strength and their need for governmental assistance. The Royal Africa Company, weak and endlessly soliciting ministerial and parliamentary assistance, was in a weaker position than the largely self-sufficient Hudson's Bay Company or the powerful East India Company. The latter's determination to preserve peaceful relations with France,[45] a policy in line with ministerial thinking, combined with its fiscal strength and influence, ensured that it was very influential. It was when a company or a pressure group advocated action that conflicted with ministerial views that the relative imperviousness of the government to mercantile pressure was revealed.

In the Walpole period Anglo-French colonial tension was strongest in the western hemisphere. In North Africa the colonial expansion of the two powers produced rivalry, particularly as each sought influence with the Indian tribes. This led to press comment[46] and diplomatic representations.[47] More serious was the position in the West Indies. The West Indian colonies of the two powers competed actively in the production of sugar for the European markets, and in trade, often illicit, with Spanish America and with the British North American colonies.[48] Furthermore relations were harmed by competing claims to several islands. Particularly serious in this period was the position of the island of St. Lucia. Granted by George I to the Duke of Montagu, it was settled, on his orders, in December 1722. The settlers were expelled the following January by the governor of Martinique, for the French also had longstanding claims to the island.[49] This French move received a lot of attention in London, particularly in the press.[50] It crystallised for many a feeling that France was weakening the British colonial and commercial position. The *London Journal* noted, 'The disappointment at St. Lucia having put people on enquiring into the state of the French power in the West Indies, it is agreed on all hands, that since the conclusion of the peace they have repair'd their old fortifications, built new ones, and increased their colonies, insomuch that they seem to have some extraordinary view that way if a war should break out again'.[51]

Similar sentiments were voiced about French intentions throughout the period of the alliance. The writer Erasmus Phillips voiced concern over French moves in North America: 'we ought to have a vigilant eye on France, who has made great encroachments since our first settlements there, and watches an opportunity to divest us of our properties in that part of the world'. In 1729 the opposition MP Captain Vernon claimed in the House of Commons that France could not be trusted to settle Anglo-Spanish differences, and spoke of 'the danger of our alliance with France, both as to the security of our commerce and government, that France dealing in the very commodities we do ourselves, namely, the woollen manufacture, 'twas a jest to think she will advantageous us that way by the mediation of peace ...'[52]

Opposition newspapers attacked the ministry by calling attention to the improvements in the French colonial and commercial position; these attacks were matched in Parliament, whilst in ministerial circles there was considerable unease over the issue.[53] And yet Anglo-French colonial and commercial rivalries were not pressed by either government, not because they were not concerned, but simply because they regarded the diplomatic benefits of the alliance as paramount. Noting the threat to British colonies from the expanding French colony of Louisiana, the *Weekly Packet* stated in 1719 that it was 'a time when other circumstances oblige us to favour the interest of France'. Four years later the French Chargé d'Affaires in London, Chammorel, ascribed the British government's passive response to the St. Lucia crisis to their need of a French alliance in order to maintain peace, essential both in order to ease the national debt and to lessen the Jacobite threat.[54] In the 1730 session, when the two old chestnuts of St. Lucia and French repairs to the harbour of Dunkirk were revived by the opposition in order to embarrass the ministry, many MPs, according to one member, Colonel Howard, though suspicious of French intentions, felt that they could not jeopardise the alliance by defeating the ministry on these points,[55] and in ministerial circles there was an unwillingness to jeopardise the Anglo-French alliance by harping on points of dispute. This was certainly so in the case of Horace Walpole (envoy in Paris, 1723-30), particularly over Dunkirk.[56] British envoys in Paris were regularly instructed to complain over commercial and colonial matters, and French envoys in London were pressed likewise, but there is an absence of urgency in these instructions, and complaints were often followed up in a perfunctory manner. This was the case both during and after the alliance of 1716-31, for in the 1730s neither government wished to convert the mistrustful neutrality of the other into outright hostility.

The failure to be seen publicly defending British commercial and colonial interests against French competition harmed the ministry domestically, and helped the opposition in its attempt to associate the Anglo-French alliance with the surrender of British interests. This was not too serious in the late 1710s when France, weakened by the War of the Spanish Succession, did not appear as a major threat. There was criticism of France for taking over some of Britain's carrying trade during the 1718-20 war with Spain, but this did not become a major issue. In the early 1720s the primacy of domestic issues, such as the South Sea Bubble and the Atterbury Plot, and the relatively uncontroversial nature of foreign policy during a period of European peace, led to a relatively low level of opposition attack on the Anglo-French alliance, but this changed in 1725, and thereafter the ministry were attacked every session over foreign policy. However, in many respects general denunciations of the ministry for following French diplomatic initiatives were less successful politically than specific attacks on supposed failures to defend British interests, and commercial and colonial issues (and the retention of Gibraltar) provided the best opportunities for the latter. Trade thus became a major issue in the public debate of foreign policy (as it rarely was in the 1720s in ministerial circles), because, unlike say the balance of power, it was a concrete issue. However, it was only in 1730, over Dunkirk, that the opposition selected an issue that could be used to seriously discredit the Anglo-French alliance. Prior to that they failed to capitalise on the general commercial (or for that matter religious and traditional) hostility to France.

In domestic political terms relations with France only seriously embarrassed the ministry in 1730. The position was very different with Spain. Anglo-Spanish commercial and colonial disputes were not noticeably different to those between Britain and France. Spanish disquiet about the new British colony of Georgia[57] was matched by Anglo-French territorial disputes elsewhere in North America; smuggling in breach of monopoly commercial privileges was a problem for all states with West Indian colonies; the British ships in the Channel that sought to prevent contraband trade with France (principally wool exports and alcohol imports) were even called in the British press *guardacostas,* [58] the term used to describe Spanish ships ordered to prevent contraband trade in the West Indies. Not only were the Anglo-Spanish disputes similar to disputes elsewhere; they were also capable of diplomatic solution, and such a settlement was reached with the Convention of the Pardo of 5 January (ns) 1739. With the important exception of quarrels over the *Asiento* and the permission ship, British contraband trade with the Spanish possessions was no different to Dutch and French trade, and both latter powers had significant quarrels with Spain over the issue. Indeed a Dutch-Spanish conflict was believed imminent in 1738.

Grievances over Anglo-Spanish commercial relations, with regard both to Spain itself and to the West Indies, had a long history. In the case of the trade with Old Spain the principal issue was the terms upon which British merchants in Spain were allowed to trade. There were frequent complaints over arbitrary Spanish fiscal demands, consular privileges, quarantine regulations and customs frauds. At times of poor Anglo-Spanish relations, as in the late 1720s, these were particularly serious, though even an easing of diplomatic relations, as that which followed the Treaty of Seville of November 1729, did not necessarily produce better conditions for British traders. In May 1730 William Cayley, Consul at Cadiz, wrote to the Duke of Newcastle, 'since my last arrival at this port, which is now two years, our trade has been subject to very great and frequent oppressions. Every article almost of the treaties have been infringed, and privileges of all kinds broke through . . .' [59]

These infringements were serious, but their political impact was limited, for several reasons. As is clear from the reports of French consular officials, such as Robin, D'Aubenton and Champeaux, the British position was not notably worse than that of other nations trading with Spain, particularly France. [60] Violence did not usually play any role in the disputes. It was easier for the Spanish government to control its agents in Spain, [61] and for redress of grievances, once granted, to be enforced than it was in the colonies. Much of the British trade to Old Spain was handled by merchants whose links with British political circles were poor: Jews, and Irish and English Catholics. Indeed, British diplomats and consuls often complained about the nature of the British mercantile community in Iberia.

The position in the West Indies was very different, and it was far easier for opposition politicians to exploit it. Compared to quarrels over the imposition of quarantine regulations at Cadiz in the late 1720s or the inspection of ships to prevent the evasion of tobacco duties in the mid-1730s, the disputes in the West Indies were often violent and spectacular. [62] The seizure of ships and the ill-treatment of sailors provided a vivid and easily grasped issue, and it is from this that the fame of Captain

Jenkins' ear, supposedly removed in the West Indies when his ship the *Rebecca* was seized in 1731, derived. These issues could be readily grasped, they provided good copy for the press and, as an issue of national pride and honour, they were most effective in Parliament. Compared to such issues as St. Lucia, confused at the Board of Trade and in Parliament with St. Vincent,[63] Spanish depredations on British commerce had a very wide emotional appeal. It was this that the opposition exploited, for the actual merits of the case were confused and difficult to grasp.

Opposition exploitation of the supposed ministerial failure to protect British trade in the West Indies was constant, both during periods when depredations were serious, and during other periods, such as 1732-6, when they were uncommon. The issue was made a more attractive one by the ministry's eagerness to claim that in their foreign policy they were taking care of British trade. This was the case both in Parliament[64] and in the ministerial press. The *St. James's Journal* in 1723 used the issue to argue that 'the event of His Majesty's measures proved, that the interests of his subjects were very safe in his care and concern for them'.[65] Ministerial defences of foreign policy initiatives, such as the Preliminaries of Paris (May 1727), the Treaty of Seville and the Second Treaty of Vienna, stressed the government's care for trade with the Spanish Empire, and it is hardly surprising that the opposition chose to attack on the issue. Furthermore, as with Dunkirk, past declarations made the ministry more vulnerable.

Claiming to defend trade, the ministry were nevertheless prepared to question mercantile grievances over the situation in the West Indies. The ministerial press attacked what they claimed to be exaggeration of the extent of depredations,[66] insisting that the Old Spain trade should not be neglected in favour of that with the colonies,[67] and the ministry, although frequently pressing Spain for redress over grievances, were nevertheless unhappy about mercantile claims. In 1728 Townshend and Walpole advocated selling the *Asiento* to Spain, a sensible move that would have eased tension, but this was resisted by important elements in the South Sea Company.[68] Three years later Benjamin Keene, Minister Plenipotentiary in Spain, criticised the Company's demands.[69] In 1731 Delafaye, Undersecretary of State in the Southern Department, the Department responsible for Anglo-Spanish diplomatic relations and for colonial issues, argued, correctly, that the petition of the Bristol mercantile community to Parliament, complaining about Spanish depredations, exaggerated the nature of the problem.[70] An ambivalence in ministerial attitudes to mercantile grievances was apparent, and this lent weight to opposition arguments. The ministry were well aware of the popularity of the opposition case, and of the political dangers it posed. In March 1730 Horace Walpole remarked that the opposition had decided at first to base their parliamentary assault on the ministry on the issue: 'The opponents of the ministers had entertained last summer such a sanguine and certain persuasion that it would be impossible to have made a peace with Spain; and consequently that the British commerce would have still continued in an uncertain and precarious state without satisfaction or revenge, that they had concerted their measures to call the ministers to an account for their indolence and neglect in suffering so patiently the insults of the Spaniards, and as this was a very popular spirit to a nation jealous of their humour, as well as of their privileges of trade, it had created a great ferment . . . all sorts of people, gentlemen as well as merchants . . .'[71] The continual press interest in the issue, and the relatively successful opposition exploitation of it in several parliamentary sessions, particularly that of 1729,[72] forced the ministry to consider how they could best avoid political difficulties over the depredations. Indeed many European commentators argued that the importance of trade with the Spanish Empire drastically limited the ministry's freedom of diplomatic manoeuvre.[73] In contrast to opposition suggestions, as in 1729, that Spain should be coerced by means of naval action – the traditional Tory 'blue water policy' – the ministry hoped to win Spanish agreement to respect existing agreements over trade (and Gibraltar) by supporting Spanish interests in Italy, and, in particular, the introduction of Spanish garrisons into Tuscany and Parma as stipulated in the Quadruple Alliance of 1718. This formed the basis of the Seville Treaty of 1729 and was a major element in Anglo-Austrian negotiations in 1730-1.[74] Britain sought, successfully, to win Austrian acceptance of the garrisons, claiming that it was essential for the sake of British commerce. Conversely Spain threatened in 1730 to limit British concessions if Britain failed to support her over the garrisons, whilst Britain threatened to withdraw support for the Spanish position in Italy if her commercial rights were infringed.[75] In March 1732 Newcastle responded to reports that Tuscany was seeking commercial concessions in the Spanish Empire by ordering Keene to tell the Spanish first minister, Patino, 'if the settlement of Don Carlos in Italy, procured singly by the King, should be followed by a Treaty of Commerce with the Florentines, prejudicial to Great Britain, it would be such a notorious mark of ingratitude, as could not fail of exasperating the whole nation against them, and of depriving them of that support, which by a strict observance of their Treatys, and by a proper behaviour towards the King and his people, they may always expect from His Majesty'.[76] This policy succeeded in the early 1730s. The Treaty of Seville prevented a resumption of the serious parliamentary attacks over depredations that had been so important in the 1729 session, the Spanish accession to the Second Treaty of Vienna in July 1731 helped to ensure a satisfactory discussion of foreign policy issues in the 1732 session, and in early 1732 the Spanish ministry made moves to limit the activities of the *guardacostas*,[77] moves that helped to reduce the extent and seriousness of depredations. The opposition continued to bring the issue up in Parliament and the press,[78] and occasional Spanish seizures of British ships, such as those collecting salt in the Tortuga Islands in 1733, kept the issue alive.

The depredations issue became serious again in 1737, and owed something to increased Spanish determination to limit contraband in the face of the terrible inroads it was making in Spanish American trade,[79] a determination that led to the capture of about a dozen British ships that year, but it owed more to the decision of the opposition to treat this as the chief topic upon which to attack the ministry. The reasons are unclear – possibly they reflect the failure of the Bolingbroke campaign with its central attack on corruption and the need for a more concrete issue, possibly the shift of relative importance within the opposition from Pulteney, Bolingbroke and the *Craftsman*, to Chesterfield, the 'Boy Patriots' such as Pitt and Lyttelton, and the opposition newspapers that were to rise to prominence in the last years of the Walpole ministry, *Common Sense* and the *Champion*. The sustained opposition campaign placed the ministry in a difficult position, for they were no longer able to play the card of supporting Spanish interests in Italy. The Franco-Austrian alliance following the Third Treaty of Vienna limited Spanish aspirations and Britain's capacity to support them, and it was not until the disintegration of this alliance in 1741 that such a policy could be rumoured or considered.[80] It was to be the basis of various tentative Anglo-Spanish diplomatic approaches during the War of the Austrian Succession.

The British ministry were well aware of the seriousness of the situation. Horace Walpole correctly argued 'that our subjects will scarce be made easy with general assurances only of a disposition in the Spanish Court to live well with us',[81] and the ministry pressed Spain to settle mercantile grievances.[82] The Spanish ministry did not want war, and, as Keene pointed out, the difficulties facing British trade were matched by those facing the French.[83] Negotiations, rendered lengthy largely by the disorganised state of the Spanish government, produced a settlement, in the negotiation of which Sir Robert Walpole played a major role. Spain agreed to pay £95,000 to satisfy British claims over depredations, whilst the points at issue were to be settled by plenipotentiaries. This agreement – the Convention of the Pardo – contained many difficulties. Spain had only signed it on condition that the South Sea Company paid £68,000 which was admitted to be owing to Spain, but which the Company, angry at Spanish conduct over the previous decade, refused to pay.

Given a peaceful domestic situation in Britain, a compromise could well have been made. The Convention of the Pardo was itself a second agreement, an initial convention (9 September (ns) 1738) having failed to satisfy the British. But in 1738-9 a diplomatic solution of commercial problems was no longer the key to the situation. The dispute was no longer a commercial one; it was rather about trade as a political weapon. The British opposition were intent upon using the issue of trade both to discredit the ministry and to provoke, if possible, the weakening or disintegration of the Spanish Empire. Wrapping themselves in the flag, they fostered unreasonable expectations. Horace Walpole commented in March.1739, 'ambition, avarice, distress, disappointment, and all the complicated vices that tend to render the minds of men uneasy, are got out of Pandora's box, and fill all places and all hearts in the nation'.[84] However, as with the Excise Crisis in 1733,[85] the crucial element was not simply the widespread agitation, but rather its relationship to strains within the ministry and doubts within ministerial ranks in Parliament. Henry Etough, a confidant of the Walpoles, noted that although the Convention won parliamentary approval, 'many of the majority in private conversation wished for war, and reproached the minister for want of courage'.[86] Trade with the Spanish Empire was the successful political issue it was because it could be used to focus widespread dissatisfaction, and because, unlike the Excise Crisis when the ministry simply withdrew the contentious legislation, the ministry's field of manoeuvre was limited. As a result the ministry felt it necessary to reverse an earlier order and to keep Admiral Haddock's squadron in Spanish waters, the final issue that wrecked the Anglo-Spanish negotiations by leading the Spaniards to abandon the path of compromise and negotiation.[87]

The Jenkins' War episode reveals, not the importance of commercial considerations in the conduct of foreign policy, but the strength of defending trade as a political issue. The opposition in 1738-9 were advocating a foolish policy. War with Spain wrecked the Old Spain trade and did not produce the expected collapse of the Spanish Empire. Anglo-Spanish commercial differences were not settled to Britain's satisfaction in the Treaty of Aix-la-Chapelle that ended the war, and Britain lost a lot of its trade during the war to other powers.[88] Many British ships were taken by privateers, insurance premiums rose, and convoying proved difficult to arrange. The war was bad for commerce, as well as being a disaster politically and fiscally.

British foreign policy in the 1730s sought to favour trade by encouraging peace. This was one of the bases of Walpole's position, and he believed that peace was beneficial to the whole economy. In 1739 he justified British neutrality in the War of the Polish Succession by claiming, correctly 'by our neutrality at this juncture, we reaped the sweets of an unrivalled, uninterrupted commerce for several years; a consideration, Sir, that, of all others, ought most to influence the conduct of a trading nation'. In the same speech he stated with regard to mercantile pressure for war with Spain, 'however some private persons might suffer, with whatever reason they might call out for justice upon Spain, yet our pacific forbearance was the safest and wisest conduct for the general interest of a trading people',[89]in which view he was justified by the succeeding war. In the long term it is possible to argue that Britain gained from her colonial struggles in the mid-eighteenth century. By the Peace of Paris in 1763 Canada was British, India in the British sphere of influence, Spain humbled. The benefits of empire are difficult to evaluate, and not all contemporaries thought these conquests worth the cost. The decision to fight Spain in 1739 was a mistake, as Britain was not strong enough to confront both Spain and her French ally successfully, and as these powers could play the Jacobite card. The opposition, with their empty boasts of national glory, ignored the Bourbon threat, and British commerce suffered from the opposition's ideology of gaining trade and empire through conflict. It was easy for the opposition to applaud such sentiments as

> Rule, Britannia, rule the waves:
> Britons never will be slaves.[90]

The reality was to be sailors rotting off Cartagena in 1741, and French warships in the Channel in 1744.

NOTES

1. Significant works on economic and fiscal matters include E. L. Jones (ed.), *Agriculture and Economic Growth in England, 1650-1815* (1967); P. G. M. Dickson, *The Financial Revolution* (Oxford, 1967); W. E. Minchinton (ed.), *The Growth of English Overseas Trade in the Seventeenth and Eighteenth Centuries* (1969); A. J. Little, *Deceleration in the Eighteenth Century British Economy* (1976); R. Davis, 'English Foreign Trade, 1700-74', *Economic History Review* (1962).

2. G. Symcox, 'Britain and Victor Amadeus II', in Baxter (ed.), *England's Rise*, pp. 151-2; G. Niedhart, *Handel und Krieg in der Britischen Weltpolitik, 1738-63* (Munich, 1979).

3. Poem, 'Probus to Philartes', in Anon., *A New Miscellany for the Year 1738* (1738), p. 16.

4. *Weekly Courant*, Nottingham opposition paper, 1 Mar. 1739; *Common Sense*, 17 Feb. 1739; *Craftsman*, 20 July 1728.

5. McLachlan, *Trade and Peace with Old Spain* (Cambridge, 1940); H. E. S. Fisher, *The Portugal Trade. A Study of Anglo-Portuguese Commerce, 1700-70* (1972); Reading, *Anglo-Russian Commercial Treaty* (New Haven, 1938); D. J. Ormrod, 'Anglo-Dutch Commerce, 1700-1760' (Ph.D., Cambridge, 1973); M. J. Jubb, 'Fiscal Policy in England in the 1720s and 1730s' (Ph.D., Cambridge, 1977); L. Sutherland, *The East India Company in Eighteenth Century Politics* (Oxford, 1952); N. C. Hunt, 'The Russia Company and the Government, 1730-42', *Oxford Slavonic Papers* 7 (1957); L. M. Penson, 'The London West India Interest in the Eighteenth Century', *EHR* 36 (1921); R. B. Sheridan, 'The Molasses Act and the Market Strategy of the British Sugar Planters', *Journal of Economic History* 17 (1957); F. G. James, 'The Irish Lobby in the Eighteenth Century', *EHR* 81 (1966); E. Hughes, *North Country Life in the Eighteenth Century* (1952), pp. 290-303.

6. *Daily Gazetteer,* 30 Oct. 1740, 25 Aug. 1735.

7. *St. James' Evening Post,* 2 Mar. 1732.

8. Anon., *The Occasional Writer,* No. 1. (1727), p. 25; Waldegrave Journal, 16 Oct. (ns) 1727, Chewton; Horace Walpole to Delafaye, 7 Sept. (ns) 1728, PRO. 78/188; Keene to Horace Walpole and Poyntz, 20 Oct. (ns) 1729, BL. Add. 32763; Count Königsegg, Austrian envoy in Spain, to Pententriedter, 7 Mar. (ns) 1728, HHStA, Frankreich, Varia, 12; Horace Walpole to Townshend, 24 July (ns) 1728, Bradfer Lawrence.

9. Townshend to William Finch, 29 Sept. 1727, PRO. 84/294; Harrington to Horace Walpole, 13 July 1739, PRO. 84/380.

10. Horace Walpole to Harrington, 18 July (ns) 1735, PRO. 84/345.

11. Horace Walpole, Stanhope and Poyntz to Newcastle, 10 Aug. (ns) 1727, BL. Add. 32757.

12. Waldegrave Journal, 10 Nov. (ns) 1727, Chewton.

13. *Political State of Great Britian* (Jan. 1739), pp. 38-9; Cobbett, IX, 808, 14 Feb. 1735; Tilson to Titley, 8 Ap., 26 July 1737, BL. Egerton Mss. 2684.

14. Allen to Delafaye, 9 Sept. (ns) 1732, PRO. 92/34.

15. Essex to Newcastle, 13 Sept. (ns) 1734, PRO. 92/35.

16. *York Courant,* 4 Jan. 1732; C. Gill, 'The Affair of Porto Novo: An incident in Anglo-Swedish Relations', *EHR* 73 (1958).

17. Finch to Harrington, 2 Jan. 1739, Harrington to Finch, 28 July 1730, PRO. 95/84, 55; Le Coq to Lagnasc, 9 Jan. (ns) 1725, Dresden, 2673.

18. M. Huisman, *La Belgique Commerciale sous l'Empereur Charles VI: La Compagnie d'Ostende* (Brussels, 1902); G. Hertz, 'England and the Ostend Company', *EHR* 22 (1907).

19. Keene to Waldegrave, 4 Dec. (ns) 1736, Chewton.

20. Tyrawly to Newcastle, 25 Sept. (ns) 1728, Tyrawly to Delafaye, 25 Feb. (ns) 1729, PRO. 89/35. Cayley, Consul at Cadiz, to Keene, 22 June (ns) 1728, PRO. 94/218; Walpole to Townshend, 2 Oct. 1725, Coxe, II, 485.

21. Bishop Downes of Meath to Bishop Nicolson of Derry, 7 Oct. 1724, *Letters on various subjects . . . to and from William Nicolson* (2 vols., 1809, cont. paginated), II, 585; Robinson to Harrington, 17 Sept. (ns) 1738, PRO. 80/131.

22. Nicholas Paxton, the Treasury Solicitor, to Lord [Harrington?], 16 May 1738, PRO. 36/45.

23. Hunt, 'Russia Company'; Russia Company memorial to Townshend, 20 Ap. 1729, PRO. 91/107.

24. Newcastle to Essex, 12 Oct. 1732, PRO. 92/34.

25. *Wye's Letter* 5 Jan. 1730; Egmont I, 341.

26. PRO. 35/56 ff. 118-23.

27. Newcastle to Burges, – Ap. 1731, 29 Ap. 1734, Burges to Newcastle, 4, 25 June (ns) 1734, representation of the merchants and sugar refiners of Bristol to George II, PRO. 99/80, 99/63, 36/31; Imberto, Venetian envoy in London, to the Senate of Venice, 14 May (ns) 1734, ASV. LM. Ing. 100.

28. Finch to Harrington, 27 Feb. (ns) 1739, 7 Oct. (ns) 1735, PRO. 95/84, 95/72; Sparre, Swedish envoy in London, to Frederick I, 13 Nov. (ns) 1733, PRO. 107/18.

29. Wych to Harrington, 25 Mar. (ns) 1737, PRO. 82/58.

30. Waldegrave to Townshend, 17 July (ns) 1728, PRO. 80/61; Waldegrave to Horace Walpole, 16 July (ns) 1728, Chewton; *Mist's Weekly Journal,* 30 July 1726; Le Coq to Augustus II, 24 Dec. (ns) 1726, Dresden, 2675.

31. Anon., *The Pretensions of Don Carlos Considered,* p. 13; Edward Finch to Townshend, 9 Ap. (ns) 1727, PRO. 88/34.

32. Hugh Thomas, Jacobite agent in London, to Earl of Mar, 22 Dec. 1718, RA. 41/13; Townshend to Poyntz, 12 July 1726, BL. Add. 49891. The suppression of Austrian industries had been discussed by the Dutch in 1731, Chesterfield to Harrington, 1 May (ns) 1731, PRO. 84/312.

33. Harrington to Robinson, 18, 21 Jan., 1, 11 Feb., 4 Ap. (quote), Robinson to Harrington, 23 Jan. (ns) 1732, PRO. 80/84-6.

34. Bladen to Waldegrave, 13 Oct. (ns) 1737, Chewton; Bladen, '. . . the Matters which gave rise to the Conferences at Antwerp, and . . . the several points discussed there', PRO. 80/136 ff. 138-47.

35. Horace Walpole to Trevor, 29 Sept. 1738, Trevor, 14.

36. P. Dickson, 'English Commercial Negotiations with Austria, 1737-1752', in Whiteman, Bromley and Dickson (eds.), *Statesmen, Scholars and Merchants*, pp. 81-112.

37. Anon., undated, 'Proposal for opening a branch of the trade betwixt Great Britain and France', SRO. GD. 135/147 No. 23; Le Coq to Lagnasc, 15 Aug. (ns) 1724, Dresden 2676, III.

38. Chauvelin to Magnan, 12 June (ns) 1730, *Sbornik Imperatorskogo Russkogo Istoricheskogo Obschchevstva* (148 vols., St. Petersburg, 1867-1916), 81, p. 47.

39. Horace Walpole to Newcastle, 7 June (ns), Newcastle to William Stanhope, 5 June (ns), Horace Walpole, William Stanhope and Poyntz to Newcastle, 10 Aug. (ns) 1728, BL. Add. 32739, 32757.

40. Chamber of Commerce to Chauvelin, 22 May (ns) 1728, AE. CP. Ang. 364; Memoir of M. Gregoire deputé du commerce de Provence, undated AN. AM. B^7 294.

41. Gill, 'Porto Novo', *EHR* 73; P. D. Hollingworth, 'A Study of the Policy of La Bourdonnais, 1735-47' (M. A. Durham, 1957).

42. Africa Company memoranda 13, 28 Feb., 4, 18 Dec. 1724, 18 Mar. 1725, 18 Mar. 1726, PRO. 35/48, 54, 55, 61; Townshend to William Finch, 10 June 1726, PRO. 84/290; Africa Company to Burchett, Secretary of the Admiralty, 28 May, 6 June, 3 Aug. 1728, PRO. ADM 1/3810.

43. Waldegrave to Newcastle, 29 Mar. (ns) 1733, BL. Add. 32781; Couraud to Waldegrave, 25 June 1733, enclosing 'Observations relating to the Gum Trade', Chewton.

44. Chavigny to Chauvelin, 24 Dec. (ns) 1735, AE. CP. Ang. 392; Admiral Wager to Newcastle, 18 Nov. 1736, PRO. 42/21; Amelot to Cambis, 16 Feb. (ns) 1738, PRO. 107/21.

45. Delafaye to Waldegrave, 10 Feb. 1732, Chewton.

46. *British Journal,* 11 July 1724, reporting a representation from the General Assembly of South Carolina; *London Evening Post,* 8 Jan., 5 Feb. 1737; Chammorel to Dubois, 21 Jan. (ns) 1723, AE. CP. Ang. 344.

47. Horace Walpole to Newcastle, 10 July (ns) 1728, BL. Add. 32756; Waldegrave to Chauvelin, 13 June (ns) 1732, Waldegrave to Newcastle, 27 June (ns) 1732, BL. Add. 32777.

48. Board of Trade to George I, 24 July 1724, PRO. 35/50; *Craftsman,* 8 Nov. 1729.

49. Dubois to Stair, 5 May (ns) 1719, J. M. Graham, *Annals and Correspondence of the Viscount and the First and Second Earls of Stair* (2 vols., 1875), II, pp. 111-12; Destouches to Dubois, 31 Aug. (ns) 1722, French memorandum, 12 Oct. (ns) 1722, AE. CP. Ang. 342, Sup. 7 f.56-8; settlement of 8 Jan. 1723, Northumberland Record Office, Delaval Papers 650/c/18/2.

50. *Loyal Observator,* 9 Mar. 1723; *Weekly Journal or Saturday's Post,* 9 Mar. 1723; *London Journal,* 13 Ap. 1723; Chammorel to Dubois, 5 Ap. (ns), Destouches to Dubois, 29 Ap. (ns) 1723, AE. CP. Ang. 344.

51. *London Journal,* 27 Ap. 1723.

52. E. Phillips, *The State of the Nation in respect to her Commerce, Debts, and Money* (2nd ed., 1726), p. 10; Egmont, III, 331.

53. Newcastle to Townshend, 13 June 1729, PRO. 43/77.

54. *Weekly Packet*, 26 Sept. 1719; Chammorel to Morville, 7 Oct. (ns) 1723, AE. CP. Ang. 346.

55. HMC. *Carlisle*, p. 67.

56. Horace Walpole to Delafaye, 14 Dec. (ns) 1729, PRO. 78/192; Horace Walpole to Newcastle, 10 Sept. (ns) 1730, BL. Add. 32769.

57. Newcastle to Keene, 24 Mar., 7 Ap., 5 May, 12 Sept. 1737, PRO. 94/129; Bussy, French envoy in London, to Amelot, 4 Ap. (ns), 20 June (ns), 5 Aug. (ns) 1737, AE. CP. Ang. 394-5; Harrington to Horace Walpole, 30 Aug. 1737, PRO. 84/367; J. T. Lanning, *The Diplomatic History of Georgia: A Study of the Epoch of Jenkins' Ear* (Chapel Hill, 1936).

58. *Daily Post Boy*, 26 Mar. 1731.

59. Cayley to Newcastle, 9 May (ns) 1730, PRO. 94/219.

60. Memoranda from French merchants in Carthagena, 4 Nov. (ns) 1715, 7 Sept. (ns) 1716, Robin to Maurepas, 24 Aug. (ns) 1724, D'Aubenton to Maurepas, 5 July (ns) 1728, 7 Ap. (ns), 4 Aug. (ns), 16 Nov. (ns) 1730, AN. AM. B⁷ 265, 268, 284, 292, 302-4; Waldegrave to Newcastle, 9 Feb. (ns) 1732, 7 Mar. (ns) 1733, BL.Add. 32776, 32780; Keene to Newcastle, 14 Oct. (ns), 11 Nov. (ns) 1737, PRO. 94/128.

61. Delafaye to Waldegrave, 3 Mar. 1733, Chewton.

62. E. G. Hildner, *The Caribbean in Anglo-Spanish Diplomacy, 1720-62* (D. Phil., Michigan, no date); F. J. Maning, *The Duke of Newcastle and the West Indies* (Ph.D., Yale, 1925); J. McLeish, *Yutcan and the eighteenth century Mosquito Shore* (M.A., London, 1926).

63. Poyntz to Delafaye, 1 Ap. (ns) 1730, PRO. 78/194.

64. Royal speech at end of session, 10 Aug. 1721; Broglie to Chauvelin, 26 Dec. (ns) 1730, AE. CP. Ang. 371.

65. *St. James's Journal*, 23 Mar. 1723; *St. James's Evening Post* 27 Aug. 1730.

66. *Hyp Doctor*, 9 Mar. 1731, 11 July 1732; *Flying Post*, 11, 20 July 1732; *Craftsman*, 15 July 1732.

67. *Whitehall Evening Post*, 5 Sept. 1728; 414 of the 666 marchantmen entering Cadiz in 1732 were British, 330 of 519 (1733), 596 of 1002 (1734): *St. James' Evening Post*, 1 Feb. 1733, *General Evening Post*, 19 Jan. 1734, *Daily Post Boy*, 21 Jan. 1735.

68. Townshend to Horace Walpole, 24 June 1728, Bradfer Lawrence; *Daily Post Boy*, 30 Mar. 1733.

69. Keene to Newcastle, 10 Jan. (ns) 1731, PRO. 94/107; Keene to Robinson, 15 Dec. (ns) 1730, BL. Add. 23780.

70. Delafaye to Waldegrave, 8 Mar. 1731, 3 Mar. 1733, Chewton.

71. Horace Walpole to Waldegrave, 13 Mar. 1730, Chewton.

72. Knatchbull, 13 Mar. 1729, pp. 91-2; Thomas Winnington MP to Hervey, 9 Ap. 1729, Dorchester, Dorset Record Office, Ilchester Papers D124/box 240.

73. Harrington to Newcastle, 4 Sept. (ns) 1735, PRO. 43/87.

74. Draft account by Sinzendorf of conference with Robinson that evening, 25 Oct. (ns) 1730, HHStA. England, Noten, 2; Harrington to Chesterfield, 5 Mar. 1731, PRO. 84/312.

75. Newcastle to Keene, 25 July 1730, BL. Add. 32769.

76. Newcastle to Keene, 16 Mar. 1732, PRO. 94/113.

77. Joint declaration signed by Keene and Spanish ministers, 8 Feb. (ns) 1732.

78. Cobbett, IX 593, 687, 29 Mar. 1734, 23 Jan. 1735.

79. Vandermeer, Dutch envoy in Spain, to the States General, 22 Dec. (ns) 1738, PRO. 84/378; G. Walker, *Spanish Politics and Imperial Trade, 1700-1789* (1979), pp. 193-209.

80. Robinson to Harrington, 25 Jan. (ns), 22 Feb. (ns) 1741, PRO. 80/144.

81. Horace Walpole to Keene, 29 Nov. (ns) 1737, PRO. 84/369.

82. Keene to Newcastle, 13 Dec. (ns) 1737, PRO. 94/128.

83. Keene to Newcastle, 14 Oct. (ns) 1737, PRO. 94/128.
84. Horace Walpole to Trevor, 16 Mar. 1739, Trevor, 17.
85. P. Langford, *The Excise Crisis* (Oxford, 1975), p. 85.
86. BL. Add. 9200 f. 63.
87. R. Pares, *War and Trade in the West Indies, 1739-63* (Oxford, 1936).
88. *Northampton Mercury,* 6 Aug. 1739.
89. Walpole 21 Nov. 1739, Cobbett, XI, 231-2.
90. J. Thomson and D. Malet, *Alfred: a masque* (1740), II, v.

A Confessional Policy? Religion and British Foreign Policy

'we Protestants are so lukewarm against fiery Catholicks that all parade, all shew, and all real unanimity should be used to convince them that we will not be tricked this time as we have been formerly.'   Tilson, 1736[1]

The influence of religion on the public's view of Europe and on the conduct of British foreign policy is a subject that has received little attention. It might not appear to be an important subject: for much of the period British foreign policy was based upon an alliance with either France or Austria, both champions of the Catholic Church, although neither was as conspicuously involved in anti-Protestant action as in the previous forty years. Louis XIV had followed a marked anti-Huguenot policy, and had been stridently denounced for it in Britain, while the Habsburg conflict with their rebellious Hungarian subjects had to a great extent been a religious struggle between Protestant Hungarians and the Emperor and had been followed with great attention in Western Europe. Religious conflict or conflict with religious elements on this scale did not recur in the age of Walpole. The violence involved in the so-called Thorn massacre of 1724, when religious disturbances in Polish Prussia led to governmental intervention and the execution of some of the leading citizens of Thorn,[2] or in the Salzburg disturbances in 1731-2, when the Prince-Archbishop of Salzburg's proselytising policies were met by popular opposition and mass emigration,[3] was minimal compared to that of the period 1680-1720. However, it would be mistaken to assume that there was little religious tension in Europe. The Counter-Reformation in the Empire was still an active process, and Catholicism appeared to be on the advance in Central Europe. Within Protestant German circles there was a sense of challenge and threat which played a major role in the spiritual revival of German Protestantism in the early eighteenth century. In the late 1710s religious tension within the Empire had nearly produced conflict.[4] Hanoverian policy, therefore, was strongly influenced by an awareness of confessional rivalry. The Protestant position in northern Germany had been greatly weakened, firstly by the conversion of the Electoral house of Saxony to Catholicism, a step that owed much to the designs of Augustus II and Augustus III on the Polish throne, and secondly by the integration of the independent ecclesiastical principalities of north-west Germany into the Wittelsbach power bloc. Klemens August, Archbishop-Elector of Cologne 1723-61, was also bishop of the Lower Saxon and Westphalian bishoprics of Münster, Paderborn, Hildesheim, and Osnabrück. These developments harmed the Protestant position in north Germany, and the Wittelsbach bloc, in particular, challenged the Hanoverian wish to dominate north-west Germany. The

Hanoverians claimed a right to protect the rights of Protestants in this area, such as those of the townspeople of Hildesheim, and they had the right to nominate every other Prince Bishop of Osnabrück. Hanoverian influence was therefore challenged when the Catholics in the area could look to the Wittelsbachs for support. As a result the Hanoverians sought to limit Wittelsbach influence, and to prevent the election of Wittelsbach prelates.[5] The resulting tension hindered attempts in 1729-30 to negotiate an Anglo-Wittelsbach alliance, and it was argued that the Hanoverian decision in 1730 to support the townspeople of Hildesheim against the Prince Bishop played a major role in wrecking the negotiations.[6]

At the Imperial Diet in Regensburg, Hanoverian diplomats championed the cause of oppressed Protestants within the Empire. Suspicion of Austrian policy within the Empire was increased by its close association with the Imperial Vice-Chancellor, Schönborn, Bishop of Würzburg. St. Saphorin's willingness to support and expound the cause of Protestants within the Empire doubtless harmed Anglo-Austrian relations: had a British diplomat handled Anglo-Austrian relations, they might well have been smoother on the religious front, though Edward Finch's conduct at Dresden suggests a need for caution in suggesting this. The destruction of Hanoverian diplomatic material makes it difficult to write on the subject with certainty, but insofar as a Hanoverian political-religious policy can be isolated, it was one of support for oppressed Protestants and the creation of a German Protestant league.[7] Good relations with Hesse-Cassel were stressed, and most, though not all, Hanoverians ministers hoped that it would be possible to create a Hanoverian-Prussian alliance that would champion the Protestant cause within the Empire. Cooperation between the two powers during the religious crisis of 1719-20 was less than perfect, but there was a shared awareness of the need to combine in the face of the Catholic advance which played a role in the Treaties of Charlottenburg (1723) and Hanover (1725) and in the response to the Thorn crisis. Prussian interest in the Hanover alliance owed much to Frederick William I's desire to obtain French and British support for his claims to the Jülich-Berg inheritance, claims contested by the Wittelsbachs. Despite the major role of France in the Hanover alliance, it could be presented in the Empire as an alliance aimed against Catholic Austrians. As Carteret had pointed out in 1722, 'la France est toujours Protestante en Allemagne'.[8]

Given this strong Hanoverian stance on confessional matters, it is necessary to supplement Hatton's portrayal of George I as a figure of the early Enlightenment by noting that he can also be presented as a Protestant crusader, and a keen supporter of the Protestant position within the Empire.[9] There is less evidence in the case of George II, possibly reflecting the relative diminution of confessional tension after the 1720s and the success of the Prussians in presenting themselves as the champions of Protestantism. The extent to which the religious attitudes and Electoral confessional policies of George I and George II influenced their policy in Britain is a topic about which it is difficult to find any information. In domestic terms there was a clear relationship with Archbishop Wake's interest in developing links with foreign churches that did not obey Papal authority, including the Gallican church of France, and with the Sunderland ministry's attempts in the late 1710s to satisfy Dissenter demands. George I was closely associated with Sunderland's policies.

However, in terms of foreign policy there was no clear confessional approach. Intervention on behalf of Protestants abroad who were being denied their rights and/or persecuted was a course of action that could be, and was, followed,[10] but it was not a diplomatic strategy. A strategy that was discussed was the concept of a Protestant league, though it is significant that it tended to be raised in British circles largely when there was a feeling that Britain was isolated (1735-40) or that she was losing the initiative to a powerful ally (early 1720s, winters of 1727-8 and 1729-30). In 1721 Whitworth, fearful that the Catholic powers sought to disunite the Protestants, argued in favour of a Protestant League of Prussia, Britain, Denmark and Hesse-Cassel: 'the occasion for it can never be more plausible and when once established the two mighty Houses of Austria and Bourbon will be obliged on every turn to have no small regards for them'.[11] The following year Townshend informed St. Saphorin that George I thought the best way to deal with confessional problems in the Empire was to create a union among the Protestant Princes.[12] In 1736 and 1737 there was a lot of press discussion in Britain about the possibility of a Protestant League.[13] It could be suggested that the idea played an important part in encouraging hopes that the succession of Frederick the Great would lead to the creation of such a league. The idea of an Anglo-Prussian alliance was a diplomatic scheme designed to act as a counterpoise to the Austro-French alliance. It was also a project whose rationale rested on untested concepts of mutual interest, in which religious factors played a major role.

The idea of a Protestant league had many weaknesses. Townshend noted in 1722 that whenever George I had taken initiatives in that direction, the particular views of princes had taken precedence over 'le Bien Public'.[14] The Protestant princes clashed over territorial and jurisdictional interests in Germany. Aside from the numerous Hanoverian-Prussian disputes, Prussia had designs on Swedish Pomerania. Also, Denmark had designs on Hamburg, most seriously in 1734-5, which British diplomats were instructed to thwart. Dutch-Prussian disputes over East Friesland and over Prussian recruiting in Dutch frontier areas were serious, the latter nearly leading to war in the spring of 1733, when George II made it clear that he would support the Dutch. Even when both Britain-Hanover and Prussia were seeking redress for oppressed Protestants, they disagreed over methods.[15]

Aside from specific quarrels between Protestant princes, their general diplomatic policies were at variance with the idea of a Protestant league. The Dutch, militarily vulnerable to France, sought a system that would prevent conflict in Western Europe. They were therefore delighted with the Anglo-French alliance, and sought to associate themselves with this pact, although they were disinclined to incur any commitments. Just as a pact with France countered Hanoverian feelings of vulnerability in the face of Prussia, so the possibility of French military aid was of great importance to the Dutch, whose exposed eastern border was threatened by the Prussian bases at Wesel and Minden. The ending of the Anglo-French alliance in 1731 placed the Dutch in a difficult position. This was made clear in the Anglo-French war panic of that summer. Chesterfield wrote from The Hague of 'the excessive fears they had here of a rupture between His Majesty and France'.[16] Awareness of their vulnerability to France, an awareness that stemmed from the 1672 French invasion and from the French occupation of the Spanish Netherlands in the early stages of the War of the Spanish Succession, greatly influenced Dutch policy in the 1730s, leading to a Dutch desire to settle the Jülich-Berg dispute and avoid the risk of a war in the Rhineland, to the neutrality agreement with France in 1733, and to pressure in 1734-5 for a negotiated end to the War of the Polish Succession. Influenced by fear of France, Dutch policy increasingly diverged from that of Britain. The long delays in acceding to the Second Treaty of Vienna – delays which so exasperated Chesterfield – were hardly novel:[17] the Dutch constitution and political system made haste difficult,[18] and the Dutch had taken some time before joining the Alliance of Hanover, whilst they had refused to join the Quadruple Alliance. More worrying for the British were signs of independent Dutch action. The 1733 neutrality agreement with France was negotiated without the British being either consulted or informed. The British ministry were very concerned about improved Franco-Dutch relations[19] and what they saw as the Francophile policies of the Dutch envoy in Paris, van Hoey.[20] The British ministerial argument that intervention in the War of the Polish Succession was impossible as the Dutch would not support such a British policy, was not simply an excuse to avoid action. Dutch neutrality would have seriously threatened British trade, and, as the United Provinces had the same treaty obligations to Austria as Britain, the British ministry could expect serious domestic criticism if the Dutch remained neutral.[21] In 1726-9 the ministry had been attacked for being duped by France and for allowing her to continue to trade with Spain, whilst British interests – Gibraltar and commerce – were challenged. In the late 1730s the Dutch refused to support the British against Spain, whilst relations were harmed by Hanoverian designs in East Friesland[22] and by continued Dutch suspicion of the consequences for Dutch politics of the marriage in 1734 of William IV of Orange and Anne, George II's eldest daughter. The Orange family, the champion of Protestantism in Whig mythology/history, was seen as a threat by the Dutch ministry.[23]

Distrust helped to ensure that the crises which began in 1739 – the Anglo-Spanish war of 1739, and the War of the Austrian Succession the following year – did not witness concerted Anglo-Dutch policy. In December 1738 Horace Walpole had been concerned about the prospect of an Austro-Dutch agreement over the Austrian Netherlands without British consent that would lead to the Dutch gaining possession of Ostend. The following April, after a meeting with George II, he wrote, 'I found His Majesty not at all contented with our Maritime freinds'.[24] The drift towards war with Spain and the prospect that France would join Spain led to British anxiety about the naval balance and determination to force the Dutch to act as allies, not wellwishers or mediators:[25] 'the Distance between approving, and even wishing well to a cause, and joining in it, is so wide that I dare not presume to argue from the one to the other; and as long as I see this state so languidly support, and enforce even their own Grievances, I dare not be over-sanguin of their duly exerting themselves in the Redress of ours'.[26] Horace Walpole, sent to The Hague in June 1739 on his last diplomatic mission, an unsuccessful attempt to gain Dutch support, told Halewyn, the Pensionary of Dort, that if France declared war on Britain and the Dutch refused the aid stipulated by treaty, 'it must be looked upon as an absolute separation of the Friendship between the two Nations'.[27]

The British argued that Dutch unwillingness to promise support or to arm encouraged France 'more to act against us; than anything else can do . . .'[28] Horace Walpole claimed in October 1740 that French military preparations and their repairs at Dunkirk, in breach of clear treaty commitments, made it 'an undoubted casus foederis' for the Dutch. And the following February, Harrington was complaining of 'the timidity and irresolution of the Dutch'.[29]

In the late seventeenth and early eighteenth centuries the Dutch alliance was regarded in Britain as the fundamental element of any confessional foreign policy, any Protestant league. The strains of the 1730s indicated that it was necessary to re-examine the concept of a Protestant league. It was not simply that Anglo-Dutch cooperation diminished because of Dutch debt and consequent Dutch inability to pursue a forceful foreign policy, as well as differing appreciations of European developments;[30] in addition, Anglo-Dutch diplomatic relations deteriorated. It has been suggested that George II and Harrington were less sensitive to Dutch interests than George I and Townshend had been.[31] The British ministry strongly disapproved of Hop, the Dutch envoy in London (1723-61), whom they claimed was anti-British and malicious.[32] Chesterfield, a success at The Hague (1728-32), was followed, after a gap in senior representation, by William Finch (1733-4), who was known not to enjoy the complete confidence of the London ministry. Horace Walpole was absent for most of 1736 and half of 1737 and was represented, and, eventually, replaced in December 1737 by Robert Trevor, a mere Secretary of Embassy. The Dutch felt slighted and ignored by the British, an attitude which helps to explain the tension between so many British and Dutch diplomats.[33] The Dutch felt that the British clung selfishly to their own interests and failed to share the wider European perspectives of the Pensionary, Slingelandt.[34] The British ministry disliked Slingelandt's suggestions, such as his proposal in 1728 that the British return Gibraltar.[35] However, Slingelandt and Horace Walpole enjoyed important good personal relations; Slingelandt's death in 1736 played a major role in the deterioration of good diplomatic relations.[36]

Anxious about Dutch developments, the British ministry was aware that the prospect of Dutch assistance depended also upon wider European perspectives. Horace Walpole noted in October 1740, 'it is impossible for us to expect from them any immediate assistance, nor indeed do I see the time when they will have courage and abilitys enough to give it, they are so terribly check'd by the proximity, and power of France; at least until they can have greater security and encouragement, from our having an alliance with other powers, proper for their accession . . .' The following April Harrington wrote, '. . . the dilatory proceedings of that divided Republick . . . together with the weak, and indebted state of their Government, and their great apprehensions of France and Prussia, have fully convinced the King of the slow and feeble assistance, that must be expected from thence, unless they shall see part of their present apprehensions removed, and such an alliance forming as may assure them of support . . .'[37]

An Anglo-Dutch alliance would not suffice. The United Provinces, like Hanover, were exposed to foreign attack and required the alliance of a power with a major army. Britain could not provide the required security, nor could she hope to find in the alliance the European influence her monarch and ministers desired. Indeed, such an alliance would be vulnerable. Just as British foreign policy in 1741 was influenced by the threat of a Franco-Prussian invasion of Hanover, so in the latter stages of the War of the Austrian Succession Britain had to prop up the weak Dutch war effort.

A confessional foreign policy restricted, therefore, to alliance with the United Provinces would not suffice, but grave difficulties faced any attempt to expand it. There was interest in a wider league in several Protestant capitals.

In September 1733 the Prussian envoy in The Hague hinted at Prussian interest in 'a more strict union and correspondence with His Majesty and the Republick so as to make a distinct party'. In 1735 Chavigny noted British interest 'à former un tiers parti en Europe fondé sur un intérêt Protestant'. Horace Walpole talked about the idea during the War of the Polish Succession and mentioned an earlier instance, the Triple Alliance of Britain, the United Provinces and Sweden of 1668.[38] To be effective any wider alliance would have to include Prussia. It was possible to conceive of an alliance that did not do so – Britain, the United Provinces, Denmark, Sweden, Hanover and Hesse-Cassel – but without Prussia such an alliance would be militarily weak and handicapped by Prussian opposition. An alliance including Prussia could be considered in George I's reign, when religious tensions ran high and when Hanover and Prussia had a joint interest in excluding Russian influence in Mecklenburg. However, the good relations of the early 1720s were replaced by hostility, partly because of personal differences between George II and Frederick William I and territorial disputes between their states, partly because of an absence of shared interests. Prussian policy was dominated by the Russian threat, and influenced by eastern European interests in a way that Hanoverian, and British policy after the fall of Stanhope, and, in particular, after the death of Peter the Great, was not. It was largely due to good Austro-Russian relations in 1726 that Prussia left the Hanover alliance to side with Vienna. Prussian willingness to consider better relations with George II in early 1730 owed much to the domestic Russian political crisis that followed the accession of Czarina Anna.

Britain and Hanover could not guarantee Prussia against Russian hostility. Whilst the British navy could hope to give some measure of protection to Sweden, nothing could be done for Prussia. Furthermore a Prussian alliance would have tied Britain and Hanover to an aggressive power, and could have led to conflict. The Prussians made it clear that any alliance would entail support for their claims to the Jülich-Berg inheritance. Hanoverian concern for the position of Rhenish Protestantism conflicted with the desire to prevent further Prussian expansion to the west of Hanover. A war over Jülich-Berg would have led to conflict with France which supported the Wittelsbach claimant to the succession, the Prince of Palatine-Sulzbach. In the second half of the 1730s, when there was considerable interest in the idea of an Anglo-Prussian alliance, such an alliance would have led to confrontation over Jülich-Berg with both Austria and France.

There was support for a Prussian alliance in the British ministry. In April 1735 Slingelandt pressed Horace Walpole on the need to secure a Prussian alliance and to offer support in the Jülich-Berg dispute. Horace noted, 'all the persons with whom I have talked here, have constantly insisted upon the necessity of His Majesty's, and the States engaging the King of Prussia in their interest; and that nothing should be left unattempted to obtain that point'.[39] That summer the ministers left in London wrote to Hanover to urge 'an immediate reconciliation between His Majesty and the King of Prussia, and, by that means, engaging that Prince to act in concert with the King, for the support of the Equilibre, and Liberties of Europe; and their Lordships humbly offer as an additional reason for taking this step, that it appears to be too probable, from Mr Walpole's Letters, that without this, no exigencys, or necessity, will ever engage the States to concurr with His Majesty, in taking the proper measures for opposing the progress of the arms of France . . .'[40]

British interest in relations with Prussia and Prussian approaches in the late 1730s[41] helped to fuel speculation about an alliance.[42] It is too easy to ascribe its failure solely to personal factors. There is no doubt that George II did not want Prussian expansion in the Rhineland.[43] However, the increasingly bitter Horace Walpole (who never seems to have comprehended Hanoverian interests as he had done those of France and the United Provinces) was guilty of excessive simplification when he wrote to Trevor in October 1738, 'What should hinder the Kings of England and Prussia from being intimately well together, not their interests, but their humour, . . . what should hinder those two great powers, from being strictly united; but little views, founded on jealousy etc: I could go on and sketch out a noble plan for opposing the power of the House of Bourbon; if the great interest of the *whole* was to take place of humour, brigues, and pitiful notions, but Providence only can make the proper disposition in the hearts of his Viceregents to answer so good and great an end'.[44]

Instead, as other British ministers and diplomats stressed, a major problem was the unpredictability of Frederick William I, the difficulty of assessing his intentions and the ambiguity of his diplomatic approaches.[45] Frederick William wished to keep open diplomatic channels with Austria and, in particular, France, and it was suggested that his approaches to Britain were sometimes zesigned to elicit French diplomatic offers. Important Franco-Prussian discussions took place in 1735 and 1739.[46] To bring Prussia to what Dickens called 'a regular system'[47] was far from easy.

Frederick William I hoped that the succession of Frederick Prince of Wales would lead to better relations; the British placed similar hopes on Crown Prince Frederick of Prussia.[48] However, the course of Anglo-Prussian diplomacy in 1740-2 was to go far towards justifying the hesitations about an alliance of the previous decade. The Prussians were dissatisfied at British unwillingness to support their expansionist schemes; the British were appalled by Prussian aspirations, and by Frederick II's propensity for violence. Horace Walpole could argue in July 1741, 'we must gain him as the only way for salvation',[49] and there was a willingness to consider supporting some Prussian expansion, but there was also an opposition to simply accepting whatever Frederick desired. George II told the Saxon envoy Utterodt in December 1740 that Frederick was a prince guided only by ambition and the desire for aggrandisement, that he negotiated everywhere, and that, if Frederick's pretexts for the invasion of Silesia were accepted, no ruler could be secure in his German possessions.[50] George was influenced by Hanoverian concerns and personal attitudes ('Family hatreds were generally more violent than others,' observed Frederick II[51]), but Prussian policy, and Anglo-Prussian relations, during the War of the Austrian Succession justified George's conclusion that Frederick could not be trusted. Prussia was to acquire a reputation for deceit and double-dealing (possibly understandable in a second-rank power trying to deal with the vagaries of war[52]) that hindered those who urged better relations with Frederick.

Whether Anglo-Prussian relations were a matter of missed opportunities, as Horace Walpole argued, or not, is difficult to say, given the absence of relevant Hanoverian documentation, but the issue is important in assessing George II. Clearly George was influenced by personal and Electoral views, but the question is whether he pushed these to an extent that made better relations impossible. George I's concern for Electoral views had not prevented good relations with Prussia in the early 1720s. The evidence can be interpreted in several ways, but George II was surely correct in arguing that Frederick II could not be relied upon. Prior to the invasion of Silesia, Frederick negotiated with Britain and France and demanded support for wide-ranging expansionist schemes. After the invasion it was difficult to feel that he could be trusted. All rulers pushed their own interests, but Frederick did so with levels of deceit and violence that did not preclude negotiation, but made it difficult to feel that any policy could be based on a Prussian alliance.

Furthermore, British and Prussian diplomatic strategies were fundamentally incompatible (not that that has ever prevented alliances). Though both powers could agree on shared interests – limiting Russian expansion in 1721, resisting Austrian attempts to increase Imperial authority until 1726 – there was a basic tension between Prussia, keen on territorial expansion and seeking allies who would support this, and Britain, unwilling to see the European system altered, disinclined to risk conflict and opposed to, or not interested in, Prussian expansionist schemes, whether in Jülich-Berg, Courland or Poland. This Anglo-Prussian difference of interests was ignored by most contemporary commentators, who preferred to concentrate on the more visible and politically sensitive Hanoverian-Prussian issue. The

Prussians, like the Russians, were also keen to argue that any differences were due to Hanoverian issues and/or the personal views of the British monarch. However, in the case of Prussia and Russia (and Spain in the period 1714-33) there was a tension between expansionist schemes and the defensive interests of Britain. Once the Stanhopian policy of intervening extensively in European affairs had been abandoned, there was a largely defensive mentality among British politicians: concern to defend the Utrecht settlement, in particular the benefits Britain had acquired, and a determination to protect the balance of power. British politicians sought no further territorial acquisitions in Europe – rumours concerning Leghorn notwithstanding – and found it difficult to accept the suppositions of most European powers: of the major states, only France was primarily interested in wielding influence rather than gaining territory. The other states sought territory and favoured alliances that would further this goal. The scheme for a confessional alliance system based on an Anglo-Prussian pact ignored the incompatible diplomatic strategies of Britain and Prussia. Hanover and Prussia could cooperate in aggrandisement – they had done so at Sweden's expense during the Great Northern War – but it was far harder to arrange a solid Anglo-Prussian alliance.

The absence of a foreign policy based upon an alliance with other Protestant states did not mean that religious issues played no role in British foreign policy. This section will consider three related issues, pressure from Catholic powers on behalf of British Catholics, British pressure on behalf of foreign Protestants, and the relationship of this pressure to British alliances with Catholic states.

Anti-Catholicism was a major part of British political culture and ideology, and yet relations with Catholics were generally good.[53] In Scotland much of the religious tension was within the Protestant community, between Presbyterians and Episcopalians. In England violence tended to be directed not against local Catholics, but against migrants, particularly Irish Catholics. The undercutting of wages by Irish Catholics in London was a particular source of tension. Foreign intercession on behalf of British Catholics had two aspects, firstly intercession on behalf of the Catholic majority in Ireland, and secondly attempts to prevent a worsening of the Catholic position in mainland Britain. Catholics in Ireland were harshly treated, and their position was viewed with concern in Catholic Europe. The Papacy pressed Catholic powers to intercede on behalf of the Irish Catholics,[54] and papal views were seconded by the extensive Irish Catholic diaspora. Catholic politicians and diplomats were genuinely shocked by the condition of their Irish co-religionists. Chammorel wrote in 1731 that Ireland was treated tyranically.[55] The British ministry was pressed by the French in particular over Ireland, but the Austrians also raised the issue.[56] Many Irishmen had emigrated to France, and the French were keen to maintain a flow of recruits to their Irish regiments, which led to a political storm in late 1730 when the British ministry, bowing to domestic pressure, withdrew permission for such recruiting and embittered Anglo-French relations in the process.[57] The French pressed the British over anti-Catholic legislation in Ireland,[58] whilst Robinson's pressure in Vienna on behalf of Protestants in Austrian lands was met by Austrian recommendation of 'the favourable treatment of the Catholicks in Ireland'.[59] The Spaniards meanwhile were concerned about the position of Catholics in Minorca and Gibraltar.[60]

Moves against English Catholics, compared to Irish or Scottish, caused the greatest difficulty due to their conspicuous nature and the close social links of Catholic envoys and the English Catholic community – the Duke of Norfolk and Kinsky, for instance.[61] Catholic envoys regarded intervention on behalf of the Catholic community as part of their duty. The exposure of the Atterbury plot in 1722 led to widespread criticism of Catholics and to a ministerial scheme to increase the fiscal burdens upon them, which was resisted by the Catholic envoys.[62]

The significance and strength of Catholic pressure is difficult to judge. British Catholics and Jacobites were dissatisfied with the help they received. In 1722 the Duchess of Gordon's Edinburgh house was searched by constables in a disrespectful fashion. The Duchess's steward, writing to complain of this and of 'the insults done here to Catholicks', noted: 'If such things were done to the Palatines or other Protestants by their Catholick sovereigns, all the Protestant powers would interest themselves for redress of their grievances, and why the Catholick potentates are not as zealous for their distressed brethren is much to be lamented . . .'[63] The Jacobite Lord Lansdowne complained that anti-Catholic parliamentary moves would not have succeeded 'If the Catholick Princes abroad had solicited as earnestly to stop this Bill, as the Protestants at home have strenuously opposed it . . .'[64]

These comments were unjustified, however, as they exaggerated the effectiveness of complaint: British politicians and diplomats were clearly unsympathetic.[65] Destouches reported Walpole and Pulteney as saying that the more France supported the Catholics, the less Britain would heed her pressure, in order to avoid setting a bad precedent, Pulteney saying publicly that as Britain was not involved in French domestic troubles, France should follow her example. Destouches found it necessary to deny that he was interfering in British domestic affairs.[66] The French were aware of the need to tread carefully, but their failure in 1723 to intercede successfully on behalf of the Catholics led Morville to conclude that nothing useful could be done at that time, bar exhorting the British Catholics to suffer persecution patiently and silently.[67]

The British ministry were regularly pressed to support foreign Protestants. Royal concern and the far-flung interests of Archbishop Wake of Canterbury were of great importance,[68] and as a result envoys were instructed to intercede on behalf of foreign Protestants. Great concern was shown about the position in Poland[69] and the Empire,[70] where Protestantism was on the defensive, and in Sardinia, where the British acted as protectors of the Waldensians.[71] Such pressure was a constant feature throughout the period, and a surprising quantity of British diplomatic correspondence was devoted to the issue. British envoys in Turin, Vienna, Poland and the Empire seem to have devoted at least as much attention to it as they did to commercial considerations.

The impact of this British pressure was limited for a number of reasons. There was a hesitation about being seen to exert pressure, and a justifiable fear that it would meet with counter-accusations. Reprisals could be threatened − in 1727 the British, seeking to have James III removed from Avignon, pointed out the position of British Catholics[72] − and British envoys found the position of British Catholics brought up when they made complaints: 'It has been sometimes argued that since we did not suffer the Roman Catholics in our Parliament, or in any other offices or places, so why should they the Protestants; I tell them that the difference between England and Poland is, that we have strong laws against the Roman Catholics, with very good reasons for them, but those laws are not put in execution with rigour, all mildness and humanity being shown to the professors of that religion; whereas in this country the laws are extremely favourable for the Protestants, who have always behaved never to deserve otherwise, notwithstanding which, they are treated with severity, and even with injustice'.[73]

Many British envoys were convinced that representations were of scant value, as they had little impact: 'I reckon our applications in favour of our distressed brethren of Salzburg will have the common fate of such applications; of being received and not minded. All we can do for them at last, I believe, will be to pray for them'.[74] Woodward was driven to suggesting that the only way to intercede on behalf of the Polish Protestants was to appeal for Russian assistance, an idea approved by Harrington.[75] Suggestions were made that the British were insufficiently zealous on behalf of their European co-religionists.[76] Certainly some envoys were less than happy about their duties in this sphere. Responding to pressure to find wives and children of European Protestants who had emigrated to Georgia and to send them after, Robinson exploded, asking a correspondent to imagine what would happen 'were 60 or 70 Papists to pass out of Ireland into Spain, and . . . M. Montijo [Spanish envoy in London] [were] to desire without naming their names that the Government in England would find out their wives and children for them and send them after them – But directors of corporations . . . sit at ease in their offices at London and have but one thing in their head. . . . As a political affair, I do not know whether the Emperor can grant it; as a private affair there are times and circumstances, when things are easier than at others'.[77]

The general policy was to temper requests with discretion,[78] although it was realised that such a policy led to a risk that nothing would be achieved.[79] The experience of cooperating with other Protestant powers in this area was disheartening, and there was particular scepticism about Prussian motives.[80] Conduct reflected the ambiguity in attitudes towards the spectre of international Catholicism. Many diplomats and politicians felt that the European situation was unstable because of Catholic schemes. There was acute tension, accompanied by talk of an imminent religious war and of a Catholic plot to extirpate Protestants, in 1719-21 and 1725-7. The Vienna alliance was regarded as extremely sinister.[81] It was also believed that Catholics in general were predisposed to support Jacobitism 'as the cause of their Religion',[82] though Jacobites were sceptical of the support they could expect on this count.[83] At the same time British ministers were aware that they could not conduct their foreign policy as though a religious war was imminent. Toland might argue that 'our first maxim is, to support the Protestant interest everywhere', but in 1726, seeking to win Wittelsbach support against the Vienna alliance, British diplomats had to argue the need for Catholic and Protestant unity against the Austrian yoke.[84] Although the ministry might proclaim their support for European Protestantism in Parliament and in print, and Walpole give £50 in 1730 towards 'the suffering Protestants at Kieydan in Poland',[85] it was necessary, as in commercial matters, to accept the consequences of alliance-diplomacy.

The French government continued its anti-Protestant domestic policies throughout the course of the Anglo-French alliance, having long done the same during the previous century, and did not believe there was any conflict between allying with Protestants abroad and acting against them at home. The French stressed their interest in supporting foreign Protestant powers against Austria,[86] and took care to exert pressure on behalf of British Catholics with tact.[87] In turn the British in 1719 pressed the French Protestants not to oppose the government,[88] and stressed the common domestic threat facing the British and French ministries in the late 1710s: Spain supported the Jacobites and opponents of the Regent Orléans.[89]

During the Anglo-French alliance there was much press coverage of the poor treatment of Protestants in France.[90] It is difficult to assess the impact of this coverage. It is notable that press reports of French persecution were rarely linked to comments on the Anglo-French alliance and that there was little criticism of the alliance on religious grounds, though 'Orator' Henley, the charismatic London preacher, 'observed to his audience, that as France is our ally, and the Pope calls the French king his son, ergo, we are in alliance with the son of the whore of Babylon'.[91]

Public criticism of the Anglo-Austrian alliance on religious grounds was also muted, though in the Commons debate on the Address in 1732 Oglethorpe suggested that Charles VI intended to destroy Protestantism in his dominions. The British ministry interceded on behalf of the Hungarian Protestants in particular, and the press devoted attention to their plight. However, criticism of Austria on religious grounds was limited until after the beginning of the War of the Polish Succession, when it became an acceptable topic for ministerial papers.[92] Dutch suggestions that the negotiation of the Second Treaty of Vienna should entail benefits for Hungarian and Bohemian Protestants met with as little success as their suggestions of including commercial provisions.[93]

Whether public support for the French and Austrian alliances was lost due to the confessional aspect is unclear. It had little impact on the parliamentary discussion of foreign policy. Possibly the absence of a positive religious element made it more difficult to achieve support, as opposed to tolerance or indifference, for these alliances. Neither alliance enjoyed the popular support that was to be achieved by the Prussian alliance during the Seven Years War, but possibly the latter reflected a different political climate within which foreign policy was discussed. 'Patriotism' as a basis of foreign policy had had little success during the 1720s and early 1730s, but the opposition use of it during the agitation over Spanish depredations in the late 1730s altered the nature of public debate over foreign policy.

> 'The connexion between the fates of Great Britain, Holland and the Protestant interest, is natural and inseparable: They compose a whole, each part of which is happy in proportion to its union with the other two.'
>
> *Hyp-Doctor,* 22 May 1733

> 'I have occasionally mentioned the tie of religion, as what should always keep this Court, and Sweden, united with us, they have assured me that the King of Denmark lays a great stress upon it . . .'
>
> Titley, 1731[94]

The impact of religious issues and attitudes is difficult to gauge, but is of importance, given the recent trend of early eighteenth-century historiography to question earlier tendencies to secularise the period and downgrade the importance of religious feelings. In terms of specific policy it is difficult to point to religious issues as being of great importance. British policy towards Sardinia was no more determined by the British desire to protect the Waldensians than it was by the wish to protect British commerce. British ministers displayed concern about the position of distant Protestant communities, such as the Courlanders, but accepted that there was little Britain could do to improve their lot. Efforts to do so, such as those that followed the Thorn massacre, were usually unsuccessful.

It is possible to suggest that sectarian awareness played a major role in shaping attitudes to British foreign policy. It was widely believed that Catholicism was on the increase in the British Isles[95] and on the advance in Europe. Suspicions of Catholic loyalty were increased by the Jacobite threat. There was an enormous amount of anti-Catholic material both in the culture of print – newspapers, pamphlets, prints and books – and in the public culture of anniversary celebrations and public ritual, much of it relating to European events: celebrations of the defeat of the Armada, or pornographic literature concerning the seduction of Mademoiselle Cadière by her Jesuit confessor.[96] The representation of Catholics was crude and violent, their intentions were diabolical, their strength and deceit frightening. The public ritual lent immediacy to the material in print, and both were further linked by sermons.[97]

Given these circumstances, it is easy to understand both the absence of widespread support for the French and Austrian alliances, and the emotional support for a Protestant alliance and/or a Protestant foreign policy. The absence of Protestant enemies was of great significance in fostering such emotion. Continued Tory stress, for example in *Mist's Weekly Journal,* on Anglo-Dutch enmity was of some importance in the early 1720s, but far less so a decade later. Whilst British foreign policy could be presented, as in 1725-33, as a choice between Catholic allies, public attitudes were of little importance beyond ensuring an absence of significant support for ministerial policy. Possibly some of the public anxiety about ministerial foreign policy reflected a wider unease. The importance of the failure to win public approval (itself impossible to measure and an ambivalent concept to discuss) for ministerial foreign policy was minor in parliamentary terms, but possibly more important in the long term. The culture of print helped to inform (and possibly widen) a political nation interested in foreign affairs, and religious issues played a major role in the way in which foreign society and culture, and therefore the activities of foreign states, were seen. This created difficulties for the ministry.

There was no equivalent in Britain of the Dutch anti-Catholic panic of 1734,[98] but a sense of religious unease was readily apparent in a society which saw the birth of Methodism. This unease and the specific concern about the growth of Catholicism, particularly acute in the mid-1730s, possibly helped to fuel the popular impression in the latter 1730s that British foreign policy was drifting and purposeless, and confronted by the new, frightening Austro-French alliance that blossomed rapidly after their peace agreement of 1735. The period saw great interest in the idea of a

Protestant alliance, which could be exploited by the opposition. The ministry were portrayed as failing to stand up to Spain and France, and as failing, in the early 1740s, to develop a solid alliance with Prussia. Confessional attitudes to European affairs played a certain role in the replacement of Bolingbroke and the *Craftsman* platform by the new politicians and new newspapers of the later 1730s. A study of attitudes to foreign policy in the 1740s and 1750s would benefit from a consideration of the role of confessional issues in the foreign policy of the age of Walpole.

NOTES

1. Tilson to Robinson, 13 Oct. (ns) 1736, BL. Add. 23799.

2. Townshend to Edward Finch, 15 Jan. 1725, PRO. 88/29.

3. G. Florey, *Geschichte der Salzburger Protestanten und inhrer Emigration, 1731-2* (Vienna, 1977).

4. K. Borgmann, *Der Deutsche Religionstreit der jahren 1719-20* (Berlin, 1937); W. R. Ward, 'Power and Piety: the origins of Religious Revival in the early eighteenth century', *Bulletin of the John Rylands Library* 63 (1980).

5. Albert to Malknecht, Bavarian foreign minister, 3 Feb. (ns), 9 Ap. (ns) 1719, 16 Jan. (ns) 1724, Munich, KS, 17072, 17083; Gansinot to Plettenberg, 13 Jan. (ns), 20 Mar. (ns) 1722, Münster, NB. 259¹; Whitworth to Townshend, 18 Mar. (ns) 1721, PRO. 90/13.

6. Törring to Plettenberg, 24 Dec. (ns) 1729, Münster, NA. 148; Chauvelin to Chavigny, French envoy at the Imperial Diet, 23 Jan. (ns), 22 Feb. (ns), 7 Mar. (ns) 1730, AE. CP. Allemagne, 376.

7. St. Saphorin to Townshend, 26 Aug. (ns) 1722, PRO. 80/47; St. Saphorin to Bothmer, 3 Ap. (ns) 1723, Hanover, Calenberg Br. 24, Nr. 4913; Thom, Wolfenbüttel envoy in London, to ---, 22 Jan. (ns) 1726, Wolfenbüttel, 1 Alt. 6, Nr. 86.

8. Cortanze, Sardinian envoy in London, to Victor Amadeus II, 6 July (ns) 1722, AST. LM. Ing. 31.

9. I have benefited from discussing this point with Professor W. R. Ward.

10. Instructions for Schaub, going to Saxony-Poland, 22 Sept. 1730, PRO. 88/38.

11. Whitworth to Schaub, 14 Jan. (ns) 1721, Whitworth to Townshend, 12 Ap. (ns) 1721, PRO. 90/13, 14.

12. Townshend to St. Saphorin, 7 Sept. 1722, PRO. 80/48.

13. *Rayner's Morning Advertiser* 14 May, *Read's Weekly Journal* 15 May, *St. James' Evening Post* 25 May, *Daily Gazetteer* 29 May, *General Evening Post* 29 May, *Fog's Weekly Journal* 5 June 1736.

14. Townshend to St. Saphorin, 7 Sept. 1722, PRO. 80/48.

15. Harrington to Woodward, 5 Mar. 1731, PRO. 88/38; Whitworth to Wake, Archbishop of Canterbury, 11 Jan. (ns) 1718, BL. Add. 37366.

16. Chesterfield to Harrington, 24 July (ns) 1731, PRO 84/314.

17. Chesterfield to Harrington, 26 Oct. (ns) 1731, PRO 84/315.

18. Whitworth to Tilson, 9 Jan. (ns), 16 May (ns), 2 Nov. (ns), Whitworth to Townshend, 19 Mar. (ns) 1721, PRO. 90/11-13, 15; Whitworth to Bothmer, 2 May (ns) 1722, BL. Add. 37388; Horace Walpole to Harrington, 10 Dec. (ns) 1734, PRO. 84/335.

19. Harrington to Slingelandt, 18 Jan. 1734, PRO. 84/297; Newcastle to Waldegrave, 30 Mar., 20 Ap. 1734, BL. Add. 32784.

k

20. Horace Walpole to William Finch, 26 Dec. 1727, BL. Add. 32753; private instructions for Waldegrave, 17 Feb. 1735, PRO. 78/207; Horace Walpole to Harrington, 29 Nov. (ns) 1735, 4 Aug. (ns) 1739, PRO. 84/342, 347, 349, 381.

21. Gansinot to Törring, 5 Jan. (ns) 1734, Munich, KS. 17326; *Thistle* 26 Mar. 1734; De Löss to Augustus III, 29 Jan. (ns) 1734, Dresden, 638 IIa.

22. Horace Walpole to Trevor, 18, 25 Nov. (ns) 1736, Trevor, 5.

23. Horace Walpole to Trevor, 21 Oct. (ns) 1736, Trevor, 5.

24. Horace Walpole to Trevor, 1 Dec. 1738, 24 Ap. 1740, Trevor, 15, 18.

25. Harrington to Horace Walpole, 3 Aug. 1739, PRO 84/381.

26. Trevor to Harrington, 26 June (ns) 1739, PRO 84/380.

27. Horace Walpole to Harrington, 7 July (ns) 1739, PRO 84/380.

28. Horace Walpole to Trevor, 4 Jan. 1740, Trevor, 20.

29. Horace Walpole to Hardwicke, 10 Oct. 1740, BL. Add. 35586; Harrington to Robinson, 27 Feb. 1741, PRO 80/144.

30. J. Aalbers, *De Republiek en de Vrede van Europe* I (Groningen, 1980); J. Aalbers, 'Holland's financial problems (1713-33) as a consequence of the French wars', in A. C. Duke (ed.), *Britian and the Netherlands* VI (1978).

31. H. Dunthorne, The Alliance of the Maritime Powers, 1721-40 (London PhD., 1978).

32. Townshend to Chesterfield, 19 Nov., 6, 17 Dec. 1728, Chesterfield to Townshend, 25 Feb. (ns) 1729, Chesterfield to Harrington, 8 Jan. (ns) 1732, PRO 84/302, 303, 316; Horace Walpole to Trevor, 17 Mar. 1741, Trevor, 26.

33. Horace Walpole to Trevor, 31 Jan. 1738, Trevor, 10; Dickens to Harrington, 1, 29 Nov. (ns) 1732, PRO 90/33; Horace Walpole to Keene, 6 Oct. (ns) 1735, BL. Add. 32789.

34. A. Goslinga, *Slingelandt's efforts towards European Peace* (The Hague, 1915).

35. Townshend to Chesterfield, 9 July, Chesterfield to Townshend, 3 Aug., Townshend to Slingelandt, 23 July 1728, PRO 84/301, 580.

36. Horace Walpole to Trevor, 16 Oct. (ns) 1736, Trevor, 5; Newcastle to Horace Walpole, 11 Ap. 1735, BL. Add. 32787.

37. Horace Walpole to Hardwicke, 10 Oct. 1740, BL. Add. 35586; Harrington to Robinson, 17 Ap. 1741, PRO. 80/145.

38. William Finch to Harrington, 29 Sept. (ns) 1733, PRO. 84/324; Chavigny to Chauvelin, 8 Feb. (ns) 1735, AE. CP. Ang. 390.

39. Horace Walpole to Harrington, 26 Ap. (ns) 1735, PRO. 84/342.

40. Undated memorandum, PRO. 36/161, f. 518-19.

41. Trevor to Dickens, 5 July (ns) 1737, 16 May (ns), 22 Nov. (ns) 1738, Trevor, 9, 12; Horace Walpole to Trevor, 31 Oct. 1738, Trevor, 15; Dickens to Harrington, 3 Aug. (ns) 1737, PRO. 90/43; Wych to Harrington, 4 Nov. (ns) 1738, PRO. 82/59.

42. *Daily Post*, 16 Feb. 1736; *Sherborne Mercury*, 7 June 1737; *London Evening Post*, 30 Dec. 1737; *Adam's Weekly Courant*, 27 Dec. 1738; *York Courant*, 23 Jan. 1739.

43. Horace Walpole to Trevor, 22 Mar., 26 Ap. 1737, Trevor, 7, 8.

44. Horace Walpole to Trevor, 24 Oct. 1738, Trevor, 15.

45. Harrington to Dickens, 24 June 1737, PRO. 90/43; Horace Walpole to Harrington, 10 Sept. (ns) 1737, PRO. 84/367; Dickens to Harrington, 16 July (ns) 1737, PRO. 90/43; Dickens to Harrington, 13, 16 Dec. (ns) 1738, PRO. 90/44.

46. Horace Walpole to Trevor, 9 Jan. 1739, Trevor, 16.

47. Dickens to Harrington, 13 Aug. (ns) 1737, PRO. 90/43.

48. Frederick William I to Borck, Prussian envoy in London, 19 Jan. (ns) 1736, BL. Add. 33064; Harrington to Rondeau, 29 Nov. 1734, *Sbornik* 76, 329.

49. Horace Walpole to Trevor, 12 July 1741, Trevor, 27.

50. Utterodt to Augustus III, 10 Jan. (ns) 1741, Dresden, 2677, III.

51. Dickens to Harrington, 4 Feb. (ns) 1741, PRO. 90/49.

52. Black, 'Anglo-Sardinian Relations', *Studi Piemontesi*, Vol. 12 (1983), p. 59.

53. Black, 'The Catholic Threat and the British Press in the 1720's and 1730's', *Journal of Religious History*, Vol. 12 (1983). I have benefited from discussing anti-Catholicism with Colin Haydon.

54. Waldegrave to Newcastle, 23 Jan. (ns) 1732, BL. Add. 32776. For pressure on the French government on behalf of the Scottish Catholics, Hay to Abbot Stuart, 30 Oct. (ns), Father Lewis Innes to James III, 2 Dec. (ns) 1726, RA. 98/128, 99/121, and re Minorca, Horace Walpole to Newcastle, 14 Oct. (ns) 1728, BL. Add. 32752, J. Shortiss to Horace Walpole, 21 Nov (ns) 1723, PRO. 35/46.

55. Chammorel to Chauvelin, 25 Ap. (ns) 1731, AE. CP. Ang. 373.

56. For Austrian pressure on behalf of Hanoverian Catholics, Charles VI to Kinsky, 26 Ap. (ns) 1732. HHStA. EK. 68.

57. Chauvelin to Broglie, 27 Ap. (ns), Chammorel to Chauvelin, 30 Nov. (ns), 11 Dec. (ns), Chauvelin to Chammorel, 10 Dec. (ns) 1730, AE. CP. Ang. 369, 371, sup. 8; Delafaye to Newcastle, 24 Oct., Newcastle to Henry Pelham, 24 Oct. 1730, PRO. 63/393; Horace Walpole to Waldegrave 26 Nov. (ns) 1730, Chewton; Waldegrave to Newcastle, 28 Nov. (ns) 1730, BL. Add. 32770; Stainville, Lorraine envoy in Paris, to Francis III of Lorraine, 10 Dec. (ns) 1730, Nancy, 86.

58. Morville to Chammorel, 14 Jan. (ns) 1724, Chavigny to Chauvelin, 29 Jan. (ns), 11 Feb. (ns) 1732, AE. CP. Ang. sup. 7, 376; Waldegrave to Delafaye, 11 Feb. (ns) 1732, PRO. 78/200.

59. Robinson to Tilson, 23 Feb. (ns) 1732, PRO 80/85; seven Irish Catholics to Philip Kinsky, 11 Dec. 1731, Vienna, Palais Kinsky, correspondence of Philip Kinsky.

60. Dodington, envoy in Spain, to Stair, 4 Oct. (ns) 1715, SRO 135/141/3A; Colonel Kane, Governor of Minorca, answer to Monteleon's memorandum to Secretary of State Addison, 1717, Maidstone, Kent Archives Office, U 1590 0152; Newcastle to Keene, 27 Jan. 1732, BL. Add. 32776. The French supported Spanish pressure, Dubois to Destouches, 13 Mar. (ns) 1723, AE. CP. Ang. 344; Horace Walpole to Newcastle, 24 Mar. (ns) 1728, BL. Add. 32754. For Spanish pressure over Gibraltarian Catholics, Keene to Newcastle, 20 Mar. (ns) 1733, PRO 94/116. Gibson supported the conversion of Minorca, Gibson to Newcastle, 17 Jan. 1730, PRO. 36/17.

61. *St. James' Evening Post*, 23 June 1733. For British Catholic requests for assistance from Catholic envoys, *Worcester Post-Man*, 6 Dec. 1723.

62. Chammorel to Dubois, 8, 29 Mar. (ns), Destouches to Dubois, 18, 22 Mar. (ns), 19, 29 Ap. (ns) 1723, AE. CP. Ang. 344; Shack, Lorraine envoy in London to Duke Leopold of Lorraine, 19 Nov. (ns) 1722, Nancy, 213; St. Saphorin to Townshend, 16 Dec. (ns) 1722, PRO. 80/47; Thomas Southcoat, Jacobite, to James III, 30 May (ns) 1723, RA. 67/44; W. King (ed.), *Memoirs of Sarah Duchess of Malborough* (1933), p. 311.

63. Steward to Duchess, 19 May 1722, BL. Add. 43347.

64. Lansdowne to James III, 31 May (ns) 1723, RA. 67/45.

65. St. Saphorin to Tilson, 28 Nov. (ns) 1722, PRO. 80/47; Polwarth and Whitworth to Carteret, 14 Dec. (ns) 1722, BL. Add. 37390.

66. Destouches to Dubois, 19, 29 Ap. (ns) 1723, AE. CP. Ang. 344.

67. Morville to Chammorel 26 Aug. (ns), 3, 17 Sept. (ns), 7 Oct. (ns), 3 Dec. (ns) 1723, AE. CP. Ang. sup. 7.

68. Wake to Newcastle, 5 Aug. 1724, PRO. 35/51; Newcastle to Horace Walpole, 21 May 1728, PRO. 78/189; Harrington to Robinson, 17 Aug. 1733, PRO 80/98; Petition to George II on behalf of Protestant churches of Hungary and Transylvania, 1 Sept., Gibson to Newcastle, 13 Sept. 1735, PRO. 36/36-7; *St. James' Weekly Journal*, 2 Jan. 1720.

69. Scott, envoy in Saxony-Poland, to Tilson, 10 June (ns) 1721, Whitworth to Townshend, 11 Nov. (ns) 1721, Harrington to Woodward, 9, 30 Mar., Woodward to Harrington, 12 May (ns) 1733, PRO. 88/28, 90/15, 88/41.

70. Townshend to Chesterfield, 14 May 1728, PRO. 84/300.

71. Molesworth to Newcastle, 21 June (ns), 1, 25 July (ns) 21 Oct. (ns) 1724, PRO. 92/31; Newcastle to Hedges, 6 July 1727, PRO. 92/32; d'Aix to Victor Amadeus 14 Aug. (ns) 1729, AST. LM. Ing. 37. [Delafaye or Newcastle] to Horace Walpole, 16 Oct. 1727, PRO 78/187.

72. Waldegrave Journal, 3 Nov. (ns) 1727, Chewton; Horace Walpole to Newcastle 14 Oct. (ns) 1727, BL. Add. 32 752. The press sometimes urged a tough attitude towards British Catholics in order to gain concessions for foreign Protestants, *London Journal,* 2 Feb. 1723. The Dutch, Prussians and Hessians closed Catholic churches in 1719-20 in reprisal for the persecution of Protestants in the Palatinate.

73. Woodward to Harrington, 5 May (ns) 1733, PRO. 88/41; Edward Finch to Townshend, 18 Feb. (ns) 1725, 22 Oct. (ns) 1726, PRO. 88/29, 88/33.

74. Chesterfield to Tilson, 18 Dec. (ns) 1731, PRO. 84/316; Woodward to Harrington, 9 May (ns) 1733, PRO. 88/41.

75. Woodward to Tilson 9 July (ns), Harrington to Woodward, 21 July (ns) 1735, PRO 88/45.

76. Chesterfield to Harrington, 15 Jan. (ns) 1732, PRO. 84/316; Robinson to Chesterfield, 26 Jan. (ns) 1732, PRO 80/84; Trevor to Horace Walpole, 11 Sept. (ns) 1736, PRO 84/359. Le Coq was sceptical about the degree of ministerial concern over the Thorn affair, Le Coq to Lagnasc, 9 Jan. (ns), 3 Ap. (ns) 1725, Dresden, 2673.

77. Robinson to Weston, 12 Aug. (ns) 1735, PRO 80/117.

78. Instructions to Woodward, 22 Oct. 1728, Harrington to Dickens, 7 Aug. 1733, PRO 88/35, 90/35; Horace Walpole to Trevor, 16 Sept. (ns) 1736, PRO 84/359.

79. Horace Walpole to Robinson, 29 Sept. (ns) 1736, PRO 80/123. Tilson was pessimistic about the Austrian stance 'unless a handle happens by want of our assistance', Tilson to Titley, 5 July 1737, BL. Eg. 2684. Whitworth agreed, Whitworth to Stanhope, 13 Jan. (ns) 1720, PRO 90/11; Tilson to Robinson, 3 Dec. (ns) 1736, BL. Add. 23799.

80. Harrington to Woodward, 5 Mar. 1731, PRO 88/38.

81. Townshend to Du Bourgay, 10 May 1726, PRO 90/20; Le Coq to Lagnasc, 12 Mar. (ns) 1725, Dresden, 2673.

82. Whitworth to Stair, 13 Feb. (ns) 1716, SRO 135/141/7; Polwarth and Whitworth to Carteret, 1 Dec. (ns) 1722, BL. Add. 37390; *St. James' Evening Post,* 29 Dec. 1733.

83. Graham to Daniel O'Brien, 15 Sept. (ns) 1727, RA. 110/60. It was claimed by the opposition that Catholics supported ministerial candidates in the 1734 elections, 13 Mar. 1734, Cobbett, IX, 440-1; *London Evening Post,* 3 Nov. 1733.

84. J. Toland, *The State Anatomy of Great Britain* (3rd ed.), 1717, p. 45; Albert to Törring, 24 May (ns), St. Saphorin to Törring, 26 Ap. (ns) 1726, Munich, KS 17091, 17433; Delafaye to Horace Walpole, Sept. 1727, PRO 78/187; Wake's speech in debate on Address, *Worcester Post Man,* 27 Nov. 1718.

85. King's speech, Lords' Address, 23 Nov. 1719; Henry Neuman to Selina Countess of Huntingdon, 17 Dec. 1730, HMC., *Rawdon-Hastings* III (1934), p. 5.

86. Chambrier, Prussian envoy in Paris, to Frederick William I, 3 Ap. (ns) 1723, AE CP Prusse 73; Prior, British envoy in Paris, to Townshend, 15 Jan. (ns) 1715, PRO 78/159.

87. Horace Walpole to Newcastle, 21 Sept. (ns) 1726, BL. Add. 32747.

88. Schulenburg to Görtz, 11 Ap. (ns) 1719; Graham (ed.), *Stair* II, 106. Atterbury claimed that deference to France led to a diminished British stress on the topic of the Protestant interest abroad, Atterbury to Hay, undated, RA 103/57. A similar claim was advanced in an undated letter to the *Craftsman's* publisher, CUL. CH. papers 74/52.

89. Craggs to Dubois, 20 Jan. 1719, PRO 100/3; *Flying Post: or Post Master*, 11 Feb. 1720.

90. *Weekly General Post*, 2 Mar. 1717; *Post Man and the Historical Account*, 4 Mar. 1718; *Evening Post*, 14 Mar. 1723; *Newcastle Weekly Mercury*, 20 Ap. 1723; *Flying Post or Post Master*, 27 June 1724; *St. James' Evening Post*, 28 Nov. 1724.

91. *The British Journal: or the Censor*, 28 Dec. 1728.

92. HMC. *Egmont* I, 215; Harrington to Robinson, 10 Aug. 1731, Harrington to Dayrolle, Resident at The Hague, 2, 20 Feb. 1733, Dayrolle to Harrington, 3 Feb. (ns) 1733, PRO 80/78, 84/321; *St. James' Evening Post*, 31 Aug; *Hyp Doctor*, 24 Sept. 1734.

93. Chesterfield to Harrington, 24 July (ns) 1731, PRO 84/314.

94. Titley to Harrington, 5 May (ns) 1731, PRO. 75/56.

95. Wodrow, May 1727, *Analecta* III, 423-4; *Egmont*, 24 Ap. 1732, I, 262; *Read's Weekly Journal*, 9 June 1733; *Weekly Miscellany*, 2 Feb. 1734; Sir William Lowther, 13 Mar. 1734, *Cobbett* IX, 440; *Norwich Mercury*, 28 Sept. 1734; *St. James' Evening Post*, 12 Oct. 1734; Philip Doddridge to Samuel Clark, 17 Jan. 1735, G. F. Nuttall, *Calendar of the correspondence of Philip Doddridge* (1979), p. 76; *Daily Post Boy*, 3 Feb. 1735; *Northampton Mercury*, 14 May 1739.

96. *Weekly Journal or British Gazetteer*, 24 Mar. 1716; *London Journal*, 25 Dec. 1725; 'Princess Elizabeth: or the cruelty of Queen Mary with the Intrigues of Bishop Gardiner', acted in Norwich in December 1730, *Norwich Mercury*, 24 Dec. 1730.

97. *London Journal*, 4 Jan. 1735. On 27 May 1722 a statement was read throughout all Scottish Presbyterian churches attacking Popery and Jacobitism.

98. W. Fryhoff, 'De Paniek van juni 1734', *Archeif voor de Geschiedenis van de Katholieke Kerk in Nederland* 19 (1977).

Jacobitism and British Foreign Policy

'I see no appearance of our being able to do anything for ourselves there without foreign force.'

James III, 1736[1]

The strength of Jacobitism in Britain in the first half of the eighteenth century has recently been a source of historical debate. This debate has had two principal components. First there has been dispute over the extent of support for the Jacobites in 1745. It has been pointed out that although overt English support was limited, there was also little sign of widespread support for George II. The Hanoverian dynasty has been shown to have enjoyed little determined support.[2] Secondly there has been a controversy, still unresolved, about the extent of Tory support for Jacobitism.[3] The last decade has also produced a series of major works on the Jacobites.[4] However, there has been no recent study of the relationship between British foreign policy and Jacobitism; Fritz's book concentrates on the period 1715-23 and is disappointingly brief thereafter. It is to be hoped that a major forthcoming work on Jacobitism by Edward Gregg will narrow this gap, but an understanding of the impact of Jacobitism on British foreign policy demands a critical evaluation of ministerial rather than Jacobite archives. As the Bishop of Chichester wrote in 1739, 'I hear the Jacobites are very sanguine, but so indeed they always are'.[5]

It is not difficult to point to sustained ministerial concern about Jacobitism. A major intelligence operation, ably described by Fritz, followed Jacobite moves. Jacobite post was intercepted and British envoys were regularly instructed to send reports on the Jacobites.[6] Newcastle ordered Waldegrave in October 1733 to 'employ all your engines to get the best intelligence you can of their proceedings; Whether any, and what encouragement, is given them by the Court where you are, and endeavour to learn who are the persons that are in the Pretender's confidence in France, and what intercourse they have with the French Ministers'.[7] It is difficult, however, to assess these instructions. In a sense the fact that there were envoys in Italy meant that the ministry might as well send them instructions to keep a close eye on the Jacobites. These instructions were far from regular. Instead they were issued during periods when rumours of Jacobite schemes were frequent, such as the spring and summer of 1731, the spring of 1732, the War of the Polish Succession, and the period of warfare that began in late 1739. There were some periods, 1728-30 for example, when such instructions were rare. This would suggest that far from being a constant fear of the British ministry, Jacobitism aroused anxiety only in relation to the international situation. This interpretation accords with Jacobite views in the 1720s and 1730s. Few Jacobites believed that it would be possible to restore the Stuart dynasty other than through violence and with foreign assistance. The majority of Jacobite leaders, and in particular the very cautious James III, argued that foreign assistance was vital.[8] It is therefore against the background of British relations with other states that the Jacobite issue should be considered.

There is no doubt of the widespread support in Catholic Europe for the Catholic cause. The Hanoverians were regarded as Protestant usurpers.[9] Molesworth reported from Turin in September 1723 that all the Italian rulers and states favoured and secretly supported the Jacobite cause.[10] Support also existed in influential circles in France and Austria, whilst in Spain Jacobites were prominent at court and their advice believed to be of some importance.[11] The Jacobite cause was patronised actively by the Papacy, a point taken up frequently by the British press, and James III resided in Papal towns, Avignon, Bologna and Rome. Aside from financing the Jacobite cause, the Papacy also provided diplomatic support. However, the Jacobites also looked to non-Catholic powers for support, to Sweden in the 1710s and Russia in the following decade. Just as Britain's principal ally in the period 1716-33 was a Catholic power, so the Jacobites argued (in non-Catholic circles) that their cause was not a religious one.

Foreign assistance to Jacobitism could most readily be given by France, the Catholic power with the largest army and navy and fewest logistical difficulties. The powerful French forces stationed along the border with the Austrian Netherlands could easily be moved to the Channel coast. In 1740 Waldegrave reported that, although there were very few French forces in Brittany and Normandy, 'certainly if the French intended to draw a body together for any attempt against us, the garrisons of Calais, Dunkirk, Gravelines, Lisle, Arras, Cambray, Bethune, etc. would supply in four or five days a considerable body of men'.[12] The speed with which the French assembled a large body of troops in the Dunkirk area in 1731 frightened the British ministry. Under the energetic guidance of Maurepas, the Secretary of State for the Marine, the French navy grew in size in the 1720s and 1730s, and in 1733 and 1738 the French were able to send a squadron to Baltic waters.

An invasion of Britain was certainly within French military capabilities. In the late 1710s and early 1720s they would only have been able to send a small force, but by the 1730s they could have put a considerable force, easily in excess of 20,000 men, on board ship. Such a concentration of manpower and shipping would, however, have alerted the British, who, quite apart from intelligence considerations, in peacetime easily enjoyed maritime superiority in home waters, and could do the same in wartime so long as large forces were not sent to the Mediterranean and/or the West Indies. As a result the Jacobites pressed potential helpers for a surprise attack with a relatively small number of men. In 1726 the Austrians were asked to provide only 6,000 men. The Jacobites claimed that the short trip from Ostend could be carried out successfully in fishing boats and small ships and that surprise would be achieved by avoiding a major naval expedition. It was argued that chances would be improved by a night crossing and by the fact that only a few British ports were guarded.[13] This and other Jacobite requests for small forces were based on the assumption that the small and dispersed British army would be unable to concentrate a large opposing force, and that the Hanoverian regime would be brought to a state of collapse by popular opposition and fiscal difficulties.[14] On the whole foreign statesmen were hesitant about accepting Jacobite claims,[15] but whatever the subsequent fate of a landing force, it is reasonable to note that a small invasion force could easily have been sent by either France or (from Ostend) Austria.

The role of the Jacobite issue in Anglo-French relations has never been studied. It is generally accepted that an important motive in British willingness to negotiate the Anglo-French alliance was a wish to prevent French support for opponents of the Hanoverian succession. This was of pressing importance in 1715-16 due to the Jacobite insurrection of those years, and was of significance again at the time of the Atterbury Plot (1722). The importance of the Jacobite factor at other periods of the Anglo-French alliance is harder to discern, as is the role it played during the dissolution of the alliance in 1731 and in Anglo-French relations in the following decade. In April 1731 the French envoy in London, Count Broglie, responded angrily to the new Anglo-Austrian alliance by claiming that France need only 'jouer le Pretendant' in order to harm Britain.[16] It is important to consider whether anxiety on this score influenced the British ministry both during the course of the Anglo-French alliance, and in the following decade. In the 1730s, although the British ministry rarely supported French diplomatic initiatives,[17] they refused to fight France during the War of the Polish Succession or to support Prussia against Franco-Austrian pressure over Jülich-Berg in 1737-8.

During the Anglo-French alliance the French ministry frequently assisted the British ministry by providing information about Jacobite schemes. In 1719 Dubois was thanked for such assistance, and in 1722 French information was of great importance in uncovering the Atterbury Plot.[18] The Regent moved the Irish regiments in the French army away from the Channel coast, in response to British fears, and the public nature of this gesture was an important overt demonstration of support.[19] In 1727 the death of George I led James III to leave Italy and to attempt to base himself north of the Alps. He first tried Lorraine, whence he was expelled by Duke Leopold in response to French pressure.[20] He then moved to Avignon, but substained British pressure led the French to persuade the Pope to tell James to return to Italy.[21]

The Jacobites argued that an alliance between the major Catholic powers, and in particular between France and Spain, was of great importance to their schemes. In May 1720 Arthur Dillon stated that James should 'pursue with fervency an entire understanding between France and Spain as the basis of his restoration'. Four months later the Earl of Orrery wrote of France, 'they must first settle their own affairs and enter into a strict friendship too I believe with Spain before we can hope for any benefit from them'.[22] The Jacobites supported schemes for Franco-Spanish reconciliation in the late 1710s, the early 1720s, 1727, and 1731-2, just as in 1735 they encouraged the idea of an Austro-French alliance,[23] because they believed that such an alliance would wean France from her pro-British stance. For this very reason the British, when allied with France, were very concerned about Franco-Spanish relations, particularly in 1718-19, 1721 and 1727. There was a danger that relatively pro-British French ministers `and courtiers, such as Orléans, Bourbon, Dubois and Morville, would be replaced by more pro-Spanish figures, such as Maine, Torcy, and d'Huxelles. The Anglo-French alliance was extremely fragile, and the Spaniards and the Jacobites hoped, with some reason, that their cause would be advanced by such events as the majority of Louis XV, the deaths of Orléans and Dubois, the falls of Bourbon and Morville, and, after the end of the Anglo-French alliance, by the death or removal of Fleury.[24] A Franco-Spanish alliance would certainly have threatened Britain. The naval and fiscal resources of the two states would have been of great assistance to the Jacobites, whilst the threat of French attack might have prevented Britain's other allies, such as Hanover, Hesse-Cassel and the United Provinces, from sending military assistance. It was very fortunate for the British ministry therefore that Franco-Spanish relations were generally poor, thus providing the French with their principal motive to ally with Britain. Even after that alliance ended, Franco-Spanish relations continued to be characterised by hostility and suspicion. The sole period of relatively good relations was 1733-5, which should be taken into account in any analysis of British neutrality in the War of the Polish Succession. Even during that war Franco-Spanish relations were strained. The two powers failed to cooperate over military operations in Italy in 1734 and 1735 and engaged independently in secret negotiations with other powers. Spanish conduct during the war helps to explain the unilateral French settlement with Austria; if she had been offered reasonable terms, Spain would have done likewise. The principal Spanish minister, Patino, was distrusted by Fleury whom the Spanish court, particularly Elisabeth Farnese, made no secret of their wish to replace. Fleury's discovery of secret negotiations between Spain and the French foreign minister, Chauvelin, played a major role in Chauvelin's replacement in February 1737. After Patino's death in

November 1736 Franco-Spanish relations thawed slightly, but Fleury's determination to maintain the Franco-Austrian alliance and his consequent resistance to Spain's Italian aspirations prevented a reconciliation between the two powers. For most of the 1730s they failed to cooperate. In the spring of 1731 Spain and France failed to coordinate their approaches to Austria. That summer Spain ignored French pressure and joined the new Anglo-Austrian pact. In 1732-3 Spain allowed Britain to try to settle her Italian differences with Austria. The unilateral French settlement with Austria in 1735 was followed by French pressure, supported by the threat of military action, that led, after considerable delay, to the Spanish evacuations of Parma and Tuscany. In 1739-40 France refused to take her support of Spain, in her war with Britain, to the point of hostilities. Thus, the First Family compact, the Franco-Spanish alliance of 1733, was far from ushering in a period of cooperation. Franco-Spanish relations paralleled Anglo-Austrian relations in the first half of the century: the 'natural' alliance portrayed by publicists, and some historians, was far from obvious to informed contemporaries.

Poor Franco-Spanish relations were of great importance both to the British ministry and to the Jacobites. They were a decisive factor in Anglo-French relations. Had France enjoyed good relations with Spain in 1717-20 and 1725-6, she would not have followed Britain in her anti-Spanish policies, and this would have wrecked both the Anglo-French alliance and British foreign policy. To a great extent Britain was able to appear very influential in European affairs on these two occasions, precisely because of Franco-Spanish differences. Furthermore it was the continuance of these differences in the 1730s that made the collapse of the Anglo-French alliance in 1731, Britain's relative isolation after 1735, and the War of Jenkins' Ear less serious for Britain, and correspondingly less propitious for the Jacobites, than they might otherwise have been. In the summer of 1731 Britain responded with major military preparations to the French army build-up on the Channel coast. In 1732 Spanish military preparations led to increased British naval armaments. In each case the Jacobites hoped for assistance. The situation would have been far more serious had France and Spain cooperated in 1731 and 1732, as was feared. The military situation in 1739-40 would have been potentially disastrous if France had joined in the Anglo-Spanish hostilities. The diversion of French and Spanish resources against Austria from 1741 onwards lessened the danger considerably, and ensured that the crisis of French military support for Jacobitism when it came, in 1744-6, was far less serious than it might have been in 1739-40.

Thus the connection between Jacobitism and Anglo-French relations has to be placed, as it was by contemporaries, in the wider international setting. The Jacobites were correct in arguing both that an improvement in Franco-

Spanish relations was of importance to their cause and that changes in the French court and ministry were crucial. In 1721 James III observed, 'till Abbe du Bois be gained of which I see little prospect or till he be removed . . . I see little hopes of our receiving much favour from that Government, although I have so many and so considerable friends in France, that I should not think it altogether impossible to gain our ends by them alone . . .'[25] Three years later he wrote, 'when C[ardinal] du B[lois] was alive our chief hopes were from Spain',[26] Jacobite hopes were to be disappointed: the deaths of Dubois and Orléans did not lead to the end of the Anglo-French alliance. Furthermore, the increased weakness of the Jacobite movement in England[27] led the Jacobite leadership to become more dependent on the prospect of foreign assistance. In May 1724 the Earl of Strafford, one of the leading Tories in the House of Lords, informed James, 'some who were bold before, are now grown so cautious. It were to be wished your friends here could procure your return home, but since that cannot be you must have recourse to your friends abroad . . .'[28] The international situation in the first half of the 1720s was far from favourable for Jacobite schemes, a point stressed by ministerial newspapers.[29] After Spain's accession to the Quadruple Alliance in 1720 her energies were concentrated on obtaining Anglo-French diplomatic support for her Italian schemes. Spanish interest in Jacobite schemes slackened and, despite some British concern over the purpose of Spanish military preparations,[30] there was no realistic prospect of Spanish support for the Jacobites. This reflected Spanish realisation of Spain's need for Anglo-French assistance, and the continuing strength of the Anglo-French alliance.[31] British and French influence in Mediterranean affairs was greatly increased by the alliance.

In June 1724 the British Ambassador in Madrid, William Stanhope, informed Newcastle that the Jacobites had lost all hope of French and Spanish assistance 'but flatter themselves with the expectation of the Czar's attempting something even this summer in their master's favour'.[32] The Jacobites certainly hoped in the early 1720s that Peter would support them. The British ministry were concerned about Russian intentions,[33] and in the early 1720s, a period that has received relatively little attention, the wish to counter Russian schemes in the Baltic was a major element in British foreign policy, proving of particular significance in Anglo-Prussian relations. However, it could be suggested that this reflected George I's Hanoverian anxieties rather than British ministerial fears about Russian support for Jacobitism, fears expressed only occasionally in the surviving documents. In 1722 Whitworth, no longer an advocate of a major British role in an active anti-Russian coalition, observed, 'the Princes whose Dominions border on the Baltick, Poland, and the Emperor, are chiefly and directly concern'd in the Czar's growing power: Tis therefore their interest to concert in time such measures, as may be sufficient for their own security, and then to solicit England to accede to the common cause on reasonable grounds . . .'[34] Whitworth's attitude reflected the more limited conception of British foreign policy that obtained after Stanhope's death. That the British ministry actually followed a more active role, particularly in 1723, was due largely to an aspect of the Baltic crisis understandably not mentioned by Whitworth, namely active Hanoverian participation.

Jacobite hopes of Russia were to be disappointed. There was no doubt of Peter's propensity for 'fishing in troubled waters',[35] and had the Jacobite cause appeared stronger in Britain, it might have received more Russian assistance. However, despite several panics, Peter, perhaps impressed by British success in organising anti-Russian measures, proved unwilling to open hostilities. Much to the relief of British diplomats, Russian attention was diverted to expansion at the expense of Persia. Tilson wrote, 'my wishes are that it may draw him [Peter] in so deep, that it may take off his thoughts in a great measure from this side of the world. For that appears the chiefest hope of ease; otherwise everything is so disjointed that I am apt to judge he might push on projects, without a sufficient formed force against him'.[36]

British fears of a Franco-Russian alliance threatening British interests[37] proved to be misplaced. They did, however, indicate the continuing importance of the French alliance during the relatively calm period between the crises of the Atterbury Plot and the First Treaty of Vienna. The alliance was of importance not so much because of any help it could provide (the French were of scant assistance in organising anti-Russian moves in the early 1720s), as because it prevented France from developing her links with Russia and Spain into an overtly anti-British alliance. The Jacobites would have sought to exploit such an alliance, and its failure to materialise in the early 1720s dashed their hopes of foreign assistance. Chammorel observed in April 1725 that the Jacobites could not hope for any European help, whilst the previous month Newcastle had written, 'either before, or since His Majesty's happy accession, there never was a greater unanimity and zeal in both Houses of Parliament for His Majesty's service, or so universal a satisfaction and tranquility throughout the nation as there is at present; so it is hardly to be imagined that the Jacobites can be mad enough to think of making any disturbance at this time'.[38]

Ministerial complacency was to be suddenly shattered and Jacobite hopes as speedily revived by a surprising new European alliance. Despite the prognostications of opposition figures in the early 1720s, France did not desert Britain. Instead, to general amazement, Austria and Spain negotiated an alliance. In July 1725 James III observed, 'the affairs of Europe seem now to be in such a situation as to promise us soon some happy turn in my favour'.[39] The Jacobites approached Spain and Austria for assistance,[40] and the British ministry were soon aware of revived Jacobite hopes.[41] Much depended on the French attitude. The British ministry were aware that the Jacobites hoped to woo France from the Alliance of Hanover,[42] and that the French stance was crucial, 'it being both the opinion of the Duke of Ormonde and the bishop [Atterbury] that all attempts in his [James III's] favour will be no effect while your alliance with France continues'.[43]

, In the late 1720s Townshend was to be criticised by the opposition for the alacrity with which he negotiated the Treaty of Hanover and engaged Britain in an alliance against Austria and Spain. He was to be accused of committing Britain without cause to the French side of the Franco-Spanish rift that followed the French rejection of a Spanish bride for Louis XV. However, it could be suggested that Townshend's determination to negotiate the Treaty of Hanover reflected a fear that the Anglo-French alliance was in danger of dissolution, and a determination to yoke France to British interests. The threat of a league of France, Austria and Spain was no fantasy in 1725, and was possibly the most serious crisis that faced Britain in the age of Walpole before 1739-40. Had France, as was feared, chosen to abandon Britain, then the latter would have been left without allies of any military consequence. Hanover could have been easily overrun, and a serious invasion of Britain might have threatened. The strident tone of ministerial propaganda about the Jacobite threat in 1725-6 was therefore justified, not so much by the terms of the Treaty of Vienna, as by the alarming international situation and the danger that France would abandon Britain. On 9 September Newcastle told a meeting of the Lords Justices (George I was in Hanover) that Britain must maintain her French alliance, '. . . France which kingdom it is now so necessary to support in order to preserve the Balance of Europe'.[44] The British ministry's argument that they were supporting France against Spain and Austria[45] was somewhat disingenuous as it failed to stress the British need for French support.

In August 1725 Fleury suggested to Horace Walpole that the British send warships into the Channel to 'prevent any sudden attempt that might be made in favour of the Pretender'.[46] The threat of a sudden invasion attempt could not be dismissed lightly, and the British ministry were well aware of the danger posed by Ostend.[47] A major reason for the massive display of naval power in 1726-7, when British fleets were deployed in West Indian, Baltic, Spanish and home waters, was the wish to intimidate Spain and Austria so that they would not attempt an invasion. In April 1726 Townshend wrote of the Spanish government, 'they have laid schemes and have it in their thoughts to give us trouble here in favour of the Pretender, if they have power and opportunity to put it in practice'.[48] Naval strength was matched by a vigilant watch on Jacobite activities,[49] and the latter was assisted by information communicated by the French ministry.[50]

The Jacobite threat was of great significance in 1725-7, but it is clear that the British ministry were most concerned about it in relation to the international situation. There was little prospect of internal disorder, though ministerial fears were revealed by the harsh response to the Glasgow malt tax riots of 1725 and to the disorders in some of the forests of southern England associated with the Waltham Blacks.[51] Possibly the most serious military threat was posed by the Jacobite scheme for an Austrian invasion of Hanover and its retention until George I renounced his British throne. The accession of Prussia and Russia to the Alliance of Vienna in 1726 left Hanover extremely vulnerable. However, Austrian caution about supporting Jacobitism and commencing hostilities in the Empire made such a scheme impossible. Sinzendorf doubtless agreed with the Jacobite envoy, Sir John Graham, 'that it never could be the interest of His Imperial Majesty to have a subject of the Empire upon the throne of England, who would always make use of that power to strengthen himself in Germany by degrees'. The papal nuncio made the same point to the Austrian ministry.[52] Nevertheless, Jacobite pressure for the movement of troops led Sinzendorf to reply that Austria could not act against George I as Elector, as there was nothing to lay to his charge.[53] Austrian caution towards the Jacobites was in keeping with the general Austrian diplomatic stance. The Austrian ministry were opposed to war, not very committed to the Spanish alliance, and ready to negotiate. When hostilities began at Gibraltar in early 1727, they proved receptive to French approaches for a negotiated settlement of the European conflict. The Austrian ministry made it clear to the Jacobites that they would not support them unless there was war. The Jacobites offered to guarantee the Pragmatic Sanction and to support the Ostend Company, but their approaches were rebuffed.[54] The Austrian Minister, Prince Eugene told Graham that foreign assistance for the Jacobite cause would be useless unless there was strong internal support, 'adding that he knew personally most of the men of quality in that country [England], but did not think any of these, who were in his time in the Jacobite interest sufficiently qualified for heading a party'.[55]

Another possible source of military pressure on George I was Russia, and the Jacobites hoped that Catherine I would be willing to send troops to attack Hanover,[56] and to invade Britain.[57] However, these hopes were minor compared to those of Austrian and Spanish assistance, being quelled by the British naval movement to Baltic waters, besides which the Jacobites themselves were sceptical about Russian intentions and capabilities. In August 1725 Hay expressed doubt about the Russian fleet: 'I have reason to believe that there will be as little use made of that equipment as the Czar had when he was alive'.[58]

British naval activity limited drastically the prospect of Spanish interventions on behalf of Jacobites. In 1726 British naval activity led the

Spaniards to fear that their Biscayan ports, from which an invasion of Britain could be mounted, would be attacked, as they had been in 1719. It is notable that Ripperda, the leading Spanish minister, proved less interested than his predecessor of the late 1710s, Alberoni, in supporting the Jacobites. In the absence of any study of Hispano-Jacobite relations in the 1720s it is difficult to account for Spanish policy. Ripperda's willingness to suggest that he would support the Jacobites might have reflected simply a wish to intimidate the British ministry into concessions. His failure to act may have been due only to the British navy, or it may have reflected a desire not to repeat the earlier failure of Spanish military assistance in 1719. Ripperda's fall in the summer of 1726 removed an unpredictable element of Spanish policy, although the Spanish attack on Gibraltar in early 1727 suggests that continued Jacobite hopes of Spanish assistance were not without substance.

In June 1726 Father Lewis Innes, principal of the Scots College in Paris, wrote, 'the resentments that both the Emperor and the King of Spain have against King George are too deep and too well grounded to think that either of them will ever make up any more with him'.[59] As with so many other Jacobite predictions, this was to prove over-optimistic. When George I died a year later, a temporary settlement of European quarrels, the Preliminaries of Paris, had already been agreed. This was one of the blows the Jacobite cause suffered in 1727; the other was the peaceful nature of George II's succession,[60] which had not been expected in Jacobite circles.[61] The peaceful succession made it clear to the British ministry and Jacobites alike that the Jacobite cause depended on European assistance. 'Nothing but troubles in Europe can be of any service to the Pretender', claimed Horace Walpole, whilst Orrery wrote to James, 'just as this accident happened your best and most powerful friends abroad seemed to have abandoned the thoughts of supporting your cause, at least for some time, and the most promising opportunity of your succeeding in an attempt this year could not probably be laid hold of . . . Your business Sir is . . . to go on and cultivate in the best manner you can the friendship of foreign princes that you may be able to take the opportunity of any favourable conjuncture that may happen for you, which considering the uncertainty and instability of human affairs is not quite to be despaired of . . .'[62]

Orrery was to be proved correct in the long term, but in the late 1720s the position was particularly bleak for the Jacobites. The Spanish government continued to listen to them,[63] but failed to provide any significant support. The Austrians, convinced that the Jacobites could not cause disturbances in England,[64] preferred to place their hopes in the parliamentary opposition, and, in particular, in the opposition Whigs. Austrian envoys, who found British policy at odds with Austrian interests, Palm, Kinsky and Strickland, turned to them and not to the Jacobites. The French ministry continued to provide the British with information on the Jacobites, and in 1728, in response to British requests, seized the entire edition of a Jacobite manifesto addressed to the Congress of Soissons.[65] Fears continued to be expressed in Britain about French intentions, particularly by members of the opposition keen to embarrass the ministry,[66] but the European situation was bleak for the Jacobites,[67] and this was reflected in a lower level of British ministerial concern. In 1728-30 there are relatively few references to the Jacobites in British diplomatic correspondence. It may have been the bleak international situation and, in particular, the Treaty of Seville of November 1729, that led James III in January 1730 to instruct his parliamentary supporters to cooperate with other opposition elements in order to 'promote a misunderstanding between the English government and any foreign power, but most especially France'.[68] Having lost the prospect of Spanish assistance, and with neither Austria nor Prussia interested in supporting Jacobitism, James saw that it was Anglo-French relations that were crucial. This was also realised by Horace Walpole, who had written in July 1728, 'our dangers from France, at all times, if we are not good friends with that Crown, are immediate, and at our door, especially as long as there is a Pretender'.[69] Broglie stressed the same point in October 1730, as did the ministry in Parliament. Anonymous notes of a parliamentary speech delivered by a ministerial speaker, probably in the state of the nation debates in 1730, included the statement that France was 'zealous against the Pretender. Their friendship useful. Might hurt us if otherwise on account of the Pretender'.[70]

Despite this argument, there is little sign that the Jacobite issue and its role in Anglo-French relations was seriously considered in the summer of 1730 when the decision was taken secretly to approach Austria. Possibly this was because it was certainly hoped that the French would accept the Anglo-Austrian reconciliation and agree to observe its terms. Possibly the issue had not been seriously considered: Jacobite quiescence since late 1727, both in Britain and Europe, would have made this understandable.

The hostile French response to the Anglo-Austrian reconciliation led to widely circulated reports of French support for Jacobitism. It was believed that both James III and Ormonde had been received in France, and it was reported that James had seen Louis XV.[71] These reports were false, and Fleury assured Waldegrave that James's request to return to France had been rejected.[72] However, the British ministry were greatly alarmed by the revival of Jacobite activity and by uncertainty over French intentions. Spying on the Jacobites was increased.[83] On 26 March Newcastle wrote to Waldegrave. He suspected that Chauvelin and the two French envoys in London, Broglie and Chammorel, were seeking to inflame Anglo-French relations 'so that one cannot be sure what party France may take upon the conclusion of our Treaty, and whether they may not underhand raise and foment difficultys and troubles in His Majesty's Dominions ...' Waldegrave was ordered to 'take notice, whether the Irish regiments in the service of France are ordered to the coasts of that Kingdom that lie nearest to England ...'

On 1 April Newcastle added darkly, 'there is reason to apprehend that there is something doing'. Waldegrave sought to calm Newcastle, claiming that French hostility to Britain would not lead to action because of the risks that would entail, particularly as France lacked allies. However, he accepted that 'this is too nice a matter not to be constantly on ones guard about it'.[74] The subsequent war panic, when a large portion of the British army was deployed on the Channel coast to prevent a feared French invasion, indicated the depth of British anxiety. Suspected French enmity ensured that the 1732 Spanish military preparations were watched with caution. The possibility of a Spanish invasion in favour of the Jacobites was widely discussed,[75] though the Spaniards had no such intentions. James III was not hopeful of Spanish support although, as he pointed out, 'the court of Spain is so unaccountable and changeable' that they might aid him.[76] The Spanish refusal to give Ormonde an audience of leave and the French refusal to let him come to France[77] were welcomed by the British ministry, but there was no disguising the dangerous nature of the international system for Britain. The possibility of Bourbon encouragement of Jacobitism could not be discounted, and this was a threat, irrespective of the real strength of domestic Jacobitism. The very belief that the Jacobite card could be used weakened Britain's international position. British diplomats argued that Jacobitism was weak, Robinson telling Eugene in 1732 'that as for the Pretender his name was, God be praised, hardly known in England'.[78] Robinson's claim was an exaggeration, though it was true that domestic willingness to intrigue and correspond with the Jacobite court had diminished, and that much of the initiative for Jacobite discussions in London lay with that exemplar of diplomatic perpetual motion, the new French envoy Chavigny.[79] Foreign estimates of British support for Jacobitism varied. In 1731 Chammorel reported that the fire of Jacobitism had not gone out, but still burnt in the embers. If James III went to France, he said, there would be public joy in Britain and a collapse of the state fiscal system.[80] Chammorel's report was no doubt coloured by French anger at the Second Treaty of Vienna. Similarly Fleury, five years later, would have been influenced by his audience when he told Waldegrave that in the event of a Jacobite invasion 'he [Fleury] was persuaded that in such a case all the opposition to [George II's] measures would cease, that those who oppose [the British government] most at present would join you against the Prince and his adherents, he [Fleury] named Mr Pulteney amongst others'.[81]

Possibly Fleury's attitude was decisive in 1733 when the French ministry rejected the Jacobite scheme, actively supported by Chavigny, for an invasion of Britain.[82] The Jacobites, pessimistic about the prospect of foreign aid in 1732 and early 1733,[83] became more optimistic in 1733 as a result of the Excise agitation, which could serve to convince them, and others, that the British ministry was very weak, and also because of signs that the Polish succession crisis would lead to a European war that might entail Anglo-French hostilities.[84] In June, James observed, 'my affairs certainly never had so good an appearance'.[85] The Franco-Spanish alliance, long desired by the Jacobites,[86] was realised in the First Family Compact. The British ministry became progressively more alarmed.[87] Rumours of an invasion became persistent in 1734.[88] Seeking to encourage Anglo-Bourbon rivalry, the Austrians pressed the British on the danger of a Jacobite invasion.[89] Newcastle was particularly concerned about the Jacobite threat. In February 1734, informing Waldegrave that the Franco-Spanish treaty stipulated the return of Gibraltar to Spain, he commented, 'It is scarce to be imagined, that they would have gone so far, without having some secret engagements, in favour of the Pretender: especially, since the court of France may think, that they can never secure that sovereignty, over all Europe, which, by this treaty, they seem to be aiming at, unless they can also place the Pretenders upon the throne of England'. He expressed his fear that once Austria had been beaten, Spain and France would 'be at liberty, to make any attempt they may think proper, against His Majesty and his dominions'.[90]

Evidence of Bourbon-Jacobite contacts increased the alarm. In Rome the French Ambassador, the Duke of St. Aignan, advised James III, despite British complaints.[91] James's eldest son, Charles, accompanied the Spanish army that invaded Naples in 1734, and Don Carlos' public demonstration of support for him outraged the British ministry.[92] It was widely believed that British entry into the War of the Polish Succession would lead to open Bourbon support for the Jacobites,[93] a reasonable supposition judging from Anglo-Spanish relations in 1718-19. The extent to which the threat of open Bourbon support for the Jacobites led the Walpole ministry to follow a policy of neutrality in the War of the Polish Succession is difficult to assess. As has been argued in other sections of this work, British neutrality in the war can be traced to several influences, and the relationship of these influences varied during its course. The prospect of successful Bourbon military action in favour of the Jacobites was strongest in the summer of 1733. The French navy had a large squadron ready for sea, and troops on the Channel coast were ready for an amphibious operation. The level of British preparedness was low. Very few warships were ready to sail, and the only force that was being prepared for a voyage, Rear Admiral Stewart's squadron designed for the Mediterranean, was tiny. Concern about Jacobite schemes was tempered by the belief that neither France nor Spain intended to support James.[94] Aware of French military preparations, the British ministry did not believe that war would break out, and they sought to prevent it by dissuading the Russians from invading Poland and the French from regarding such an invasion as a *casus belli* with Austria. Unaware of the nature of Franco-Spanish relations, the British ministry hoped that their mediation of Austro-Spanish differences in Italy would keep Spain allied to Britain.

The destruction of these hopes by the Franco-Spanish alliance led to an upsurge of British ministerial concern about Jacobitism in early 1734. However, the massive naval armament of this period made the prospect of a Bourbon-supported invasion unlikely. In a sense the Jacobites had been correct in 1726 to argue that a surprise attack was best. The prospect of the Bourbon – French and Spanish – fleets defeating the British navy in 1734-5 was scant. The British fleet, by contrast with 1739-48, was concentrated in home waters, whilst the Bourbons had to have a large Mediterranean force for Italian operations. Not only was a successful invasion unlikely in 1734-5; the Bourbons also could not spare the troops. The Austrian ability to mount an Italian counter-attack in 1734 and the French failure to triumph in the Rhineland made the prospect of Bourbon military support for the Jacobites unlikely. Furthermore, it increased the Bourbon need to maintain British neutrality. This neutrality should not be viewed simply as a matter of British inaction. The British ministerial response to the war was affected by Bourbon actions, and the Bourbons sought to persuade the British of their good intentions. Fleury did not follow Chavigny's recipe of intimidation and intervention. Based in 1733 upon an inaccurate assessment of British political stability, this recipe was down-right foolish in 1734-5 when the massive British naval armament – far outnumbering the Bourbon in terms of ships that could be readily put to sea – gave the British the capacity to influence Bourbon schemes. Fleury claimed in 1734 that he was intimidated by the British naval preparations into failing to send the required forces to the relief of Danzig.[95] In 1735 the dispatch of Admiral Norris and a fleet to the Tagus discouraged Spain from attacking Portugal.

To have risked provoking British entry into the war by supporting the Jacobites would have been very foolish. The Spaniards apologised for Carlos' reception of Prince Charles; Fleury assured the British that France would not support the Jacobites.[96] The connection between British neutrality and Bourbon-Jacobite relations was far from simple. Neither Britain nor the Bourbons wanted to fight each other, and it was the unwillingness of the Bourbons, particularly of France, to fight that effectively thwarted Jacobite hopes. British neutrality in the War of the Polish Succession was a major diplomatic achievement of the French, an achievement they failed to repeat, to their cost, in the War of Austrian Succession. Waldegrave's perceptive summary of the situation, penned before the outbreak of the War of the Polish Succession, was equally appropriate for the period of conflict: 'I am firmly persuaded that several of the French ministers espouse the Jacobite party, and even the Cardinal himself does not discourage it as much as he pretends to do. In case of a rupture, between our two courts, the Pretender would certainly be made use of to distress us, but as long as we remain upon the foot we are they will never think of him in earnest, knowing that a war must inevitably be the consequence'.[97]

The war ended with an alliance the Jacobites had actively sought, one of Austria and France.[98] The Jacobites sought in the late 1730s to benefit from improved relations among the Catholic powers, but their hopes were to prove unfounded until the outbreak of Anglo-Spanish hostilities in 1739, a war that Spain did not seek. Austria preferred to attempt Balkan aggrandisement, Spain to plot for Italian acquisitions, and Fleury to enjoy his new position as most influential European statesman. There were scares, particularly reports that Prince Charles was to be received in France or Spain,[99] and there was British ministerial anger at the courtesies extended to the Jacobites by foreign powers and their envoys. In 1737 this led to a breach of diplomatic relations with Venice that was to persist until 1744.[100] St. Aignan continued to see James III regularly and Fleury to reassure the British about Franco-Jacobite relations.[101] However, in general, the situation was far from alarming. Trevor, commenting on Dutch information about Jacobite schemes, observed, 'the [information] entrusted to me, seemed rather to prove the alertness of the Jacobites, than the least impression, which their intrigues had found at any of the courts'.[102] There is an absence of concern about Jacobitism in British diplomatic correspondence in 1736-8 that is very marked, particularly in contrast to that of the years on either side. Possibly this should be taken into account when discussing the relative lack of drive behind the policy for a Protestant league in the late 1730s. It is interesting to contrast the widely expressed public anxiety in Britain about the strength of British Catholicism in this period and the relative lack of ministerial concern about Jacobitism.

As was only to be expected, estimates of the strength of British Jacobitism in the late 1730s varied greatly, and the relationship between Jacobites and other opponents of the Walpole ministry created as much disagreement among contemporaries as it was latter to do among historians. Walpole's manager for Scottish affairs, the Earl of Islay, wrote from Scotland: 'The Jacobites and Papists exert themselves more than ever I knew them, since the Queen Anne's death, and though the most of those who foment this

Patriot spirit here are not Jacobites, yet I plainly forsee that, if they shall find that all their fancied hopes are blasted by a different turn in England, Jacobitism will be their next resource . . .'[103] Commentators on the situation in England tended to stress Jacobite weakness. Possibly the foreign observers, who knew little of the situation outside London, were over-impressed by the Patriots in London (as they had been earlier by Boling-broke's Country platform), and underrated Jacobite strength.[104] Whatever the strength of Jacobite sentiment in the late 1730s, there was scant interest in plotting among the British Jacobites. Bagshaw, the Consul in Genoa, provided a summary of the position in 1737: 'At Rome they hold several conferences . . . to see if they could possibly put the Pretender into England securely, in which they find a great deal of difficulty, by reason, that a great many noblemen who were of his party, are now otherwise, and have altered their minds although had declared fidelity, others are grown cold about the matter, others say that it is not yet time to undertake any such thing, of bringing the Pretender into England, but that they still hope to see that day, these are the answers that the expresses have brought to Rome, from England'.[105]

Deteriorating Anglo-Spanish relations and the belief that France would support Spain gave new strength to Jacobite hopes in 1738-40.[106] The Jacobites approached both powers. The Spanish government was willing to make promises to the Jacobites and to threaten to assist them,[107] but the extent of their help was limited, and the Jacobites preferred to seek French assistance. After the fall of Chauvelin, the British ministry had been reasonably satisfied with the state of Franco-Jacobite relations,[108] but concern about French policy increased in 1739 as it became likely that war with Spain would break out. Waldegrave, who was no alarmist, either about French intentions in general or about Franco-Jacobite relations, warned in June 1739, 'I do not believe the Cardinal [Fleury], unless we were at open war with France, would give into all the trifling Jacobite schemes the Court of Spain might be proposing to him, but I am firmly of opinion that nobody would go [to] greater lengths to help the Pretender than the Cardinal, were he satisfied of a probability of success in an undertaking of this nature . . .'[109]

That same month a French diplomat in London reported that as soon as the first orders were sent for hostilities to be commenced against Spain, England was swept with rumours that James III had already landed with a French force.[110] The connection between confrontation with the Bourbon powers and an increase in the Jacobite threat was clear, but how far this affected British policy in 1739 is far from obvious. If it is argued that the threat of Bourbon support for the Jacobites led to neutrality in 1733-5, why did it not have a similar effect in 1739? Possibly Walpole's opposition to conflict in 1739 can be related to this issue, although there is no sign that

Newcastle, in pressing for a tougher stance towards Spain, argued that the Jacobites did not present a threat. 'It is impossible in case of a war to suppose they will not endeavour to put the Pretender upon us', observed the Bishop of Chichester in June 1739,[111] but Jacobitism was but one of issues at stake that year.

The French refusal to support the Jacobites in 1739-43 was crucial, since Spanish support alone was inadequate.[112] Fleury preferred not to push Anglo-French tension to the point of actual war. He threatened to fight, particularly in order to preserve Spain's American Empire, and to that end sent a squadron to the Caribbean, and these threats served France's purpose better than actual hostilities. In 1741 France attacked Austria, and Britain gave Austria financial and diplomatic support (and the movement of troops in 1742 to the Austrian Netherlands) that far exceeded British assistance in 1733-5. However, in 1741-3 the French ministry were not prepared to commit major resources to the Jacobite cause. As in the 1730s, the desire to defeat and permanently weaken Austria was the first French priority, and the Jacobite cause a diversion. The French ministry did not provide appreciable support for the Jacobites until after the death of Fleury, when Carteret's aggressive diplomatic strategy made limiting French power the prime British concern, in marked contrast to the position in the 1730s. As a result the Jacobites benefited from French support, particularly in 1744, although, with the exception of 1744, Britain remained a sideshow as far as the French were concerned.

A consideration of the role of Jacobitism in British foreign policy, and, in particular, in Anglo-French relations suggests that it reflected the international situation rather than the strength of the movement in Britain. This was hardly surprising: the latter was difficult to evaluate, and assessments varied widely. Ministerial comments varied. In 1733 Delafaye wrote: 'Jacobitism must, in the nature of things, be rooted out by the long continuance of a Government under which no man can say that he has been injured in his liberty or property'.[113] And yet on other occasions ministerial spokesmen claimed that Jacobitism was a potent threat. Given the variation in ministerial comments, it is hardly surprising that foreign observers also arrived at differing conclusions. The extent to which powers opposing the British Ministry were encouraged to do so by the existence of Jacobitism is open to question: possibly they only listened to the Jacobites when they were at odds with Britain. This was certainly true of Austria, and arguably so of France. Spain harboured Jacobites throughout the period but could combine this with a British alliance, as in 1731-3. The primacy of the international situation was observed by Robethon in 1715, when he argued that the death of Louis XIV would extinguish Jacobite hopes more than any parliamentary action.[114] To a certain extent the Jacobites were unlucky in that France, under both Orléans and Fleury, was unwilling to confront Britain. In 1732 Fleury told Waldegrave that Orléans had for 'his own views' done 'whatever we [Britain] desired'.[115]

In fact Orléans, contrary to what his critics claimed, was no British puppet, though it was true that he sought to avoid clashes with Britain. The French refusal to aid the Jacobites was fortuitous. Had the French ministry wished, they could have threatened Britain without much expenditure or the movement of large forces. They succeeded in doing this in 1731, 1733-5 and 1739-43. To threaten Britain successfully, it was not therefore necessary for the French ministry to make that their prime goal. This was of great importance, and it also harmed the Jacobites, for the French did not need to support them openly in order to threaten Britain. Troop movements on the Channel coast were less expensive, easier to control, and likelier to succeed.

Jacobitism made relations with France even more important for Britain than they might otherwise have been. It did not have a comparable impact upon France. For the French the Jacobite option bore certain similarities to their old policy of allying with the German princes against the Emperor. It is interesting to note that the period 1714-41 saw significant departures from this policy, particularly in 1728 and 1735-40. French foreign policy in the early years of Louis XV's reign was more fluid and less uncompromising than has often been appreciated. Britain played a key role in French policy in the late 1710s, but it had lost this position by the 1730s, and, arguably (bar a reversal in 1725-6), by 1721. A limited war with Britain, comparable to wars declared by France against Spain in 1718 and Austria in 1733, was not impossible, but it would have served no particular French interest. The commercial and maritime lobby had few advocates at Versailles, bar Maurepas. There was no particular reason why France should support the Jacobite cause. It was to be later in the century, particularly after the Diplomatic Revolution of 1756, that French ministers increasingly looked on Britain as the prime threat. Invasion plans were seriously canvassed in 1744-5, 1759 and 1779. Had France been an enemy of Britain during the Walpole period and seriously contemplated pro-Jacobite action, then Jacobitism in its international context would have been continuously one of the major preoccupations of British foreign policy. French attitudes ensured that this was not the case.

NOTES

1. James III to the Duke of Ormonde, a leading Jacobite, 3 Oct. (ns) 1736, RA. 190/25.

2. B. Lenman, *The Jacobite Risings in Britain 1689-1746* (1980); F. McLynn, *The Jacobite Army in England, 1745: The Final Campaign* (Edinburgh, 1983).

3. E. Cruickshanks, *Political Untouchables. The Tories and the '45* (1979); L. Colley, *In Defiance of Oligarchy. The Tory Party, 1714-60* (1982).

4. G. V. Bennett, *The Tory Crisis in Church and State, 1688-1730* (Oxford, 1975); P. Fritz, *The English Ministers and Jacobitism Between the Rebellions of 1715 and 1745* (1975); F. McLynn, *France and the Jacobite Rising of 1745* (Edinburgh, 1981); E. Cruickshanks (ed.), *Ideology and Conspiracy: Aspects of Jacobitism, 1689-1759* (Edinburgh, 1982).

5. Francis Hare to Francis Naylor, 14 June 1739, HMC., *Hare Mss* p. 248.

6. Newcastle to Brinley Skinner, in charge of affairs in Florence, 31 Mar. 1732, PRO. 98/84; Newcastle to Waldegrave, 1 Ap. 1731, Chewton; Newcastle to Allen, Secretary in Turin, 31 Mar. 1732, PRO. 92/11; Newcastle to Waldegrave, 5 Feb. 1734, BL. Add. 32784.

7. Newcastle to Waldegrave, 9 Oct. 1733, BL. Add. 32783.

8. Memorandum by James III, – Sept. (ns) 1720; Earl of Orrery to James, 30 June 1727, RA. 49/25, 107/150.

9. Whitworth, envoy at the Imperial Diet in Regensburg, to Stair, 17 Oct. (ns) 1715, SRO. GD. 135/141/4; undated memorandum by the Duc d'Antin, influential French courtier, c. 1735-6, AE. MD. France 504 f.6; Horace Walpole to [Delafaye], 17 Sept. (ns) 1724, BL. Add. 32740; St. Saphorin, Relation Secrette de la Cour Imperiale, 6 June (ns) 1721, BL. Add. 61706; Edward Southwell to Earl of Nottingham, 26 Nov. 1723, Leicester, County Record Office, Finch Mss. DG/7/4950.

10. Molesworth to Carteret, 15 Sept. (ns) 1723, PRO. 92/31.

11. Keene to Horace Walpole, 6 Oct. (ns), Horatio Walpole to Keene, 6, 20 Oct. (ns) 1727, BL. Add. 32752; Waldegrave Journal, 29 Oct. (ns), 10 Nov. (ns) 1727, Chewton.

12. Waldegrave to Newcastle, 10 Aug. (ns) 1740, PRO. 78/223.

13. Memorandum presented by Graham, Jacobite envoy in Vienna, to Eugene on 17 May (ns) 1726, HHStA., England, Noten, 2.

14. Memorandum presented by the Duke of Wharton, Jacobite agent in Vienna, 1 Jan. (ns) 1726, HHStA., England, Noten, 2.

15. O'Rourke, Jacobite envoy in Vienna, to Graham, Jacobite Secretary of State, 29 Oct. (ns) 1727, HHStA., England, Varia, 8; Anon. French memorandum, 5 July (ns) 1736, AE. MD. Ang. 6.

16. Newcastle to Waldegrave, 1 Ap., Broglie to Chauvelin, 9 Ap. (ns) 1731, BL. Add. 32772.

17. The highpoint of cooperation was 1735: the abortive peace talks at The Hague, and joint pressure on their allies to avoid a Portuguese-Spanish war.

18. Craggs to Dubois, 20 Jan. 1719, PRO. 100/3.

19. Sparre to Frederick I of Sweden, 22 May (ns) 1722, Marburg, 184.

20. Jacquemin, Lorraine envoy in Paris, to Leopold, 28 July (ns) 1727, Nancy 139; Graham to Atterbury, 12 Sept. (ns) 1727, RA. 110/38.

21. Horace Walpole to Newcastle, 27 Dec. (ns) 1727, BL. Add. 32758.

22. Dillon to James, 21 May (ns), Orrery to James, 27 Sept. 1720, RA. 47/9, 49/15.

23. O'Rourke to James III, 22 Jan. (ns), 12 Feb. (ns) 1735, RA. 177/37, 177/136; G. H. Jones, *The Mainstream of Jacobitism* (Cambridge, Mass. 1954), p. 193.

24. James to Ormonde, 22 Mar. (ns) 1723, RA. 66/110.

25. James to Orrery, 22 Ap. (ns) 1721, RA. 53/49.

26. James III to Ormonde, 5 Feb. (ns) 1724, RA. 72/76.

27. E. Hughes, *North Country Life in the Eighteenth Century: The North-East, 1700-50* (1952), p. 24; *Applebee's Original Weekly Journal* 11, July 1724.

28. Strafford to James III, 10 May 1724, RA. 74/60.

29. *Weekly Journal or British Gazetteer*, 2 Jan., *Flying-Post: or, Post Master*, 4 Feb. 1720. Molesworth to Carteret, 30 Dec. (ns) 1722, 29 July (ns) 1723, PRO. 92/31.

30. *Wye's Letter*, 8 May 1722; *Flying-Post: or Post Master*, 30 Oct. 1722; Chammorel to Morville, 4 Oct. (ns) 1722, AE. CP. Ang. 343.

31. Horace Walpole to Newcastle, 20 Nov. (ns) 1723, BL. Add. 32686.

32. Stanhope to Newcastle, 10 June (ns) 1724, BL. Add 32739.

33. James III to John Menzies, 11 Jan. (ns) 1722, RA. 57/31.

34. Whitworth to Scott, 17 Mar. (ns) 1722, BL. Add. 37388.

35. Tilson to Whitworth, 2 Mar. 1722, BL. Add. 37388.

36. Tilson to Whitworth, 1 May 1722, BL. Add. 37389.

37. Tilson to Whitworth, 3 Aug. (ns), Whitworth to Tilson, 23 Aug. (ns) 1723, BL. Add. 37392.

38. Chammorel to Morville, 16 Ap. (ns) 1725, AE. CP. Ang. 350; Newcastle to Horace Walpole, 11 Mar. 1725, CUL. CH. corresp. 1199.

39. James to Lord Garleys, 11 July (ns) 1725, RA. 84/7.

40. Memorandum presented by Wharton, 23 Aug. (ns) 1725, HHStA., England, Noten 2.

41. Anon. to _____, 24 June (ns) 1725, Horace Walpole to Delafaye, 1, 15 Dec. (ns) 1725, PRO. 35/56, 78/182.

42. Anon. to Horace Walpole, 21 Dec. (ns) 1725, PRO. 78/182.

43. John Sample, informer on Atterbury, to Horace Walpole, 4 June (ns) 1725, CUL. CH. corresp. 1215.

44. Memorandum by Newcastle of meeting on previous day, 10 Sept. 1725, BL Add. 32687.

45. Horace Walpole to Townshend, 14 Aug. (ns) 1725. BL. Add. 46856.

46. Horace Walpole to Townshend, 14 Aug. (ns) 1725, BL. Add. 46856.

47. Anon., 'The second report upon the Treaty of Vienna', 26 July 1725, copy sent to Townshend, 30 July, PRO. 103/107.

48. Townshend to William Finch, 29 Ap. 1726, PRO. 84/290.

49. Newcastle to British consuls in Italy and Spain, 24 Jan. 1726, PRO. 99/63.

50. Newcastle to Horace Walpole, 23 May 1726, BL. Add. 32746.

51. E. P. Thompson, *Whigs and Hunters* (1975). In forthcoming work Dr. Cruickshanks is to underline the Jacobite affiliations of the Blacks.

52. Graham to Hay, 7 Sept. (ns), 16 Nov. (ns) 1726, RA. 97/7, 99/31.

53. Graham to Hay, 30 Nov. (ns), 7 Dec. (ns) 1726, RA. 99/103, 130.

54. Instructions for Wharton, 22 Aug. (ns) 1725, Graham to Hay 16 Feb. (ns), 5 Oct. (ns) 1726, RA. 85/81, 90/121, 97/139.

55. Graham to Hay, 2 Nov. (ns) 1726, RA. 98/132.

56. Daniel O'Brien to Hay, 23 Sept. (ns) 1726, RA. 97/81.

57. Hay to Captain William Hay, agent in St. Petersburg, 14 July (ns), Admiral Gordon, Scottish admiral of Russian fleet, to Hay, 6 Aug. (ns) 1725, RA. 84/39, 85/42.

58. Hay to General George Hamilton, 11 Aug. (ns) 1725, RA. 85/42.

59. Innes to Hay, 17 June (ns) 1726, RA. 94/125.

60. Lord Advocate Duncan Forbes to Newcastle, 29 July 1727, PRO. 54/18.

61. De Büy, Saxon agent in Madrid, to Count Flemming, Saxon minister, 14, 21 July (ns) 1727, Dresden. 3105, I.

62. Horace Walpole to Keene, 10 Nov. (ns) 1727, BL. Add. 32752; Orrery to James, 30 June, Graham to O'Rourke. 1 Sept. (ns) 1727, James to Colonel Bret, 26 Mar. (ns) 1732, RA. 107/150, 109/145, 152/107.

63. Keene to Newcastle, 9 Feb. (ns) 1728, BL. Add. 32754; Poyntz to Delafye, 29 Jan. (ns) 1729, PRO. 78/190.

64. Berkentin, Danish envoy in Vienna, to _____, 17 Mar. (ns) 1728, PRO. 80/326.

65. Horace Walpole to Newcastle, 3, 14 Aug. (ns), Horace Walpole and Stanhope to Newcastle, 25 Sept. (ns) 1728, BL. Add. 32757, 32758.

66. Vernon, 21 Jan. 1729, HMC. Egmont III, 332.

67. *London Evening Post,* 8 May 1729; O'Rourke to James III, 23 Oct. (ns) 1728, HHStA., England, Varia. 8.

68. R. R. Sedgwick (ed.), *The House of Commons, 1715-54* (2 vols., 1970), I, 68; Jones, *Mainstream,* pp. 178-9.

69. Horace Walpole to Townshend, 1 July (ns) 1728, Bradfer Lawrence.

70. Zamboni to Marquis to Fleury, 24 Oct. (ns) 1730, Bodl. Rawl. 120; notes of speech, PRO. 36/21, f. 219.

71. Waldegrave to Newcastle 22 Mar. (ns) 1731, BL. Add. 32772; Chesterfield to _____, 10 Ap. (ns), Delafaye to Waldegrave, 10 Ap., Horace Walpole to Waldegrave, 24 Ap., Colman, envoy in Florence to Waldegrave, 26 May (ns) 1731, Chewton; *York Courant,* 6 Ap. 1731; Dayrolle to Harrington, 29 May (ns) 1731, PRO 84/317; Allen, Consul in Naples, to Newcastle, 1 June (ns) 1731, PRO. 93/5.

72. Waldegrave to Newcastle, 22 Mar. (ns) 1731, BL. Add. 32772; Diemar to William VIII, 6 July (ns) 1731, Marburg, 204.

73. Newcastle to Colman, 18 Mar., 3 June, Thomas Pelham to Delafaye, 2 May (ns) 1731, PRO. 98/83, 78/198.

74. Newcastle to Waldegrave, 26 Mar., 1 Ap., Waldegrave to Newcastle, 10, 19 Ap. (ns) 1731, BL. Add. 32772.

75. Robinson to Harrington, 10 Mar. (ns), 'Le Connu' to Tilson, 11 Mar. (ns), Newcastle to Allen, envoy in Turin, 31 Mar., Bagshaw, envoy in Genoa, to Newcastle, 11 May (ns), Newcastle to Keene, 6 July 1732, PRO. 80/86, 84/581, 92/33, 79/16, 94/113.

76. James to St. Quintin, 26 Feb. (ns) 1732, RA. 151/167.

77. Keene to Newcastle, 21 Mar. (ns), Newcastle to Keene, 31 Mar., Waldegrave to Newcastle, 16 Ap. (ns) 1732, PRO. 94/111, BL. Add. 32776.

78. Robinson to Harrington, 10 Mar. (ns) 1732, PRO. 80/86.

79. O.X. to Newcastle, 28 Aug. 1732, BL. Add. 32778; Chavigny to Chauvelin, 17 July (ns) 1733, AE. CP. Ang. 381; Weston to Robinson, 11 Jan. 1734, BL. Add. 23790.

80. Chammorel to Chavelin, 25 Ap. (ns) 1731, AE. CP. Ang. 373; James to O'Brien, 4 Mar. (ns) 1733, RA. 159/182.

81. Waldegrave to Robert Walpole, 3 Nov. (ns) 1736, Chewton. Sparre, the Swedish envoy in London, agreed, Sparre to Horn 16 Oct. (ns) 1733, PRO. 107/17.

82. Colonel William Cecil, Jacobite agent in London, to James, 8 Mar. 1733, James to O'Brien, 28 Ap. (ns) 1733 RA. 160/4, 161/32; Chavigny to Chauvelin 23 Ap. (ns), 1, 17 July (ns) 1733, AE. CP. Ang. 380-1; Marquis de Vogüé (ed.), *Mémoires du Maréchal de Villars* (6 vols., Paris, 1884-1904), 6 May 1733.

83. James to Bret, 26 Mar. (ns) 1732, James to O'Brien, 25 Feb. (ns) 1733, RA. 152/107, 159/136.

84. Skinner to Robinson, 10 May (ns) 1733, BL. Add. 23788; O'Rourke to James, 4 July (ns) 1733, RA. 163/20.

85. James to O'Brien, 16 June (ns) 1733, RA. 162/100.

86. 'Instructions for the Earl Marishall of Scotland upon his going our minister to the Court of Spain', [Feb.-Mar. 1733], RA. 159/159.

87. Essex to Newcastle, 7 Ap. (ns), Newcastle to Essex, 23 July 1733, PRO. 92/35, 36.

88. Skinner to Newcastle, 20 Mar. (ns) 1734, BL. Add. 23790; Essex to Newcastle, 30 June (ns), Cayley to Newcastle, 6 July (ns) Consul Allen to Newcastle, 24 July (ns) 1734, PRO. 92/37, 94/220, 93/9; Couraud to Waldegrave, 31 May (ns) 1735, Chewton.

89. Dayrolle to Harrington, 29 Jan. (ns) 1734, Robinson to Harrington, 18 Sept. (ns) 1734, 5 July (ns) 1735, PRO. 84/338, 80/110, 116. The Sardinians made the same point, Essex to Newcastle, 17 Ap. (ns) 1734, Villettes to Newcastle, 4 Feb. (ns) 1735, PRO. 92/37, 38.

90. Newcastle to Waldegrave, 5 Feb. 1734, BL. Add. 32784; Essex to Newcastle, 30 June (ns) 1734, PRO. 92/37.

91. Essex to Waldegrave, 21 Jan. (ns) 1733, Chewton; Newcastle to Waldegrave, 1 Feb., Waldegrave to Newcastle, 28 Feb. (ns) 1734, BL. Add. 32784; Robinson to Harrington, 7 Ap. (ns), Essex to Newcastle, 18 June (ns), 1734, PRO. 80/105, 92/37.

92. Hervey, pp. 317-18.

93. Villettes to Newcastle, 16 Jan (ns), Skinner to Robinson, 13 Mar. (ns) 1734, PRO. 92/37, 80/105; James to Innes, 17 Mar. (ns), James to O'Brien, 11 Aug. (ns) 1734, RA. 169/3, 172/85.

94. Newcastle to Essex, 23 July 1733, PRO. 92/36.

95. This was also claimed by Hervey, p. 339.

96. Keene to Waldegrave, 21 Aug. (ns) 1734, Chewton; Waldegrave to Newcastle, 24 Feb. (ns) 1735, BL. Add. 32784.

97. Waldegrave to Newcastle, 25 Mar. (ns) 1733, BL. Add. 32781.

98. O'Rourke to James, 2 July (ns) 1735, RA. 180/144.

99. *Nottingham Post*, 16 June 1737; Newcastle to Keene, 11 July 1737, PRO. 94/129.

100. Newcastle to Keene, 11 July, Keene to Newcastle, 12 Aug. (ns) 1737, PRO. 94/128-9; Villettes to Newcastle, 11 May (ns), 4 June (ns) 1737, PRO. 92/41; Amelot to Bussy, 9 July (ns) 1737, AE. CP. Ang. 395.

101. Bagshaw to Newcastle, 5 Jan. (ns) 1737, PRO. 79/18; Newcastle to Waldegrave, 5 May, 9 June 1737, BL. Add. 32795.

102. Trevor to Harrington, 22 Jan. (ns) 1737, PRO. 84/363.

103. Islay to Robert Walpole, 16 Sept. [1737 or '38], CUL. CH. corresp. 2710.

104. 'Situation de L' Angleterre,' anon. memorandum, 27 June (ns) 1739, AE. MD. Ang. 8; Hop to Fagel, 31 July (ns) 1739, PRO. 107/30.

105. Bagshaw to Newcastle, 21 Feb. (ns) 1737, PRO. 79/18.

106. John Parker, Consul in Corunna, to Wager, 13 July (ns) 1738, CUL. CH. corresp. 2785; Admiral Gordon to Mr Williams, 15 June (ns) 1739, HMC, *Charles Stirling – Home – Drummond MSS.*, p. 189; Cruickshanks, *Political Untouchables*, pp. 22-3.

107. Waldegrave to 'Madam', 1, 5 May (ns) 1738, Chewton; Waldegrave to Newcastle, 16 May (ns) 1738, BL. Add. 32798.

108. Newcastle to Waldegrave, 5 May 1737, Waldegrave to Newcastle, 31 May (ns), Waldegrave to Stone, 31 May (ns) 1738, BL. Add. 32795, 32798.

109. Waldegrave to Newcastle, 5 June (ns) 1739, BL. Add. 32801.

110. DeVismes to Amelot, 25 June (ns) 1739, AE. CP. Ang. 404.

111. Bishop to his son Francis, 14 June 1739, HMC. *Hare*, p. 248.

112. Villettes to Horace Mann, Resident in Florence, 1 June (ns) 1740, PRO. 105/281.

113. Delafaye to Robinson, 27 July 1733, BL. Add. 23789.

114. Robethon to Stair, 19 Aug. (ns) 1715, SRO. GD. 135/141/4.

115. Waldegrave to Newcastle, 27 Dec. (ns) 1732, BL. Add. 32779; the Whigs saw Orléans' role in 1715 as crucial, Duke of Bolton to Townshend, 12 Oct. 1715, Bl. Add. 63093.

CHAPTER 8

The Press and Foreign Policy

'As times go now tis in vain for any public writer to pretend not to be on one side or another in their opinion of things.' *Whitehall Evening Post*, 29 November 1718

One of the most important social, cultural and political developments in early eighteenth-century Britain was the growth of a large, well-informed, influential and relatively free newspaper press. The fortunes and pre-occupations of the press were intimately involved with the political conflicts of the period, and the press played a major role in the education of the political nation. Particularly important was the role of the press in spreading information about Europe and European affairs.[1]

In the early eighteenth century the press expanded both in the number of titles and in circulation. This process commenced with the lapsing of the Licensing Act in 1695. Within ten years there was a large and active metropolitan press and the beginnings of a provincial press. By the end of George I's reign newspapers were being, or had been, produced in most of the major cities of Britain, including Edinburgh, Glasgow, Manchester, Leeds, Liverpool, Cirencester, York, St. Ives, Canterbury, Reading, Exeter, Bristol, Northampton, Newcastle, Worcester and Gloucester. Some towns, such as Norwich, boasted more than one newspaper. Further expansion took place in 1727-42, papers being founded in such towns as Hereford, Hull, Derby and Kendal.[2] The large number of London newspapers attracted comment.

It is difficult to gauge the circulation of the press, as there is an absence of printers' account books. However, the price was such that newspapers could be afforded by many skilled artisans. Most major London and provincial newspapers cost 1½d before and 2d after the second Stamp Act of 1725. Newspapers could be hired from hawkers for ½d, or read for free at coffee houses, barbers and taverns, whilst in London there was an important illicit press that avoided stamp duty and sold newspapers for ¼d or ½d. A sizeable readership is suggested by the large number of titles. If a 1718 claim that the *Weekly Medley's* circulation of 1,200 was too small to make it profitable was correct, the large number that lasted for some time would suggest a circulation of at least 1,200.[3] The sale of London newspapers was not restricted to London. 'King George's news-papers' were read in Moreton in Devon, and on the back of a London newspaper of March 1718 now in the Library of All Souls' College, Oxford is the endorse-ment 'For Coll: Howe at his house in Great Stoughton, Huntingdonshire by the Kimbolton Bag'.[4] In general, however, country readership of the London press owed less to direct subscription than to the mediating position of the provincial press. Provincial newspapers printed little local news. Instead they carried London and European news transcribed from London newspapers and newsletters. Thus the *Suffolk Mercury and Bury Post* of 5 December 1731 carried material from the *London Evening Post* and the *St. James' Evening Post*, and the *Leeds-Mercury* in June 1727 material from *Mist's Weekly Journal*, the *Evening Post* and *Wye's Letter*. This pattern was true of all provincial newspapers, and it helped to ensure a national readership for London news. It is very difficult, however, to ascertain the size of the provincial readership. The few indications there are suggest lower circulation figures for provincial than for London newspapers.

News concerning foreign affairs constituted a large portion of the news reports carried by British newspapers. This was the case for both manuscript newsletters and printed newspapers, whether the item in question was a daily, a tri-weekly, or a weekly. The major source of foreign news was plagiarism from other newspapers, either British or European. Particularly significant were Dutch newspapers, which could be obtained readily in London. The dominance of foreign news reflected the political sensitivity of British foreign policy, the influence of European events upon the British economy, particularly in the field of overseas trade, and public interest. Assessing the contents of the previous day's papers, the author of the *Grub Street Journal* of 12 December 1734 noted that, 'In the *Daily Advertiser* . . . there are but eleven lines of domestic news; in the *Courant* and *Daily Post Boy* not one'.

Three years earlier the ministerial *London Journal* referred to 'the close alliance with France, which the writers against the court own to be the chief cause of their papers, and that which gave rise to their numerous productions'.[5] Whether these papers had any direct influence upon the 'close alliance with France' or other elements of policy is impossible to establish. Horace Walpole, replying in December 1729 to ministerial fears about French works at Dunkirk that had been prompted by a piece in the most influential opposition paper, the *Craftsman*, complained that the ministry 'are transported and frightened with the least good or bad thing and without considering the real state of the matter we call for help from abroad upon trifles'.[6] However, in general it is difficult to point to newspapers directly prompting diplomatic moves. It is easier to suggest that the press helped to create a climate of opinion that was of importance in two respects, in influencing foreign views of British strength and in affecting the views held on foreign policy by the British political nation.

Newspapers were regularly forwarded, usually in translation, to their home governments by foreign diplomats in London. This was true of a large number of powers including the Dutch, Prussians and French. In the case of the last they were sent to the Secretaries of State for the Army, Foreign Affairs and the Marine. It is unclear to what extent they were read, though Keene reported that Philip V read the *Craftsman*.[7] What is clear is that the overwhelming majority of newspapers sent abroad, or mentioned in diplomatic reports, were those of opposition sympathies. It is difficult to assess the consequences of this, but it probably helped to fortify the widely held belief that the British ministry was weak and that Britain was a bitterly divided and unstable country. Such a belief had obvious implications for British foreign policy, for to a great extent international relations involved persuading other states of one's resolve and stability. British diplomats complained frequently of the impact of British domestic developments on the effectiveness of British foreign policy, and cited newspapers often. In November 1730 Robinson reported a recent conversation with the Austrian Chancellor, Sinzendorf, in which Sinzendorf had complained of 'the credit a Protest in time of Parliament, and a Craftsman, or any such impertinent libel has at Vienna all the year long, of which they are not sparing in their applications, when they are pleased to descant upon what they call the true interest and disposition of the people'.[8]

The British ministry were well aware, thanks to their excellent postal interception and decyphering system, of the importance attached to the press by foreign diplomats. The point was further enforced by a series of incidents, when newspaper reports led to official complaints. Some did not relate to foreign policy. The French complained about a report that Louis XV had shot dead a dog that he had been given as a present,[9] the Dutch about reports of Dutch government corruption[10] and their handling of the buggery showtrials in 1730.[11] None of these issues was as serious as the attack upon Charles III of Spain in 1770, but they reflect the concern of foreign diplomats to maintain the reputation of, and respect for, their sovereign and country.[12] There was also a determination to prevent the publication of items that cast an unfavourable light upon national policy. Prince Cantemir of Moldavia, the Russian envoy, was very concerned about a report in the *Evening Post* in 1732 concerning Russian diplomatic intentions, whilst the Swedes formally complained six years later about a report that they were supplying arms to the Turks.[13] That autumn a pamphlet that defamed the French Secretary of State for the Army, Dangervilliers, caused difficulties.[14]

The British ministry themselves complained about foreign press reports they regarded as anti-British. In 1717 concern about Dutch press reports was expressed at the highest ministerial levels.[15] In 1728 reports in the Hamburg press that George II did not oppose the Altena Company, the Danish East India Company, led to formal British complaints.[16] British envoys were sensitive about foreign press reports, particularly any that revealed sympathy for the Jacobites, or suggested that James III was the rightful monarch. Furthermore they were aware that foreign press material unfavourable to the ministerial interpretation of European affairs and British foreign policy could be reprinted by opposition British newspapers and could both vindicate the opposition stance and limit legal action against British newspapers. The summer of 1727 was marked by great uncertainty as to the Preliminary Articles that would lead to a Congress for the pacification of Europe. Several versions of such Articles were printed, and some claimed that the British ministry were willing to concede points on such sensitive subjects as the retention of Gibraltar, and the restitution of ships seized by Spanish privateers. *The Flying Post: or Post Master* reported, in an article under a Paris byline, 'We have had a very surprising copy of Preliminary Articles handed privately about here this week, they are said to be sent from London, by some persons disaffected to the administration there, who have paid for their being inserted by the writers of the *Paris a la main*, in order to come back to you; they are exploded here as fallacious . . . the author of the *Paris a la main* will be severely punished'.

The same newspaper, in its London section, reported, 'Several persons concern'd in publishing a translation of preliminary articles out of the *Paris gazette a la main* examin'd in order to find out who were the contrivers of them; they are in several particulars false and very scandalous; such as are highly injurious to the conduct of the Hanover allies and the British administration; and so disadvantageous for England, that had we been constantly beaten in a ten years war, we might have hoped for peace upon better terms. They sunk our stocks to the detriment of a multitude of families; and a general uneasiness and dissatisfaction began to appear . . .'

Foreign envoys in London reported that the publication of the Articles led to a terrible uproar in London.[17] The ministry took the matter sufficiently seriously to make diplomatic representations in Paris and to ensure that these were reported in the press: 'We hear that orders will be sent to His Excellency, Mr Walpole, at Paris, to complain of the author of the *Paris Gazette Alamaine,* for inserting certain scandalous propositions in his paper, and imposing them on the world for the Articles of Pacification lately signed'. Newcastle wrote to Horace, 'we have been forced to print in the *Daily Courant,* but in an article from The Hague, so that it can't be charged upon the government, a true translation of our Preliminarys in order to remove the impression the publication of the false ones may have made here; and indeed it appears from the intercepted correspondence of almost all the foreign ministers, that bringing of the affair of Gibraltar to the Congress was so far misunderstood, that it was necessary to set that matter right'.[18]

Four months later Gibraltar was raised again in the foreign press. The *Suite des Nouvelles d'Amsterdam du 24 Octobre 1727,* in a London letter, reported a project to settle Anglo-Spanish differences by razing the fortifications. Action was swift: William Finch, Envoy Extraordinary at The Hague, had the newspaper 'reprimanded for the article relating to Gibraltar'.[19] Townshend revealed ministerial fears over foreign press reporting during the Altena episode. Herman, envoy in Copenhagen, was instructed to wait 'on the Great Chancellor to let him know the evil tendency of printing such falsities, which, if spread here by ill-disposed persons, are enough to inflame the Parliament and the nation, as if the King were indifferent in a point which so nearly concerns the trade of his subjects, and you will leave it to his consideration whether such proceedings are not very unfriendly, when His Majesty's sense as to that company, must be very well understood at Copenhagen'.

Although British ministers and diplomats were disinclined to accept liability for the attacks of the British press, pleading the law as their excuse, they believed that all foreign newspapers could be readily controlled and therefore should be.[20]

Whether the press could 'inflame the Parliament and the nation' is a contentious issue. It is unclear how influential newspapers and other printed works, such as pamphlets, were. Establishing the wide range of the culture of print is different from establishing its impact, but the *Flying Post: or Post Master* could state in 1729, 'all the three kingdoms have reason to rejoice that the darkest corners are illuminated with the works of celebrated news writers, and that there is no part so obscure, but every week or oftener, it is illustrated with some rays of these shining lights'.

Thanks to the press the diaries of Derbyshire ministers and Somerset doctors could include references to European affairs, and people without much wealth could read about them.[21] The *English and French Journal* of 12 September 1723 referred to a tobacconist reading in a coffee house press reports about Rusco-Swedish relations. It is very difficult to comment on the extent to which the press influenced opinion. In 1726 one newspaper reported: 'on Monday night a Barber and a Porter being discoursing of the present posture of affairs in Europe, at an alehouse in Chancery Lane, they quarrelled . . . the Porter stabb'd his antagonist . . . so dangerously, that his life is despair'd of'.[22] Happily popular interest rarely took such violent forms, but it was generally believed that the press was of considerable importance. The tradesman, artisan or gentleman who neglected his affairs in order to follow the news was a standard object of satire, and it is interesting to note that usually the news in question was that of foreign affairs. In 1724 the *Universal Journal* printed what was ostensibly a letter from a country reader, Francis Careless, attacking a neighbouring landlord, the young Mr Novel. This 'errant coxcomb' ignored his steward's accounts in order to read newspapers and indulged in incessant political speculation, 'beginning with the Persian rebels, makes the tour of the whole world, settles treaties, unhinges governments, and reforms our state'. In August

1732 the London monthly, the *Comedian or Philosophical Enquirer,* attacked 'these mechanical Machiavilians, the inferior tradesmen' who assiduously read the press.[23]

The importance attached by politicians to the press is clear. The press was the chief means of political communication. Important books and pamphlets were summarised in the newspapers, which also printed petitions, corporate deliberations, such as those of the London Common Council or the Court of the South Sea Company, and, albeit intermittently and at times with much difficulty, parliamentary transactions. The opposition could attach considerable importance to the press. This was not true of all major opposition politicians – Carteret had little to do with newspapers – but it was certainly true of the opposition led by Cowper and Wharton in the early 1720s, and that associated with Bolingbroke and Pulteney in the latter 1720s and early 1730s and with Chesterfield in the later 1730s. The Jacobites sought to insert material in the press.[24] In turn the ministry invested money, effort and talent in founding and maintaining a series of papers, whilst leading ministerial figures, including Walpole, Horace Walpole, Hervey and Yonge, wrote pamphlets in defence of government policy.

To some extent press warfare was very artificial. The conventions of political behaviour in the first two decades of the century had allowed for well-developed press warfare on political lines. Possibly the political attention devoted to the press reflected a habit that had arisen from the fact that print was an area where political warfare was permitted, cheap, and stimulating: The law – and care had to be taken in criticising royal concerns – provided bounds within which an exciting but safe contest could take place. The artificiality and limited value of the struggle were discussed by very few, but some ministerial figures were very sceptical about the political impact of opposition propaganda. Tilson, a much underrated figure, was particularly so, observing in 1722, 'I can't reason . . . [that] because the mob is poisoned, women and parsons rail, and the grumblers put about libels and ballads, that therefore the whole nation will join and take up arms in favour of the Pretender . . . But such are the hopes hot and zealous people encourage one another to'. In 1730 he observed that 'the spawn of the authors of the *Craftsman* . . . will make little or no impression on people of sense', and commented, 'the Ministers as usual wade through a great deal of dirt and scandal'.[25]

Few within the ministry believed that the government should not launch a press offensive of its own. In many senses the opposition press was encouraged by the ministry's willingness to reply, and the press war had a self-sustaining life of its own. The government's efforts were extensive and expensive. Ministerial newspapers and pamphlets were distributed in large quantities, often without charge, and newspaper production was subsidised.[26]

M

The role of foreign news and of discussion of British foreign policy in the press is not surprising, given the importance of these issues in domestic political debate and their newsworthy character. It is perhaps significant that in general when the newspapers sought to advertise their value and to obtain more readers, they stressed the quality of their foreign news. The *Post Boy* in May 1728 drew attention to the quality of its printer's foreign news, and 'the extraordinary expense he is at in furnishing a Hague letter, which gives the best account we have of transactions in the different courts of Europe, the interests of Princes . . .' Announcing in August plans to become a daily, it stated that the new paper would include, 'as usual, the Original Hague letter, confessedly superior to anything extant of that kind: which has never fail'd to give general satisfaction, and which can be procured by none but the proprietors of this paper'. Three months later the new paper printed a letter supposedly sent in by an enthusiastic reader: 'Your Hague letter I always read with pleasure. The writer of it is an able, and, what is more, an uncommon and impartial man. His observations on the present state of affairs in Europe are curious, judicious and useful; and his intelligence is as remarkable for veracity, as for its superiority in every other respect to anything of that kind extant'.

The first number of the *British Observator,* a London paper founded in 1733, proclaimed, 'Our constant care shall be to procure the best foreign advices, to digest them into a proper method, and to cloath them with a convenient stile'.[27]

The quality of this press coverage has recently been questioned. J. R. Jones portrayed a press that was guilty of 'wilful misrepresentation of facts, sensationalism and pandering to popular prejudices, partisanship and appeals to xenophobia', and continued: 'Newspapers published a good deal of information about events in Europe, much of it biased or inaccurate'.[28] I would adopt a different position, based on eight years of reading both metropolitan and provincial newspapers and comparing them with the diplomatic reports available to the government. A certain amount of inaccurate information was printed, reflecting the difficulty of obtaining, and still more important, checking, information, in an age when policy was often a 'mystery of state' and poor communications were a serious hindrance. Similar problems were encountered by the governments of early modern Europe. The British ministry found it very difficult in early September 1733 to discover whether the Russians had invaded Poland, a difficulty both shared and admitted by the press. Newspapers often indicated the contradictory and unreliable nature of the information they were receiving.[29]

Press treatment was often xenophobic, and it was rare for the Catholic church to receive favourable coverage, but the predominant impression is one of a measured treatment of European affairs that was on the whole reasonably accurate and attempted to discern the 'true springs of policy'. A contributory reason for this was that reporting of European affairs took place within a context of partisan rivalry between newspapers. Reports were frequently challenged by rival papers, and it was important to maintain a reputation for accuracy and for reliable news, partly in order to lend credence to the paper's interpretation of the news. News and comment were usually, though not always clearly, distinct, though few papers went as far as the *London Observator or, Collin's Weekly Journal,* a paper of 1723, that distinguished clearly between a news section and a 'remarks' section. Newspapers also sought to provide background information in order to aid readers to understand the news, and possibly also to fill space. The educational value of this information may well have been significant. The *Weekly Journal or British Gazetteer* printed an account of Sweden in March 1717, as Swedish events had become a major topic of interest. In the same month the *St. James' Post* printed an account of the Electorate of Hanover. The Spanish invasions of Sardinia (1717) and Sicily (1718) led the press to print many accounts of the islands, whilst Peter the Great's Persian campaigns led to descriptions of the contested area. In 1723 the *Northampton Mercury* produced a description of contested St. Lucia. The following year the *Flying Post: or Post Master* supported its news of Turko-Persian relations with a description of Erivan. In 1735 accounts of Mantua and Syracuse were printed to provide background to Italian war news.[30] If the comment was often partisan, that is no different from the position in any other period, and it is important not to adopt unrealistic standards when judging the eighteenth-century press.

The care taken by foreign envoys to insert material in the press reflected their view of its importance, and possibly also a habit of emulation.[31] Given the belief in the importance of public opinion in Britain, it was clearly necessary to influence this opinion. However, some foreign envoys were aware that the opposition press was of limited effect. Transmitting a French translation of the *Craftsman* of 2 February 1734, de Löss wrote that it was worthy of attention, as it revealed opposition thinking, but that the ministry were not disturbed by such criticism as they were used to it and as they enjoyed a secure parliamentary majority.[32] Nevertheless the opposition press was still widely read in Europe. Sinzendorf was not the only major figure who read British pamphlets in translation,[33] whilst British envoys noted the attention paid to the press.[34]

Although the extent to which the press affected the views of the political nation on foreign policy is difficult to evaluate, it may well be that reiterated opposition attacks on ministerial foreign policy played a role in turning opinion against the Walpole ministry. The interminable negotiations of the

1720s and the unsuccessful Congresses at Cambrai and Soissons permitted attacks on the conduct of British foreign policy, and indeed its very substance. The indecisive and expensive armaments of the late 1720s, the confrontation with Britain's old ally, Austria, the alliance with the former enemy, France, and the alleged threat to national interests resulting from the government's supposed failure to stand firm over Spanish depredations, Gibraltar and French works at Dunkirk, all provided issues upon which the ministry could be challenged. It was not necessary to present the issues as complex diplomatic problems; they could be represented more vividly as challenges to national honour and national interests. The ambivalence present in any alliance, the subtle and, necessarily, far from public contest for predominance could be readily exploited. Opposition publicists displayed great skill in selecting those foreign policy issues in which the government could be made to appear weak, unsuccessful, foolish and dishonest. Bolingbroke's knowledge of foreign affairs might be held to account for the particularly sophisticated handling of foreign policy in the *Craftsman*, but in fact it was not necessary to have any profound knowledge of foreign affairs in order to attack the obviously vulnerable foreign policy of the ministry.

The attempts to use issues of foreign policy to precipitate the fall of Walpole failed. The major public attacks mounted upon the French alliance in 1728-31, and upon Britain's Spanish policy in 1738-9, probably played a certain role in the decisions to alter policy, but neither provoked the fall of the first minister. The *London Journal* referred in 1731 to 'the close alliance with France, which the writers against the court own to be the chief cause of their papers, and that which gave rise to their numerous productions'.[35] The *Craftsman* claimed that the Second Treaty of Vienna had been negotiated as a result of the newspaper's call for an Austrian alliance; though it also managed to condemn the new alliance for sacrificing British interests to those of Hanover.[36] However, it is necessary to draw attention to longstanding royal and ministerial dissatisfaction with the French alliance, and to suggest that these were the key elements, although doubtless public opinion affected the ministry. It is impossible to segregate 'high' from 'low' politics and to suggest that the former operated in a vacuum. In the summer of 1730, when the decision to break with France was taken, Walpole was greatly concerned about the French failure to fulfil recent promises over Dunkirk, and opposition press attention to this issue probably exacerbated his concern about the forthcoming session. However, bitter public criticism of the French alliance was hardly novel, and it is mentioned comparatively infrequently in ministerial correspondence. The Anglo-French alliance collapsed when bankrupt diplomatically. It had been attacked in Parliament and the press for several years, and this influenced ministerial conduct of foreign policy, but it did not determine it.

In the late 1720s the opposition attempt to exploit Spanish treatment of British commerce seriously embarrassed the ministry, particularly in 1729, but it never succeeded in making it the prime topic of political debate. However, in 1738-9 the opposition achieved this, and precipitated a serious crisis both within the ministry and in Parliament. There are many diplomatic and political reasons which help to account for this, but it could be suggested that developments in public opinion were of some significance. There is no doubt that the opposition campaign of 1738-9 was more sustained, popular and effective than the attack on foreign policy in the late 1720s. The increased sophistication of opposition politicians in mobilising public pressure is apparent,[37] and over this issue the opposition succeeded in tapping popular urban radicalism as they had not done in the late 1720s. The extent of the popularity of the opposition case may be questioned: public support was largely, though not exclusively, confined to the major trading towns. However, what is clear is that there was no countervailing popular support for the ministerial policy, a feature reflected in the manner in which government papers, such as the *Daily Gazetteer*, and ministerial politicians attacked the role being claimed for public opinion. Speaking in the Lords, Lord Hervey said: 'in this debate, as well as a great many others of the same nature, I find the opinion of the populace without doors is very much insisted on, as if this House were obliged to enquire, and to censure, as often as the giddy multitude takes it into their heads, that the administration have been deficient in their duty, or mistaken in their politics. If this were the case, no minister could ever be easy, nor could any one session pass over without an enquiry and censure: every session would give the populace the diversion of seeing a sacrifice made of some of the ministers or magistrates of the preceding, till at last, we should have neither minister nor magistrate in the kingdom; for what man of common sense would accept a post in our government, if he were certain, that, before the end of year he would be sacrificed to the resentment of those, whom by the duty of his office he must disoblige? We should at this rate have nothing but anarchy and confusion amongst us; and therefore your lordships must see, that the opinions, the suspicions, or the clamours of the people without doors, can be no rule for your conduct in this House'.[38]

Lord Hervey's stance – and it is noteworthy that the speech was made in a debate that related to the war with Spain – reflected the position that the ministry increasingly adopted in the last years of Walpole's ministry. In the 1720s and early 1730s ministerial speakers and newspapers had condemned the ease with which the opposition could manipulate opinion, but they had been, on the whole, cautious about attacking the role of public opinion. In the late 1730s there was a discernible shift. In particular the *Daily Gazetteer*, the ministerial paper founded in the summer of 1735, and the leading pro-government publicity organ in the latter years of the Walpole ministry, betrayed a deep suspicion of the public's interest in politics, arguing at one point that press discussion was equivalent to 'the mob ready to sit in judgement on the legislature'.[39]

The shift in the ministerial position may partly have reflected a change in the ministerial spokesmen, from men who had had experience of being in opposition, to others, such as Hervey, whose political experience was that of Walpolean ascendancy. Power produced a different political ideology. The extent to which the ministerial position was under challenge was also probably of great significance, and the role of the press in sustaining and publicising this challenge cannot be underestimated. The press, through its interest in the coverage of foreign events and in diplomatic activity, had helped to develop among the political nation a strong interest in and knowledge of the outside world. Such a development was not solely due to the press, nor did it begin in the Walpolean period. The experience of two major European wars in which Britain had been directly involved, and the connection between these wars and the strife of British political groups, had done much to develop an interest both in foreign affairs and in foreign policy, an interest that was encouraged by the accession of a foreign dynasty. The incessant criticism in the opposition press had little direct effect upon foreign policy, but it helped shape public understanding of that policy. In the 1720s the ministry replied to opposition criticisms with energy and skill, but by the late 1730s the position had changed. The ministry found it harder to persuade people that they were defending national honour and national interests. It is difficult to say whether this was cause or effect (or both) of their increasing reliance on their parliamentary majority and their willingness to ignore the debate outside Parliament. To a certain extent ministerial apologists were correct in arguing that the opposition did not enjoy the support of the bulk of the population, but the ministerial failure to sway in particular metropolitan opinion was of great importance in enabling the opposition to represent themselves as the voice of the political nation. The ministerial failure reflected their loss of the propaganda battle in the 1730s, and the opposition affiliations of urban radical elements. Valuable work on the latter has been produced in recent years,[40] and there is no doubt of their importance, particularly in the Spanish depredations agitation. However, the events of 1742, the Whig reshuffle that marked the end of the Walpole ministry, suggest that it is necessary, as with the press, not to over-state the direct political importance of these elements. The hostile climate of opinion that faced the Walpole ministry in the late 1730s was less powerful, and possibly less significant, than has been supposed, though one may agree with a newspaper comment of 1727: 'such is the depravity of the age we live in, that tho' manifest falshood be both in the facts and arguments insinuated, yet a libel seldom falls absolutely short of its aim, and generally works some degree of mischief'.[41]

NOTES

1. G. C. Gibbs, 'Newspapers, Parliament and Foreign Policy in the Age of Stanhope and Walpole', *Mélanges offerts à G. Jacquemyns* (Brussels, 1968), pp. 293-315; Black, 'The British Press and European news in the 1730s: the case of the *Newcastle Courant', Durham County Local History Society Bulletin* 26 (1981); Black, 'The Press, Party and Foreign Policy in the reign of George I', *Publishing History* XIII (1983); M. R. Harris, The London Newspaper Press, 1725-46 (London, Ph.D., 1974).

2. G. A. Cranfield, *The Development of the Provincial Newspaper, 1700-1760* (Oxford, 1962); R. M. Wiles, *Freshest Advices. Early Provincial Newspapers in England* (Columbus, Ohio, 1965); Black, 'Manchester's First Newspaper: The Manchester Weekly Journal', *Transactions of the Historical Society of Lancashire and Cheshire* 130 (1981); Black, 'The Cirencester Flying-Post, and Weekly Miscellany; Reflections on the English Press in the first half of the eighteenth century', *Cirencester Archaeological and Historical Society. Annual Report and Newsletter* 25 (1982-3); *Oedipus: or the Postman Remounted,* 5 Mar. 1730.

3. *Weekly Journal or British Gazetteer,* 29 Nov. 1718.

4. *St. James' Weekly Journal; or Hanover Post Man,* 19 Jan. 1720; *St. James' Evening Post,* 1 Mar. 1718; *Flying Post or the Postmaster,* 4 Ap. 1717; *Weekly Journal or Saturday's Post,* 30 Jan. 1720; *Leeds Mercury,* 20 Jan. 1730; *Mist's Weekly Journal,* 23 Ap. 1726; Accounts of Sir John Swinburne of Capheaton, 3rd Bt., Newcastle, Northumberland County Record Office, ZSW 455; Grey Longueville to Thomas Pelham of Stanmer, 28 June 1726, BL. Add. 33085.

5. *London Journal,* 6 Nov. 1731.

6. Horace Walpole to Delafaye, 14 Dec. (ns) 1729, PRO. 78/192.

7. Keene to Delafaye, 20 May (ns) 1731, PRO. 94/107; Edward Finch to Newcastle, 24 June (ns) 1730, PRO. 95/55.

8. Robinson to Harrington, 18 Nov. (ns) 1730, PRO. 80/69.

9. Destouches to Dubois, 9, 19 Nov. (ns) 1722, AE. CP. Ang. 343.

10. William Finch to Newcastle, 31 Aug. (ns) 1725, PRO. 84/579; Finch to Tilson, 24 Oct. (ns), Tilson to Finch, 20 Oct. 1727, PRO. 84/294; *Daily Post Boy,* 30 May 1735, Horace Walpole to Newcastle, 8 July (ns), Horace to Harrington, 12 Aug. (ns) 1735, PRO. 84/344, 346.

11. *Daily Journal* 17 June, *St. James' Evening Post* 18 June, *Daily Post* 4 July, *Whitehall Evening Post* 4 July 1730.

12. Black, '"A Contemptible Piece of Ribaldry": *The Gazetteer and New Daily Advertiser* Offends the Bourbons', *Publishing History* XII (1982).

13. R. J. Morda Evans, Antiokh Kantemir: A study of his Literary, Political and Social life in England, 1732-8 (Ph.D., London, 1959), pp. 75-6; *Daily Post,* 3 July 1738; Wasenberg, Swedish Secretary, to Harrington, 6 July 1738, PRO. 100/64; Alt to William VIII of Hesse Cassel, 7 July 1738, Marburg 221; legal reports and documents, PRO. 36/46 f. 11-95.

14. Couraud to Waldegrave, 4 Sept. 1738, Chewton; Paxton, Solicitor of the Treasury, to Harrington, 6 Sept. 1738, PRO. 36/46.

15. Whitworth, envoy at The Hague, to Wolters, agent in Rotterdam, 15 Dec. (ns) 1717, Sunderland to Whitworth, 17 Dec., Whitworth to Sunderland, 21 Dec. (ns) 1717, BL. Add. 37366.

16. Wych to Townshend, 4 June (ns) 1728, Glenorchy, envoy in Copenhagen, to Townshend 7, 24 Aug. (ns), 5 Oct. (ns) 1728, PRO. 82/45, 75/51.

17. *Flying Post; or Post Master,* 10 June 1727; Zamboni to le Coq, 17 June (ns) 1727, Bodl. Rawl. 120; l'Hermitage, Dutch agent in London, to the States General, 20 June (ns) 1727, BL. Add. 17677; *Daily Post* 5 June, *Post Boy* 6 June, *Wye's Letter* 10 June 1727; Newcastle to Horace Walpole, 12 June 1727, BL. Add. 32750.

18. *Whitehall Evening Post* 10 June, *Wye's Letter* 10 June 1727; Newcastle to Horace Walpole, 12 June 1727, BL. Add. 32750.

19. Finch to Tilson, 18 Nov. (ns) 1727, PRO. 84/294.

20. Townshend to Herman, 7 May 1728, PRO. 75/51; Cope, envoy in Hamburg, to Harrington, 20 Oct. (ns) 1741, PRO. 82/63.

21. *Flying Post; or Post Master,* 29 July 1729; V. S. Doe (ed.), *The Diary of James Clegg of Chapel en le Frith, 1708-55* I (Derbyshire Record Society, 1978); E. Hobhouse (ed.), *The Diary of a West Country Physician* (1934); Anon., *Sir Robert Brass* (1731), p. 14.

22. *St. James' Evening Post,* 1 Sept. 1726.

23. Black, 'Political allusions in Fielding's "Coffee-House Politician"', *Theoria* 62 (1984); *Universal Journal* 13, 20 June, *Whitehall Journal* 2 Ap. 1723.

24. James III to Daniel O'Brien, 31 Mar. (ns) 1733, RA. 160/85.

25. Tilson to Whitworth, 8 May 1722, BL. Add. 37389; Tilson to Waldegrave, 6, 27 Jan. 1730, Chewton.

26. *Craftsman,* 31 July 1731, 20 Oct. 1733; *London Evening Post,* 3 Nov. 1733, 3 June 1736; Accounts for ministerial pamphlets CUL. CH. papers 75/10-13; *A Report from the Committee of Secrecy appointed to enquire into the conduct of Robert Earl of Orford* (1742).

27. *Post Boy,* 7 May, 29 Aug. 1728; *British Observator,* 10 Mar. 1733; *General Evening Post,* 17 Nov. 1733.

28. J. R. Jones, *Britain and the World, 1649-1815* (1980), pp. 13, 184. For 'the confused medley of false sentiments and reflections' in the press, *London Journal,* 24 Nov. 1722; du Bourgay to Tilson, 9 Dec. (ns) 1724, PRO. 90/18.

29. *Daily Post Boy,* 11, 13 Oct. 1733; *Wye's Letter,* 16 July 1734.

30. *St. James' Post* 15 Mar., 11 Sept., *Weekly Journal or British Gazetteer* 16 Mar., 14 Sept., *Flying Post; or Post Master* 12 Sept., *St. James' Weekly Journal* 14 Sept. 1717; *Northampton Mercury,* 18 Mar. 1723; *Flying Post; or Post Master,* 10 Dec. 1724; *London Evening Post* 17 June, *General Evening Post* 19 June 1735; Black, 'An early account of Louisiana', *Louisiana History* 24 (1983). Plan of Cartagena in *Northampton Mercury,* 19 May 1740. Description of Jülich in *Dublin Newsletter,* 22 Jan. 1737.

31. Petkum, Holstein envoy, to Görtz, Swedish minister, 25 Sept. (ns) 1716, PRO. 107/1B; Chavigny to Chauvelin, 17 July (ns), 28 Aug. (ns) 1733, AE. CP. Ang. 381; Bunau to Count Wackerbarth, Saxon minister, 24 July (ns) 1733, PRO. 107/14; de Löss to Augustus III, 15 Jan. (ns) 1734, Dresden, 638 IIa; Bothmer to Cadogan and Whitworth, 9 Sept. (ns) 1718, BL. Add. 37369.

32. De Löss to Count Brühl, Saxon minister, 26 Feb. (ns) 1734, Dresden, 638 IIa; de Löss to Augustus III, 21 Jan. (ns) 1738, Dresden, 639 VIa.

33. Graham to Hay, 8 Feb. (ns) 1727, RA. 103/42.

34. Horace Walpole and Stanhope to Newcastle, 17 Nov. (ns) 1728, BL. Add. 32759; Keene to Newcastle, 17 Mar. (ns) 1734, PRO. 94/119; Kinsky to Eugene, 23 June (ns) 1733, HHSt.A. GK. 94(b).

35. *London Journal,* 6 Nov. 1731.

36. *Craftsman,* 24 Ap. 1731.

37. N. Rogers, 'Resistance to oligarchy: the city opposition to Walpole and his successors, 1725-47', in J. Stevenson (ed.), *London in the Age of Reform* (Oxford, 1977).

38. Cobbett XI, 739, 1 Dec. 1740. Lords' debate on motion for Admiral Vernon's instructions; R. Browning, *Political and Constitutional Ideas of the Court Whigs* (Baton Rouge, 1982); Carteret, Cobbett, XIII, 326, 9 Dec. 1743.

39. *Daily Gazetteer,* 2 July 1735, 18 Oct., 8 Dec. 1740.

40. L. Colley, 'Eighteenth-Century English Radicalism before Wilkes', *TRHS* 5th Sept., 31 (1981); G. S. de Krey, 'Political Radicalism in London after the Glorious Revolution', *Journal of Modern History* 55 (1983); N. Rogers, 'The Urban Opposition to Whig Oligarchy, 1720-60', in M. and J. Jacob (eds.), *The Origins of Anglo-American Radicalism* (1984).

41. *British Journal,* 23 Dec. 1727.

The Debate over Policy; Conclusions

'I had an opportunity of touching upon the principles of the Whigs and Torys, that indeed the first had been during the last war against France as absolutely necessary for preserving the present establishment of their government, but that the Peace at Utrecht and the treaties since made in consequence of it had made and must make upon that foot the Whigs for keeping well with France, and particularly friends to His Royal Highness and the Torys must of consequence as far as they were Jacobites be against his interest . . .'

Horace Walpole reporting on audience with Duke of Orléans, 1723

'For though the Parliament has approved the measures and engagements taken with foreign powers, and particularly with France, yet the nation in general, high and low, are of a contrary opinion, the close understanding with France, and the hostile proceedings towards Your Imperial Majesty being disapproved by them.'   Palm, 1726[1]

'The universal Monarchy we have so long dreaded, thanks to our own supineness, is nearer being accomplished than ever.'   *Champion,* 27 Oct. 1741

Eighteenth-century British discussion of foreign policy has not enjoyed a good press. Professor Baxter, in his powerful essay, 'The Myth of the Grand Alliance in the Eighteenth Century', presented a generation of policy-makers obsessed by the legacy of the wars against Louis XIV and unable to appreciate changes in the European system. Dealing with a later period, Professor Roberts condemned the discussion of foreign policy in Parliament and the press, and the absence of informed opinion among the politicians: '. . . no sign that anyone contemplated the possibility that the norms of policy might not be immutable . . . Outside Parliament, if one may judge by their private correspondence, leading statesmen brought their minds to bear upon foreign affairs only at long intervals . . .' Dr. Scott has recently restated Roberts' views in a significant unpublished paper.[2]

Clearly there is something to be said for this interpretation. Discussion of foreign affairs could be foolish and based on inadequate or inaccurate information. Contemporaries drew attention to such failings with some frequency, usually when they were displayed by those of differing political views. However, it will be the contention of this chapter that the discussion of foreign policy in the Walpole period was of a higher standard than might be expected from reading the secondary literature. There is a major historical problem in assessing the sophistication of such discussion: what standard is it reasonable to expect? This problem is linked to the difficulty of evaluating speeches, pamphlets, newspaper articles or letters of a period where conventions of argument and expression were different to those of today, but where the difference is obscured by the use of the same language and similar means of expression. In assessing the correspondence of politicians it is essential to remember the circumlocutions often produced by the role of the Crown. A similar effect can be discerned in Parliament, where, furthermore, foreign policy matters often arose in debates on other issues, such as the army and navy estimates, which affected the nature of the discussion. In assessing the press and pamphlet literature it is necessary to consider the nature of their readership. The discussion of foreign policy issues in the successive newspapers produced by the Jacobite Nathaniel Mist, *The Weekly Journal or Saturday's Post, Mist's Weekly Journal* and *Fog's Weekly Journal,* was more clear-cut and pithy and less cerebral than that in the *Craftsman.* This probably reflected differences in their readership, on which there is unfortunately no information. The existence of sustained public debate over British foreign policy – of debate in Parliament and print – reflected both a rapidly changing international system and the fact that changes in British foreign policy were both obvious and controversial. The obvious nature of the changes was of particular importance: however much the details of negotiations were kept secret, there was no attempt by the ministry to conceal the basic thrust of foreign policy. The ministry defended the French alliance, the confrontation with Austria and Spain in 1725-9, the Austrian alliance of 1731, and, with less clarity and enthusiasm, neutrality in the War of the Polish succession and the handling of the Spanish negotiations in 1738-9. The debate over policy was well-informed, perceptive and vigorous, and a comparison between the public debate and the actual course of foreign policy reveals that the former was in no way remote from the preoccupations of the policy-makers. Furthermore, the public debate itself can be shown to have developed in response to international events and changes in British foreign policy, and to have been far from arid in terms of the issues raised and the progress of the debate. To a certain extent the debate was restricted by party attitudes. The Tories were forced to defend the Utrecht settlement against ministerial attack. This was also an instance of the continued potency in the debate of past events. The treaty was defended by Tories, such as Stratford and Trevor in 1718 and Wyndham in 1739, and by opposition Whigs wooing Tory support, such as Pulteney in 1739 and Argyle in 1740, and vilified by Whigs such as Peterborough in 1730 and Walpole in 1739, who declared that it was 'a treaty that has been the source of all the divisions and distractions in Europe ever since'.[3] In 1741 the *Champion* asked, 'shall the treaty of Utrecht be eternally railed at by those very persons, who have been so long negociating away every one of the advantages left in our possession by that very treaty?'[4]

Another good example of the continued prominence in political debate of the past actions of British governments was the Quadruple Alliance. The decision to permit the reintroduction of Spanish influence in Italy was condemned during the 1720s. The Tory Lord Bathurst claimed in the 1730

Lords debate on the Treaty of Seville that the change might cause 'a dangerous and expensive war' and 'destroy the balance of power in Europe'. In 1731 the British navy convoyed Spanish troops to Leghorn. The opposition claimed that this threatened the balance of power and blamed Austria's Italian defeats of 1733-5 on this step.[5]

The international situation was too complex to permit an unchanging analysis of foreign policy on simply defined party lines. The need for the Whig ministry to explain the French alliance posed particular difficulties. As the *British Journal* pointed out in 1722, 'The very name of France us'd to be an abomination to the Whigs: They hated the country, for the sake of its government; and were eternally upbraiding the Tories with a fondness for that government'.[6] Discussion of British foreign policy in the period 1716-31 was dominated by the French alliance and its supposed consequences. This alliance represented an obvious reversal of the Anglo-French hostility that had dominated foreign policy from 1688 and heavily influenced discussion of foreign policy since the early 1670s. That hostility had been closely associated with the Whigs. Duke-Evans has suggested that 'the Whigs, who during the Exclusion crisis had accepted money from Louis XIV and were to re-establish an Entente Cordiale under Stanhope, only fortuitously became identified with Francophobia in the years preceding the War of the Spanish Succession'.[7] However fortuitous this identification was – and it was probably necessary if only because of Whig determination to cast themselves as the party opposed to Jacobitism, then supported by France – it became a major plank in the Whig programme. The Anglo-French alliance therefore posed major difficulties for the Whigs. It was necessary for the Whig leadership to attempt an education of the political nation that would explain the new policy of alliance with France. This was particularly important as the Tories selected the alliance as a major topic for attack. The Anglo-French alliance could be held to indicate the manner in which the Whig ministry and the Hanoverian dynasty were supposedly abandoning national interests and traditions. It could also serve as a defence against Whig attacks on the Tory ministry of 1710-14 for supposedly abandoning national interests by their unilateral peace with France in 1713. The debate over the Peace of Utrecht had been of great significance before the accession of George I, and played a major role in the Whig propaganda onslaught in George's early years. Indeed the early period of George's reign, before the negotiation of the Anglo-French alliance, represented a continuation in propaganda terms, of the conflict of Anne's last years. Louix XIV (who did not die until 1 September (ns) 1715), was distrusted by the new Whig ministry, who suspected French support for the Jacobites. The Whig propaganda of the period before and after George's accession was strongly anti-French, particularly so as, for electoral reasons, the Whigs sought to discredit the achievements of the Tory ministry. Richard Steele's

1714 pamphlet, *The French Faith represented in the present state of Dunkirk*, is a good example of the sort of literature the Whigs were soon to reject.

Contemporary discussion of the Anglo-French alliance of 1716-31 was of a reasonably high standard. The closeness of the alliance varied, as did its importance in political debate. It was most significant as a matter of discussion in the period 1725-31; in 1716-21 the impact of Hanoverian interests and Baltic questions played a role they were not to repeat a debate later, and in 1722-4 a generally peaceful European situation led to less interest in foreign policy. The ministry stressed the difference between French policy in the reign of Louis XIV and subsequently, alterations in the European system that made Austria and/or Spain more threatening than in the past, and their care in ensuring that the alliance served British interests. It was necessary for the ministry to defend foreign policy against two related, though differing, opposition charges: that Britain should be wary of continental commitments, a wariness associated with the Tories and expressed in Mist's papers, and that the ministry should not ally with France, a criticism associated with the opposition Whigs. A ministerial paper summarised the views of William Pulteney, the leading opposition Whig, in a poem 'The Yorkshire Patriot',

> 'That France was formerly our Foe,
> and must eternally be so.'

The same newspaper, *The British Journal: or, The Censor,* claimed in December 1728, 'France was never our enemy but under Lewis the Fourteenth; at which time she was a foe to the whole world. She seeks not universal Empire now, she does not invade the rights of her neighbours, she has done signal benefits to us since the regency of the late Duke of Orleans . . . Must we hate a powerful neighbour when he may be useful, because we feared him when he was dangerous? Why should we not accept his friendship when it may be of service . . . We never made them arbiters of our Differences . . .'[8] The ministerial stance was a reasonable one, given the willingness of successive French governments to consider British wishes. Several aspects of the French alliance, most significantly its role in the defence of Hanover, could not be publicly discussed, and care had to be taken in mentioning French assistance in countering Jacobite schemes. This led to a less than full ministerial defence of the Anglo-French alliance, but that situation would be true for all periods of the alliance. With these important exceptions, ministerial defence of the French alliance reproduced views expressed in diplomatic or private correspondence. France was not seen as a present threat, though uncertainty was expressed about her future conduct. Newcastle, a minister not later noted for his French sympathies in matters other than food, referred in 1727 to France, 'where the present administration appears to act upon different maxims from those which may have been produced in a former reign'.[9]

There was, however, an awareness of transience in the ministerial defence of the alliance. The rapid changes in the international situation lent weight to a strong sense of the lack of permanence of diplomatic arrangements. A ministerial pamphlet of 1727 noted, 'Nothing is more usual than this changing of sides, with the change of times and the situation of things; nothing is more politick . . . France . . . has since been reduced; and Spain has revived: yet people are still alarmed with the sound of France, which for a great while was wont to terrify them; and they think Spain and the Emperor still very weak and contemptible, because some years ago, they were really so . . . We [must] accept such Alliance as we can find, tho it were not what we could wish'.[10] Forced to defend the French alliance in the face of opposition stress on the 'natural' character of Anglo-French enmity,[11] the ministry resorted to the concept of expedience. France under its present ministry could be allied with. There was no attempt to argue that an Anglo-French alliance was 'natural'.[12] This ministerial approach did not differ essentially from that of the opposition: 'we are not to depend upon being always in friendship with any Prince, those people who well and truly consider the interests of two nations, will be of opinion, that a true and lasting amity is not to be expected,' argued *Mist's Weekly Journal* in 1726. In the following year this, the leading Tory newspaper, returned to the theme. Citing Heraclitus, it argued that mutability, discord and changing alliances were natural to the international system. In May 1727 it produced one of the best expositions of this theme: 'We have said in this paper before, that there can be no such thing as national friendship, for it is not only contrary to the maxims of government, but against the duty and trust of ministers to employ the blood and treasure of the people to any purpose, but for their peculiar interest and preservation; and therefore when men exclaim against this republick, or that prince, for their ingratitude, it is only the mark of an ignorant and weak judgement . . . Interest then being the great machine which puts all in motion, we are not to wonder if we see republicks and states often change their measures, and embrace interests quite contrary to what they had espoused before . . . Every treaty therefore is to be religiously observed till the purposes proposed by it shall take effect; but when those points are obtained it is no wonder to see the parties united before, begin to be jealous of each other . . .'[13]

This Tory stance was shared by Walpole himself, and it characterised the policies of his ministry: the decision not to commit Britain in 1729 to the Franco-Wittelsbach schemes in the Empire, the decision in 1730 to approach Austria, and three years later not to observe Britain's commitments to her. The British ministry did not regard any power as a 'natural' ally, bar the Dutch who were treated as a subordinate power that should follow the British lead and whose failure to do so was due to stupidity, obduracy or weakness. Thus the argument that eighteenth-century British foreign policy was obsessed by the French threat and treated an anti-French alliance as natural is inaccurate for this period. In addition, the claim that eighteenth-century British ministries regarded Austria as a natural ally is unfounded. Newcastle was keen to present such a view in the 1730s,[14] but this had not prevented him from serving as the Secretary of State responsible for instructing the British envoys who participated in the conferences held in France in 1727 and 1730 to plan military operations against Austria.

Ministerial attitudes were not uniform. Alongside the isolationist stance, represented most clearly by Sir Robert Walpole, who favoured only minimal commitment to European diplomacy, there was a marked interventionist standpoint. Several overlapping groups and attitudes constituted this standpoint. It tended to be held strongly by those, such as Carteret, Chesterfield and Horace Walpole, who possessed diplomatic experience. It also represented the Stanhopian legacy, that of Britain as the policeman-arbiter of Europe. As such it reflected the traditional Whig commitment to European issues, a commitment well reflected in a ministerial pamphlet of 1727: 'Even in the movements of Europe, which are farthest from us, it becomes us not to be idle spectators: we know not how far the issue and progress of them may affect us. The interests of Christian princes are strangely blended and intermixed; and either through mutual fear, or trade, or the necessity of a balance, it so happens, that the concerns of no considerable state can be indifferent to another'.[15]

In the 1720s interventionist sentiments were expressed freely by the ministry, though not to the extent that had characterised the Stanhope years. This persisted in 1730-2; Britain continued to attempt to settle European disputes, devoting much energy in 1732-3 to Austria's disputes with Sardinia and Spain, and the ministry proudly proclaimed the success of their diplomacy, and in public took the credit for European peace.[16] The royal speech at the beginning of the 1732 session drew attention to 'the general Tranquillity of Europe' and declared that Britain 'could never stand by, and be an idle spectator' of changes in the European system. *An ode to his Grace the Duke of Newcastle written on the present tranquility of Europe, established by the Influence of British Power* was published in June 1732, and one of the most fatuous pamphlets of the period, *The Natural Probability of a Lasting Peace in Europe,* was distributed through the Post Office and excerpted in the ministerial press that summer.

However, a shift in attitude was revealed by the War of the Polish Succession. Partly this was probably due to the fact that 1733 saw the first war in western Europe since 1720 and the first serious conflict since 1714. The interventionist stance of the 1720s had been made relatively easy by the care shown by the powers to avoid war. The period was one of intimidation, not conflict, and this encouraged a display of willingness to intervene whilst avoiding the actual costs of war. Subsidy treaties and naval armaments were not cheap, but their expense was far lower and more predictable than that of war. The outbreak of a major European war in 1733 posed major problems for the British ministry. As we have seen, British neutrality can be traced to a number of factors. The public defence of this neutrality drew heavily on many of the themes associated with the traditional Tory stance. The ministerial *Daily Courant* wrote, 'while the posture of affairs in Europe renders her dreaded and respected; and while the situation of things at home afford no room for reasonable men to complain: what hinders us from enjoying that tranquility we possess; or why must we like splenetic persons, because we are undistress'd by real evils, frame imaginary grievances to ourselves . . .' The ministrial *London Journal* wrote, 'England can never be under an obligation to go to war but for one of these two reasons, either to protect our trade, or preserve the balance of power in Europe . . . We ought not to strike till we have good reason to apprehend that we shall suffer by not striking . . .'[17]

Contrasting diplomatic strategies were advocated within the ministry. The Stanhopian legacy was represented by Horace Walpole and his attempts to end the conflict by British good offices, and by those who sought to commit Britain to support her treaty commitments to Austria. The Tory stance was best exemplified by Sir Robert Walpole, though he was not alone in his views. Hervey supported his case at court, whilst various diplomats, some exasperated by Austrian policy in 1732-3, were opposed to intervention. Tyrawly wrote in January 1734, 'I think we act very wisely in keeping ourselves out of the present war, and if we would concern ourselves with no business but our own, we should of consequence have fewer difficulties to work through. I am not even clear, that even that old beaten topic of the Balance of Europe, ought at this time, to make us engage in foreign broils. If our friends would perplex themselves less about the Balance of Europe, and think a little more seriously of the Balance of Trade, it might be better for us all'.[18]

Walpole's willingness to consider an Austro-Spanish marriage in early 1734 represented a dramatic shift of British policy from 1725, whilst the dispatch of a fleet to the Tagus in 1735 was a classic instance of the 'Blue Water' strategy. Walpole's opposition to the war with Spain in 1738-9 could be related to Tory opposition during the War of the Spanish Succession to conflict for the benefit of London fiscal and commercial interests.

The opposition were also divided over foreign policy. The Tories contested the interventionist foreign policy which the opposition Whigs were more prepared to accept. In the late 1720s this fundamental division within the ranks of the opposition was concealed in their shared hostility to the direction and conduct of foreign policy. The pro-French policies of the ministry and the interminable unsuccessful negotiations were attacked with vigour. The War of the Polish Succession destroyed this apparent unity which, like so much of the 'County' platform expounded by Bolingbroke, had no secure foundations. The opposition Whigs, particularly Stair and Chesterfield, clamoured for support for Austria and the preservation of the balance of power. This was in accord with opposition Whig policy since 1725, for the group had condemned the anti-Austrian policy of 1725-30 and had intrigued with successive Austrian envoys. Some Tories, such as Bathurst in 1730, had been willing to support Austria. This led Dayrolle to observe, 'I admire how the same people who cryed so much formerly against the Imperialists, call them now our best friends and Allies . . .'[19] Wyndham's moderate stance towards France in the War of the Polish Succession was not shared by the opposition Whigs.

The Tory failure to support the opposition Whigs in the mid-1730s prefigured the clash over policy in the 1740s. Both Tories and opposition Whigs could agree in 1738-9 in embarrassing the ministry by pressing for conflict with Spain, although there is little sign that they had thought out the consequences for Anglo-French relations. Until the spring of 1739 there seems to have been little expectation that war with Spain would actually take place. The secession of a large group of opposition MPs from the Commons suggests that the opposition had not expected hostilities. The manner in which a successful campaign of political obloquy was translated into the foreign policy priorities of the nation, without any informed debate of their consequences for British foreign policy and the international system, reflected little credit on the standards of political debate. The wider perspective was mentioned by some ministerial spokesmen, such as Hervey.[21] The consequences were to become readily apparent in the division of opposition opinion once the War of the Austrian Succession began. The opposition Whigs, some of whom entered the ministry in 1742, pressed, in and out of government, for help for Austria. In November 1742 Stair wrote, 'I am sure it is both the interest and the glory of the King our master and of our country, to remain firmly united, according to our engagements, with the Queen of Hungary. If we continue to govern ourselves by that plain and simple politick, we shall have all the weight that we can desire to have in Europe . . .'[22] Tory propaganda condemned the concentration on the continental struggle at the expense of maritime conflict.[23]

Thus there was a division of opinion over foreign policy within both ministerial and opposition ranks. This adds interest to a study of the public debate over policy. Although labels such as Tory can be used with profit to describe particular stances, the debate was one of great complexity, and it deserves further study. Particularly interesting is the question of the contribution of the debate to the decision to abandon the French alliance.

Differences within the opposition over foreign policy were concealed in the late 1720s (as in 1738-9) by a common opposition to ministerial foreign policy. The opposition claim that the French alliance was no longer in Britain's interest was substantiated by an intelligent, well-informed discussion of the Alliances of Vienna and Hanover. The ministry were accused, possibly with reason, of overreacting to the formation of the Alliance of Hanover, and ministerial claims that the Vienna alliance included secret provisions in favour of the Jacobites were derided. The pamphlets produced in defence of and in opposition to ministerial foreign policy in the late 1720s reveal a very high standard of debate, one which persisted in the 1730s. This partly reflects their authorship, which included senior politicians such as Horace Walpole, Robert Walpole, Bolingbroke and Pulteney.

Much of the opposition attack in the late 1720s centred on the French alliance.[24] The unreliability of France as an ally was stressed, and the opposition made much of the issue in the press. In parliamentary terms, the opposition attack had little impact until 1730, but the same cannot be said about public opinion, however difficult that term is to define and assess. The French government believed that public opinion was a significant factor in Anglo-French relations. Morville wrote to Chammorel in June 1727, 'Vous vivez au milieu d'un peuple qui ne souffre pas patiemment qu'on le croye conduit par qui que ce soit, et toute apparence de vanité à cet égard seroit d'une dangereuse conséquence. Vous devez donc envisager l'heureux succes de nos démarches communes pour la paix comme le fruit de l'union qui subsiste entre la France et l'Angleterre, et vous pourrez en tirer une preuve pour établir autant qu'il sera possible l'opinion que le maintien de cette bonne intelligence est également convenable aux intérêts réciproques'.[25]

However, it was very difficult for French envoys, or anyone else, to judge changes in public attitudes. Chammorel reported in April 1728 that opposition press attacks on foreign policy were having little impact. Indeed, he claimed that French policy was being praised by 'tout ce qu'il y a de gens dont le sentiment mérite quelque attention'.[26] Such nebulous phrases were standard, and it is difficult to advance further in assessing public opinion in an age when all could assert its importance, but none define its extent and character or the processes by which it influenced policy. Evidence for newspaper and pamphlet circulation and readership is sparse. The extent to which the ministry sponsored and subsidised production would suggest political literature was believed to be of importance in influencing attitudes. There are certainly suggestions that the press did play such a role. Richard Buckner, estate agent to the Duke of Richmond, wrote in 1728 from Sussex to his master, then holidaying in Iberia: 'Politicks is the only prevailing conversation at present, and there is no company, or sett of men of what degree soever, who does not take upon them to decide matters as peremptorily as if they were at the very bottom of the secret . . . They loudly complain of stagnation of Trade, the capture of so many merchant ships, the dilatory proceedings of the Congress, and such general topicks extracted from the Craftsman and Fog'.[27]

The importance of public knowledge and discussion of foreign policy is ill-defined, not that that makes it any less important to study. It is all too easy for historians to use public opinion as an explanatory device where it is difficult to find evidence for other influences. The War of Jenkins' Ear is a good instance. An examination of the British decision in 1730 to approach Austria would suggest that, although good diplomatic reasons could be advanced for the step, domestic pressures should not be discounted. However, it does not follow that these pressures were predominant, and it is in the assessment of the respective importance of various pressures that the historical debate will continue.

'Surely that's been done already' was the reaction of several scholars when I started this project all too many years ago. It is indeed true that the diplomatic 'story' was partly complete, although, as I showed in my thesis, important fresh material, from British and foreign archives, could alter dramatically the established picture even for so oft-studied a period as 1727-31. The same is also true for the time of the War of the Polish Succession, whilst very little work has been done on the periods between the death of Stanhope and the signature of the First Treaty of Vienna, and between the Second Treaty and the Russian invasion of Poland. Furthermore, with the exception of Anglo-Spanish relations, there has been little study of British foreign policy between the Third Treaty of Vienna and the accession of Frederick the Great. I hope to fill some of these gaps in future work; the purpose of this book has been, not to provide a narrative, but to open up debate on some of the factors affecting the conduct of foreign policy.

A general conclusion would be that the influence of the crown was more important than has usually been thought, and commercial factors less so. Walpole has been better, and Stanhope worse, treated here than is normal. Much work still remains to be done on some of the topics discussed. Closed archives are a major hinderance, as are simple gaps in the surviving documentation. I hope this survey has shown that foreign policy cannot simply be studied from the diplomatic archives. In order to appreciate foreign policy in the Age of Walpole it is necessary to consider not only British diplomacy but also domestic British history, and the relationship between domestic developments and debates and foreign policy. It is too easy to treat the international system as the sum of the diplomacies of the various European powers, and to present foreign policy in a monolithic interpretation in which the actors are the 'British', the 'French' *et al.* Instead it is clear that during this period policy options were debated and discussed within each country, not just Britain, but also every major European nation. Furthermore, these discussions were not simply concerned with diplomatic options. Rather, the debates about foreign policy were intertwined with struggles over power, patronage and domestic politics. This process was encouraged by the fact that the formulation and execution of foreign policy was generally not the job of a distinct bureaucratic institution unrelated to the strife of domestic politics. Instead foreign policy was shaped in the courts of Europe and was a victim of the indistinct nature of much eighteenth-century government. It would be helpful to reassess the process by which foreign policy was created in most of the European states of this period. I hope this work will encourage further studies on the subject.

NOTES

1. Horace Walpole to Newcastle, 20 Nov. (ns) 1723, BL. Add. 32686; Palm to Charles VI, 13 Dec. (ns) 1726, CUL. CH. corresp. 1379.

2. P. R. Sellin and S. B. Baxter, *Anglo-Dutch Cross Currents in the Seventeenth and Eighteenth Centuries* (Los Angeles, 1976), pp. 43-59; M. Roberts, *Splendid Isolation, 1763-1780* (Reading, 1970), p. 10; H. M. Scott, paper on eighteenth-century Anglo-Austrian relations given at Anglo-Austrian Historical Symposium, London, Nov. 1983.

3. Wyndham, Walpole, Pulteney, Cobbett XI, 217, 228-9, 241, 21 Nov. 1739; notes in Newcastle's hand of (?) parliamentary speech, undated [1730], PRO. 36/21 f.217; Perceval newsletter, 21 Mar. 1730, BL. Add. 27981; *Flying Post; or, the Post Master,* 2 Jan. 1718, 1 Aug. 1732; *London Journal,* 24 Ap. 1725; *Mist's Weekly Journal,* 12 Mar. 1726, 27 May, 3 June, 7 Oct. 1727; *Norwich Mercury,* 7 Mar. 1730, 30 Mar. 1734; *Fog's Weekly Journal,* 16 Jan. 1731; *Hyp Doctor,* 19 Jan. 1731, 15 July 1735, 26 Ap. 1737; *Daily Courant,* 2 Ap., 11 July 1734; *Daily Gazetteer,* 12 May 1736; *Northampton Mercury,* 8 Oct. 1739; *Craftsman,* 2 Aug. 1740; Anon., *The False Patriot. An Epistle to Mr. Pope* (1734), p. 6; Christian Cole (ed.), *Historical and Political Memoirs* (1735).

4. *Champion,* 27 Oct. 1741.

5. Bathurst, 27 Jan. 1730, Wyndham, 25 Jan. 1735, James Erskine, 14·Feb. 1735, opposition speaker, 6 Mar. 1735, Barnard, 29 Nov. 1739, Cobbett VIII, 773, 775-6, IX, 225, 822, 869, XI, 291; Sandys, 13 Feb. 1741, I. G. Doolittle, 'A First-hand Account of the Commons Debate on the Removal of Sir Robert Walpole', *Bulletin of the Institute of Historical Research* 53 (1980), p. 129.

6. *British Journal,* 22 Sept. 1722; *London Journal,* 17 Nov. 1722.

7. J. Duke-Evans, 'The Political Theory and Practice of the English Commonwealthsmen, 1695-1725' (D. Phil., Oxford, 1980), p. 150.

8. *The British Journal: or, The Censor,* 10 Aug., 28 Dec. 1728.

9. Newcastle to John Hedges, Envoy Extraordinary in Turin, 27 May 1727, PRO. 92/32.

10. Anon., *Clodius and Cicero* (1727), pp. 15-17.

11. *True Briton,* 7 June 1723; *Clodius and Cicero,* pp. 10, 14; *London Journal,* 3 June 1727.

12. Account of Council meeting, 11 Aug. 1729, PRO. 43/80.

13. *Mist's Weekly Journal,* 4 June 1726, 4 Mar., 27 May 1727.

14. Newcastle to Robinson, 19 Ap. 1732, Newcastle to Waldegrave, 5 Jan. 1738, BL. Add. 32776, 32800.

15. *Clodius and Cicero,* p. 21.

16. *Hyp-Doctor,* 4 Jan., *Free Briton,* 17 Feb., *The Flying Post; or Post-Master,* 27 July 1732.

17. *Daily Courant,* 19 Jan., *London Journal,* 16 Feb. 1734; *Hyp-Doctor,* 7 Jan. 1735.

18. Tyrawly to Delafaye, 15 Jan. (ns) 1734, PRO. 89/37.

19. Dayrolle to Tilson, 21 Feb. (ns) 1730, PRO. 84/310; Broglie to Chauvelin, 19 Feb. (ns) 1730, AE. CP. Ang. 369.

20. Chavigny to Chauvelin, 15 Mar. (ns) 1734, 14, 28 Jan. (ns) 1735, AE. CP. Ang. 384, 390; Diemar to Eugene, 8 Feb. (ns) 1735, HHStA. GK. 85a.

21. Hervey, 15 Nov. 1739, Cobbett, XI, 53.

22. Stair to Trevor, 2 Nov. (ns) 1742, Trevor, 32.

23. Fielding, *A Dialogue Between a Gentleman from London . . . and an honest Alderman of the County Party* (1747); *Newcastle Courant,* 23 Jan. 1748; Anon., *Good Queen Anne vindicated and the ingratitude, insolence, etc. of her Whig ministry and the allies detected and expos'd in the beginning and conducting of the war. The Englishman's memorial: containing a short history of the land wars we have been engaged in* (2nd ed., 1748).

24. Le Coq to Augustus II, 5 Feb. (ns) 1726, Dresden, 2674; Knatchbull, 17 Feb. 1726, 17 Jan. 1727, pp. 52, 59; Chammorel to Chauvelin, 18 Mar. (ns) 1726, AE. CP. Ang. 354.

25. Morville to Chammorel, 12 June (ns) 1727, AE. CP. Ang. sup. 8.

26. Chammorel to Chauvelin, 19 Ap. (ns) 1728, AE. CP. Ang. 362.

27. Buckner to Richmond, 25 Nov. 1728, Earl of March, *A Duke and his Friends. The Life and Letters of the Second Duke of Richmond* (2 vols., 1911), I, 165.

Bibliography

i. Manuscript Sources

For reasons of space only a select list of sources consulted have been given. Material of value solely for domestic developments has not been mentioned.

1. Foreign Holdings

Columbus
: Ohio State University Library
Maurepas Papers.

Cornell
: *University Library*
Maurepas Papers.

Darmstadt
: *Staatsarchiv*
El M. Austria, Britain, France, Hanover, United Provinces. Görtz Archive: of particular interest is correspondence with Schulenburg and Whitworth.

Dresden
: *Sachsisches Hauptstaatsarchiv*
Geheimes Kabinett, Gesandschaften. All relevant diplomatic series were consulted. The following were of particular importance:
le Coq, Watzdorf, de Löss, Zamboni and Utterodt's reports from London.
le Coq's correspondence with Marquis de Fleury.
Reports from de Brais (United Provinces), de Büy (Spain), le Coq (France), Sühm (Prussia), Wackerbarth (Austria).

Florence
: *Archivio di Stato*
Lettere Ministri: Britain.

Genoa
: *Archivio di Stato*
Lettere Ministri: Britain, France.

Hanover
: *Niedersachsisches Hauptstaatsarchiv*
All relevant diplomatic material in Calenberg Brief Archiv and Hanover Des. 91 was consulted. In addition to the material cited by Hatton, Calenberg. Brief Archiv. 11 El. 342, and St. Staphorin material in Hann. 91 was found of value.

Lucca
: *Archivo di Stato*
Documents 'al tempo della liberta' – relevant instructions and reports.

Marburg
: *Staatsarchiv*
series 4f. Britain, France, Hanover, Prussia, Sweden, United Provinces.
series 4g. newsletters.

Modena
: *Archivio di Stato*
Lettere Ministri: Britain.

Munich
: *Bayerisches Hauptstaatsarchiv*
Kasten Blau: Britain, France, Hanover.
Kasten Schwarz: Austria, Britain, France, Prussia, Saxony, United Provinces.

Münster	*Staatsarchiv* Dep. Nordkirchen, Papers of Count Plettenberg.
Nancy	*Archives de Meurthe-et-Moselle* Fonds de Vienne, series 3F. diplomatic reports. Of particular use were reports from Schmidman (Britain), Jacquemin (Austria) and Stainville (France).
Osnabrück	*Staatsarchiv* Rep. 100. Newsletters to the Prince-Bishop.

Paris	*Archives Nationales*
	a) Archives de la Marine
	   1) B3 Service Général. Correspondance.
	   2) B7 Pays Etrangèrs
	   3) AE.BI. Correspondance Consulaire
	b) Archives Privée: entrée Fleury.

Bibliothèque de L' Arsenal
Gazette d' Utrecht
Nouvelles Ecclésiastiques
Archives de la Bastille: Gazetins secrets de la Police.

Bibliothèque Nationale
a) Nouvelles Acquisitions Françaises 349 Blondel-Remarques
9399 Mémoire sur la marine de Louis XV
9511 D'Aube, Réflexions sur le gouvernement de France.
10125 correspondence of Hoym
10672 Torcy memoirs.
10681 correspondence of Groffery.
b) Manuscrits Français
7149 Cambis correspondence
7177-98 Villeneuve papers.

Quai d' Orsay Archives du Ministère des Affaires Etrangères
a) Correspondance Politique
Germany, Britain, Austria, Bavaria, Brunswick-Hanover, Cologne, Spain, Hesse-Cassel, United Provinces, Prussia, Turkey.
b) Mémoires et Documents
Austria, Germany, Britain, Spain, France, United Provinces.

Vincennes. Archives de la Guerre
A¹, Diplomatie

Parma	*Archivio de Stato* Carteggio Farnesiano Lettere Ministri: Austria, Britain, France.
Stuttgart	*Staatsarchiv* Gravanitz's mission to London 1727.
Turin	*Archivio di Stato* Lettre Ministri: Austria, Britain, France, Spain, United Provinces.
Venice	*Archivio di Stato* Lettere Ministri: Britain, France.

Vienna	*Haus-, Hof-, und Staatsarchiv*
	a) State Chancellery.
	   Britain: korrespondenz, noten, varia
	   France: varia
	   Interiora: intercepte

b) Grosse korrespondenz
Of particular interest was Eugene's correspondence with
Ferdinand Albrecht, Kinsky and Pentenridter.
c) Nachlass Fonseca.
Palais Kinsky.
correspondence and papers of Count Philip Kinsky.

Wolfenbüttel	*Staatsarchiv* All relevant diplomatic correspondence. Of particular interest were the reports of Thom (London) and the correspondence of Ferdinand Albrecht with Frederick I and Seckendorf.

2. British Archives

Aylesbury	*Buckinghamshire Record Office* Trevor Papers.
Bedford	*Bedfordshire Record Office* Lucas papers.
Bury St. Edmunds	*West Suffolk Record Office* Hervey papers.
Cambridge	*University Library* Cholmondeley Houghton papers. Not all the catalogue entries to the correspondence are accurate. Edward Harley's parliamentary journal.
Chelmsford	*Essex Record Office* Mildmay papers.
Chewton Mendip	*Chewton Hall* Waldegrave papers.
Chichester	*West Sussex Record Office* Richmond papers.
Dorchester	*Dorset Record Office* Fox-Strangways papers.
Edinburgh	*Scottish Record Office* Stair papers.
Hertford	*Hertfordshire Record Office* Panshanger papers.
Hull	*University Library* Hotham papers.
Ipswich	*East Suffolk Record Office* Leathes papers.
Leicester	*Leicestershire Record Office* Finch papers.
London	*Bank of England* Stock Ledger Books. *British Library* Egerton Mss: Bentinck papers. Stowe Mss: Jacobite correspondence. Loans: Portland and Bathurst papers.

Additional Mss: Blenheim, Bolingbroke, Burnet, Caesar, Carewe, Carteret, Coxe, Blakeney, Dayrolles, Egmont, Essex, Gualterio, Hardwicke, Hatton-Finch, Holland House, Keene, Mitchell, Newcastle, Norris, Pulteney, Robinson, Secker, Skinner, Strafford, Townshend, Tyrawly, Wager, Wilmington, transcripts from Dutch archives.

Microfilm 687: Stair-Sarah Malborough correspondence.

History of Parliament Trust
Ryder transcripts.

House of Lords Record Office
Proxy Books.

Post Office Archives
General Accounts.

Public Record Office
State Papers: Domestic, Naval, Regencies, Scotland, Ireland, Miscellaneous, Austria, Denmark, Dunkirk, Flanders, France, German States, Hamburg, Holland, Malta, Poland, Portugal, Prussia, Russia, Sardinia, Spain, Turkey, Tuscany, Venice, Drafts, Royal Letters, Treaties, Confidential, Foreign Entry Books, Foreign Ministers in London, Foreign News Letters, Treaty papers.

Wellcome Institute
Diary of Dr. Wilkes.

Maidstone	*Kent Record Office* Sackville, Stanhope, Sydney papers.
Newcastle	*Northumberland Record Office* Delaval papers.
Newport	*Public Library* Hanbury-Williams papers.
Northampton	*Northampton Record Office* Isham, Finch-Hatton papers. Notebook of William Hay.
Norwich	*Norfolk Record Office* Bradfer Lawrence, Ketton-Cremer, Townshend papers.
Oxford	*Bodleian Library* Weber letter book. Carte, Dashwood, Zamboni papers. *Christ Church* Wake papers.
Petworth	*Petworth House* Wyndham papers.
Sandon	*Sandon Hall* Harrowby papers.
Stafford	*Staffordshire Record Office* Dartmouth, Leveson-Gower papers.
Trowbridge	*Wiltshire Record Office* Savernake papers.

Windsor   Windsor Castle
                   Royal Archives: Stuart papers.

Newspapers

The London newspapers of the period, held in the British Library and the Bodleian Library, have been used, and, due to the number of titles, are not listed separately. In addition, the following provincial newspapers have been consulted (in order of first date of publication).

Worcester Post Man
Newcastle Courant
Weekly Courant (Nottingham)
Norwich Courant
Suffolk Mercury: or, St. Edmund's-Bury Post
Kentish Post
Leeds Mercury
Cirencester Post
York Mercury
Northampton Mercury
Ipswich Journal
Derby Postman
Chester Weekly Journal
Newcastle Weekly Mercury
Reading Mercury
Farley's Bristol Newspaper
York Courant
Nottingham Post
Manchester Weekly Courant
Kendal Weekly Courant
Derby Mercury
Adam's Weekly Courant (Chester)

ii. *Documents, Correspondence, Memoirs etc.*

Acts of Assembly, Passed in the Island of Jamaica, 1681-1737 (1738).
R. Beatson,   *A Chronological Register of Both Houses of the British Parliament, 1708-1807* (3 vols., 1807).
R. Beatson,   *Naval and Military Memoirs of Great Britain from 1727 to 1783* (6 vols., 1804).
The Works of Lord Bolingbroke (4 vols., 1844).
The Letters and Correspondence of Henry St. John, Lord Viscount Bolingbroke, (ed.) G. Parke (4 vols., 1798).
A. Boyer,   *The Political State of Great Britain* (1725-1731).
British Diplomatic Instruction, 1689-1787 (London, edited for the Royal Historical Society).
                    I. *Sweden, 1689-1727,* (ed.) J. F. Chance, Camden Third Series, vol. XXXII (1922).
                    III. *Denmark, 1689-1789,* (ed.) J. F. Chance, Camden Third Series, vol. XXXV (1925).
                    IV. *France, 1721-1727,* (ed.) L. G. Wickham Legg, Camden Third Series, vol. XXXVIII (1927).

V. *Sweden, 1727-1789,* (ed.) J. F. Chance, Camden Third Series, Vol. XXXIX (1928).

VI. *France, 1727-1744,* (ed.) L. G. Wickham Legg, Camden Third Series, Vol. XLIII (1930).

J. Chamberlayne, *Magnae Britanniae Notitia; or The Present State of Great Britain* (28th ed., 1727).

Chesterfield, Philip, Fourth Earl of, *The Letters of Philip Dormer Stanhope, Fourth Earl of Chesterfield* (ed.). B. Dobrée, (6 vols., 1932).

W. Cobbett, *Parliamentary History of England* (36 vols., 1806-20).

G. Colman the younger (ed.), *Posthumous letters from various celebrated men addressed to Francis Colman and George Colman the elder* (1820).

Diary of Mary, Countess Cowper, 1714-1720, (ed.) J. Cowper (2nd ed., 1865).

Culloden Papers, (ed.) H. R. Duff (1815).

More Culloden Papers, Vol. 3, *1725-1745,* (ed.) D. Warren (Inverness, 1927).

M. Eyre-Matcham, *A Forgotton John Russell being letters to a man of business, 1724-51* (1905).

Memoirs of Frederica Sophia Wilhemina Margravine of Bareith (2 vols., 1829).

Die Memoiren des Kammerherrn Friedrich Ernst von Fabrice, 1683-1750, (ed.) R. Grieser (Hildesheim, 1956).

E. Hermann, *Diplomatische Beiträge zur Russischen Geschichte aus dem königlich Sächsischen Haupstaatsarchiv zu Dresden, 1728-34* (St. Petersburg, 1870).

Hervey, John, Earl of Bristol, *Letter-Books of John Hervey, First Earl of Bristol, 1651-1750* (3 vols., Wells, 1894), III.

Hervey, John Lord, *Some Material towards Memoirs of the Reign of King George II by John, Lord Hervey,* (ed.) R. Sedgwick (3 vols., 1931).

Historical Manuscripts Commission:
    Carlisle, Onslow, Polwarth, Portland, Stuart, Townshend, Trevor Papers.
    Egmont Diary.

History and Proceedings of the House of Commons from the Restoration to the Present Time (14 vols., 1742-1744), printed for Richard Chandler.

C. Höfler, *Der Congress von Soissons, nach den Instructionen des Kaiserlichen Kabinetts und den Berichten des Botschafters Stefen Grafen Kinsky* (2 vols., Vienna, 1871, 1876).

Journal of the Commissioners for Trade and Plantations:
    From January 1723 to December 1728 (1928).
    From January 1729 to December 1734 (1928).

The Private Correspondence of Sir Benjamin Keene, (ed.) Sir R. Lodge (1933).

King, Peter Lord, 'Notes of Domestic and Foreign Affairs, during the last years of the Reign of George I and the early part of the Reign of George II', appendix to Peter, Lord King, *Life of John Locke* (1830), Vol. 2.

The Parliamentary Diary of Sir Edward Knatchbull, 1722-1730, (ed.) A. N. Newman, Camden Third Series, XCIV (1963).

Liria, Duque de, *Diario del viage a Moscovia del Duque de Liria y Xerica* (Madrid, 1889).

G. Lockhart, *The Lockhart Papers,* (ed.) A. Aufrère (2 vols., 1817).

Lettres d'Elizabeth Charlotte D' Orléans, Duchesse de Lorraine to Antoinette-Charlotte de Lenoncourt, Marquise d'Aulède (Nancy, 1865).

Memoirs and Correspondence of George, Lord Lyttelton, (ed.) R. Phillimore (2 vols., 1845).

Marini, R. A.,   *La Politica Sabauda alla Corte Inglese* (Chambéry, 1918).

M. Maris,   *Journal et mémoires de Mathieu Marais . . . sur la Régence et le règne de Louis XV (1715-1737)*, (ed.) M. de Lescure (4 vols., Paris, 1836-1868).

C. A. Montgon,   *Mémoires de Monsieur l' abbé de Montgon, publiez par lui-même. Contenant les différentes négociations dont il a été chargé dans les cours de France, d'Espagne, et de Portugal; et divers évènemens qui sont arrivés depuis l' année 1725 jusques à présent* . . . (8 vols., Lausanne, 1748-1753).

Mémoires Politiques et Militaires, pour servir à l' histoire de Louis XIV et de Louis XV composés sur les pièces originales recueillies par Andrien-Mauric Duc de Noailles, (ed.) M. L. Abbé Millot (2nd ed., Lausanne, 1778).

The Orrery Papers, (ed.) E. C. Boyle, Countess of Cork and Orrery (2 vols., 1903).

M. Percival,   *Political Ballads Illustrating the Administration of Sir Robert Walpole* (Oxford, 1916).

Recueil des instructions données aux ambassadeurs et ministres de France depuis les traités de Westphalie jusqu'à la Revolution Française (Paris):

    I. *Autriche*, (ed.) A. Sorel, 1884.

    II. *Suède*, (ed.) A. Geffroy, 1885.

    III. *Portugal*, (ed.) Le vicomte de Caix de Saint-Aymour, 1886.

    IV, V. *Pologne*, (ed.) L. Farges, 1888.

    VII. *Bavière, Palatinat, Deux-Ponts*, (ed.) A. Lebon, 1889.

    VIII. *Russie I*, (ed.) Q. Rambaud, 1890.

    X. *Naples et Parme*, (ed.) J. Reinach, 1893.

    XIII. *Danemark*, (ed.) A. Geffroy, 1895.

    XIV. *Savoie-Sardaigne et Mantoue*, (ed.) H. De Beaucaire, 1818.

    XVI. *Diète Germanique*, (ed.) B. Auerbach, 1912.

    XIX. *Florence*, (ed.) E. Driault, 1912.

    XXV. *Angleterre III*, (ed.) P. Vaucher, 1965.

    XXVIII. *Etats Allemands*, (ed.) G. Livet:

        I. *L' Electorat de Mayence* (1962).

        II. *L' Electorat de Cologne* (1963).

        III. *L' Electorat de Treves* (1966).

Sir G. H. Rose,   *A Selection from the Papers of the Earls of Marchmont in the Possession of the Right Honorable Sir George Henry Rose, Illustrative of Events from 1685 to 1750* (3 vols., London, 1831).

Saussure, César de,   *A Foreign View of England in the Reigns of George I and George II*, (ed.) Madame van Mugden (1902).

Sbornik Imperatorskago Russkago Istoricheskago obshcestva (St. Petersburg), relevant volumes.

Briefwisseling tussen Simon van Slingelandt en Sicco van Goslinga, 1697-1731, (ed.) W. A. van Rappard (The Hague, 1978).

Annals and correspondence of the Viscount and the first and second Earls of Stair, (ed.) J. M. Graham (2 vols., Edinburgh, 1875).

The Autobiography of William Stout of Lancaster, 1665-1752, (ed.) J. D. Marshall (Manchester, 1967).

Letters to and from Henrietta, Countess of Suffolk . . . from 1712 to 1767, (ed.) J. W. Croker (2 vols., 1824).

C. L. H. Villars, duc le, *Mémoires du Maréchal de Villars*, (ed.) le Marquis de Vogüé (6 vols., Paris, 1884-1904).

The Wentworth Papers, 1705-1779, (ed.) J. J. Cartwright (1883).

R. Wodrow,   *Analecta, or Materials for a History of Remarkable Providences Mostly Relating to Scotch Ministers and Christians,* III (Edinburgh, 1842).

iii. *Secondary Sources*

J. Aalbers,   'Holland's financial problems (1713-33) as a consequence of the French Wars', in A. C. Duke (ed.), *Britain and the Netherlands,* VI (1978).

M. S. Anderson,   *Peter the Great* (1978).

M. S. Anderson,   'Great Britain and the Growth of the Russian Navy in the Eighteenth Century', *Mariner's Mirror* (1956), pp. 132-146.

C. M. Andrews,   'Anglo-French Commercial Rivalry, 1700-1750: the Western Phase', *American Historical Review,* XX (1914-15), pp. 539-556.

Anon.,   Review of P. Vaucher, 'Robert Walpole et la politique de Fleury (1731-1742)', *Times Literary Supplement,* 1224 (1925), p. 439.

Anon.,   Records relating to Ministerial Meetings in the Reign of George I (no date). Typescript in the Public Record Office.

E. Armstrong,   *Elisabeth Farnese, 'the Termagant of Spain'*

E. Armstrong,   Review of G. Syveton, *Un cour et un Aventurier au XVIIIe siècle: Le Baron de Ripperda* (Paris, 1896), *EHR,* XII (1897), pp. 796-800.

A. Arneth,   *Prinz Eugen von Savoyen* (3 vols., Vienna, 1858).

T. S. Ashton,   *Economic Fluctuations in England, 1700-1800* (Oxford, 1956).

S. E. Åström,   *From Stockholm to St. Petersburg* (Helsinki, 1962).

H. M. Atherton,   *Political Prints in the Age of Hogarth* (Oxford, 1974).

L. Auer,   'Das Reich und der Vertrag von Sevilla, 1729-1731' *Mitteilungen des Österreichischen Staatsarchivs,* 22, 1969, pp. 64-93.

B. Auerbach,   *La France et le Saint Empire romain germanique depuis la paix de Westphalie jusqu' à la Révolution française* (Paris, 1912).

H. Bagger,   *Ruslands alliancepolitik efter freden i Nystad* (Copenhagen, 1974). English summary.

C., Comte de Baillon, *Lord Walpole à la Cour de France, 1723-1730* (Paris, 1868).

A. Ballantyne,   *Lord Carteret, a Political Biography 1690-1763* (1887).

A. Baudrillart,   *Phillippe V et la cour de France* (5 vols., Paris, 1890-1901).

A. Baudrillart,   'Les prétentions de Philippe V à la couronne de France', *Séances et travaux de l' Académie des sciences morales et politiques,* CXXVII (1887), pp. 723-743, 851-897.

S. Baxter,   'The Myth of the Grand Alliance', in P. R. Sellin and S. B. Baxter (eds.), *Anglo-Dutch Cross Currents in the Seventeenth and Eighteenth Centuries* (Los Angeles, 1976).

S. Baxter (ed.),   *England's Rise to Greatness, 1660-1763* (Berkeley, 1983).

A. Beer,   'Zur Geschichte der Politik Karls VI, *Historische Zeitschrift* 19 (1886).

H. Benedikt,   *Das königreich Neapel unter kaiser Karl VI* (Vienna, 1927).

G. V. Bennett,   *The Tory Crisis in Church and State, 1688-1730* (Oxford, 1975).

G. V. Bennett,   'Jacobitism and the rise of Walpole', in N. McKendrik (ed.), *Historical Perspectives: studies in English Thought and Social History in honour of J. H. Plumb* (1974).

A. Béthencourt Massieu, *Patino en la política internacional de Felipe V (Valladolid, 1954).*

J. M. Black, 'The British Press and European News in the 1730s: The Case of the Newcastle Courant', *Durham County Local History Society,* 26, 1981, pp. 38-43.

J. M. Black, 'Manchester's First Newspaper: The Manchester Weekly Journal', *Transactions of the Historical Society of Lancashire and Cheshire,* 130 (1981).

J. M. Black, 'British Travellers in Europe in the Early Eighteenth Century', *Dalhousie Review* 61 (1982).

J. M. Black, '1733 – Failure of British Diplomacy?', *Durham University Journal* 74 (1982).

J. M. Black, 'Russia and the British Press, 1720-40', *British Journal for Eighteenth-Century Studies* 5 (1982).

J. M. Black, 'George II Reconsidered', *Mitteilungen des Österreichischen Staatsarchivs* 35 (1982).

J. M. Black, 'The theory of the balance of power in the first half of the eighteenth century: a note on sources', *Review of International Studies* 9 (1983).

J. M. Black, 'An "ignoramus" in Eurpropean affairs?', *British Journal for Eighteenth-Century Studies* 6 (1983).

J. M. Black, 'The Development of Anglo-Sardinian Relations in the First Half of the Eighteenth Century', *Studi Piemontesi* 12 (1983).

J. M. Black, 'Richard Rolt, "Patriot" Historian', *Factotum* 16 (1983).

J. M. Black, 'Russia and the British Press in the Early Eighteenth Century', *Study Group on Eighteenth-Century Russia Newsletter* 11 (1983).

J. M. Black, 'The Cirencester Flying-Post, and Weekly Miscellany', *Cirencester Archaeological and History Society Annual Report* 25 (1983).

J. M. Black (ed.), *Britain in the Age of Walpole* (1984).

J. M. Black, 'Parliament and the Political and Diplomatic Crisis of 1717-18', *Parliamentary History Yearbook* 3 (1984).

J. M. Black, 'France and the Grand Tour in the Early Eighteenth Century', *Francia* 12 (1984).

J. M. Black, 'The British Navy and British Foreign Policy in the first half of the eighteenth century', *Studies in History and Politics* (forthcoming).

J. M. Black, 'The Catholic Threat and British Press in the 1720s and 1730s', *Journal of Religious History* 12 (1983).

J. M. Black, 'British Neutrality in the War of the Polish Succession, 1733-1735', *International History Review* (1985).

J. M. Black, 'Press and Politics in the Age of Walpole', *Durham University Journal* 77 (1984).

J. M. Black, 'The Press, Party and Foreign Policy in the Reign of George I', *Publishing History* xiii (1983).

P. Boyé, *Un roi de Pologne et la couronne ducale de Lorraine: Stanislas Lexzczynski et le troisième traité de Vienne* (Paris, 1898).

M. Braubach, *Versailles und Wien von Ludwig XIV bis Kaunitz* (Bonn, 1952).

M. Braubach, *Die Geheimediplomatie des Prinzen Eugen von Savoyen* (Cologne, 1962).

M. Braubach, *Prinz Eugen von Savoyen* (5 vols., Vienna, 1963-65).

V. L. Brown, 'Contraband Trade: A Factor in the Decline of Spain's Empire in America', *Hispanic-American Historical Review,* VIII (1928), pp. 178-189.

194 *British Foreign Policy in the Age of Walpole*

R. Browning,	*The Duke of Newcastle* (New Haven, 1975).
J. Carswell,	*The Old Cause: Three Biographical Studies in Whiggism* (1954).
A. C. Carter,	*Neutrality or Commitment: the Evolution of Dutch Foreign Policy, 1667-1795* (1975).
D Carutti,	*Storia Della Diplomazia della Corte di Savoia* (Turin, 1880).
J. F. Chance,	*The Alliance of Hanover* (1923).
L. J. Colley,	*In Defiance of Oligarchy: The Tory Party, 1714-60* (Cambridge, 1982).
S. Conn,	*Gibraltar in British Eighteenth-Century Diplomacy* (1942).
W. Coxe,	*Memoirs of the Kings of Spain of the House of Bourbon* (2 vols., 1788).
W. Coxe,	*Memoirs of the Life and Administration of Robert Walpole* (3 vols., 1789).
W. Coxe,	*History of the House of Austria* (2 vols., 1807).
W. Coxe,	*Memoirs of Horatio Walpole* (2nd edn., 2 vols., 1808).
G. A. Cranfield,	*The Development of the Provincial Newspaper, 1700-1760* (Oxford, 1962).
E. Cruickshanks,	*Political Untouchables. The Tories and the '45* (1979).
E. Cruickshanks (ed.)	*Ideology and Conspiracy: Aspects of Jacobitism, 1689-1759* (Edinburgh, 1982).
M. Dall'Acqua,	'Dorothea Sophia von Pfalz-Neuburg', *Zeitschrift für Bayerische Landesgeschichte,* 44, 1 (1981), pp. 302-316.
R. Davis,	*A Commercial Revolution; English Overseas Trade in the Seventeenth and Eighteenth Centuries* (1967).
H. T. Dickinson,	*Bolingbroke* (1970).
H. T. Dickinson,	*Walpole and the Whig Supremacy* (1973).
R. Drogereit,	'The Testament of King George I and the problem of the personal union between England and Hanover', *Research and Progress,* V (1939), pp. 83-6.
J. Dureng,	*Mission de Théodore Chevignard de Chavigny en Allemagne, Septembre 1726-Octobre 1731* (Paris, 1912).
K. Ellis,	'The Administrative Connection between Britain and the Hanover', *Journal of the Society of Archivists* II (1965-9).
P. Fould,	*Un Diplomate au XVIIIe siècle: Louis-Augustin Blondel* (Paris), 1914).
P. S. Fritz,	*The English Ministers and Jacobitism between the Rebellions of 1715 and 1745* (Toronto, 1975).
T. Gehling,	*Ein europäischer Diplomat am Kaiserhof zu Wien: Francois Louis de Pesme, Seigneur de Saint-Saphorin* (Bonn, 1964).
M. D. George,	*English Political Caricature to 1792: A Study of Opinion and Propaganda* (2 vols., 1959).
H. Gerig,	*Die Memoiren des Lord Hervey als historische Quelle* (Freiburg, 1936).
P. Geyl,	'William IV of Orange and his English Marriage', *TRHS,* fourth series, viii (1925), pp. 14-37.
G. C. Gibbs,	'Britain and the Alliance of Hanover, April 1725-February 1726', *EHR,* lxxiii (1958).
G. C. Gibbs,	'Parliament and Foreign Policy in the Age of Stanhope and Walpole', *EHR,* lxxvii (1962), pp. 18-37.
G. C. Gibbs,	'Newspapers, Parliament and Foreign Policy in the Age of Stanhope and Walpole', *Mélanges offerts à G. Jacquemyns* (Brussels, 1968), pp. 293-315.

G. C. Gibbs,	'Laying Treaties before Parliament in the Eighteenth Century', in R. Hatton and M. S. Anderson (eds.), *Studies in Diplomatic History: Essays in Memory of D. B. Horn* (1970).
G. C. Gibbs,	'Parliament and the Treaty of Quadruple Alliance', in R. Hatton and J. S. Bromley (eds.), *William III and Louis XIV* (Liverpool, 1968).
C. Gill,	*Merchants and Mariners of the eighteenth century* (1961).
A. G. Gonzalez,	*Cadiz y el Atlantico, 1717-1778* (2 vols., Seville, 1976).
A. Goslinga,	*Slingelandt's Efforts towards European Peace* (The Hague, 1915).
R. Halsband,	*Lord Hervey, Eighteenth-Century Courtier* (Oxford, 1973).
L. Hanson,	*Government and the Press, 1695-1763* (1936).
H. Hantsch,	*Reichsvizekanzler Friedrich Karl Graf von Schönborn* (Augsburg, 1929).
P. C. Hartmann,	*Geld als Instrument Europäischer Machtpolitik im Zeitalter des Merkantilismus* (Munich, 1978).
R. Hatton,	*War and Peace, 1680-1720* (1969).
R. Hatton,	*George I* (1978).
R. Hatton,	'New Light on George I of Great Britain', in S. Baxter (ed.), *England's Rise* (Berkeley, 1983).
A. F. Henderson,	*London and the National Government, 1721-174* (Durham, N. Carolina, 1945).
G. B. Hertz,	'England and the Ostend Company', *EHR*, xxii (1907), pp. 255-279.
B. W. Hill,	*The Growth of Parliamentary Parties, 1689-1742* (1976).
G. Hills,	*Rock of Contention: A History of Gibraltar* (1974).
C. Hinrichs,	*Friedrich Wilhelm I* (Darmstadt, 1974).
G. Holmes,	*The Electorate and the National Will in the First Age of Party* (Lancaster, 1976).
D. B. Horn,	*The British Diplomatic Service, 1689-1789* (Oxford, 1964).
D. B. Horn,	*Great Britain and Europe in the Eighteenth Century* (Oxford, 1967).
W. G. Hoskins,	'Harvest Fluctuations and English Economic History, 1620-1759', *Agricultural History Review*, XVI (1968), pp. 15-36.
M. Huisman,	*La Belgique Commerciale sous l' Empereur Charles VI: La Companie d' Ostende* (Brussels, 1902).
C. Ingrao,	'The Pragmatic Sanction and the Theresian Succession: A Re-evaluation', *Topic*, XXXIV (1980), pp. 3-18.
G. H. Jones,	*The Mainstream of Jacobitism* (Cambridge, Mass., 1954).
G. H. Jones,	'Inghilterra, Granducato di Toscana e Quadruplice Alleanza', *Archivio Storico Italiano* (1980), pp. 59-87.
G. H. Jones,	'La Gran Bretagna v la destinazione di Don Carlos al trono di Toscana, 1721-32', *Archivio Storico Italiano* (1982), pp. 47-82.
J. R. Jones,	*Britain and the World, 1646-1815* (1980).
P. Langford,	*The Excise Crisis* (Oxford, 1975).
P. Langford,	*Modern British Foreign Policy: The Eighteenth Century, 1688-1815* (1976).
W. T. Laprade,	*Public Opinion and Politics in eighteenth-century England to the fall of Walpole* (New York, 1936).
B. Lenmann,	*The Jacobite Risings in Britain, 1689-1746* (1980).
A. J. Little,	*Deceleration in the eighteenth-century British Economy* (1976).
Sir R. Lodge,	*Great Britain and Prussia in the eighteenth century* (Oxford, 1923).

Sir R. Lodge,   Review of P. Vaucher, *Robert Walpole et la politique de Fleury (1731-1742), EHR,* XL (1925), pp. 438-441.

Sir R. Lodge,   'English Neutrality in the War of the Polish Succession', *TRHS,* fourth series, xiv (1931), pp. 141-174.

Sir R. Lodge,   'The Treaty of Seville, 1729', *TRHS,* fourth series, xvi (1933), pp. 1-45.

Sir R. Lodge,   'The Anglo-French Alliance, 1716-31' in A. Coville and H. Temperley, (eds.), *Studies in Anglo-French History during the eighteenth, nineteenth and twentieth centuries* (Cambridge, 1935), pp. 3-18.

P. H. S. Lord Mahon, *History of England from the Peace of Utrecht to the Peace of Versailles, 1713-1783* (5th edition, 7 vols., London, 1858).

P. Mantoux,   *Comptes rendus des séances du Parlement anglais* (Paris, 1906).

P. Mantoux,   'French Reports of British Parliamentary Debates in the eighteenth-century', *American Historical Review,* XII, 2 (1906-7), pp. 244-269.

Earl of March,   *A Duke and his Friends: The Life and Letters of the Second Duke of Richmond* (1911).

M. Martin,   'The Secret Clause, Britain and Spanish ambitions in Italy, 1712 31', *European Studies Review,* 6 (1976), pp. 407-25.

D. McKay,   *Prince Eugene of Savoy* (1977).

D. McKay,   'The Struggle for Control of George I's Northern Policy, 1718-19', *JMH* (1973).

D. Mckay and H. Scott, *The Rise of the Great Powers, 1648-1815* (1983).

J. McLachlan,   *Trade and Peace with Old Spain, 1667-1750* (Cambridge, 1940).

F. McLynn,   *France and the Jacobite Rising of 1745* (Edinburgh, 1981).

G. Mecenseffy,   *Karls VI Spanische Bündnispolitik, 1725-29* (Innsbruck, 1934).

W. Mediger,   *Moskaus Weg nach Europa* (Brunswick, 1952).

W. Mediger,   *Mecklenburg, Russland und England-Hannover, 1706-21* (Hildesheim, 1967).

W. Michael,   *Englishe Geschichte im 18. Jahrhundert* (Berlin, 1896-1955).

P. Muret,   *Le prépondérance anglaise, 1715-1763* (Paris, 1949).

J. Murray,   *George I, the Baltic and the Whig Split of 1717* (1969).

M. Naumann,   *Österreich, England und das Reich, 1719-1732* (Berlin, 1936).

G. Oestreich,   *Friedrich Wilhelm I* (Göttingen, 1977).

W. Oncken,   'Sir Charles Hotham und Friedrich Wilhelm I. im Jahre 1730', *Forschungen zur brandenburgischen und preussischen Geschichte,* VII (1894), pp. 377-407; VIII (1895), pp. 487-522; IX (1896), pp. 23-53.

J. B. Owen,   'George II Reconsidered', in A. Whiteman, J. S. Bromley and P. G. M. Dickson (eds.), *Statesmen, Scholars and Merchants* (Oxford, 1973), pp. 113-134.

N. W. B. Pemberton, *Carteret, the brilliant failure of the Eighteenth Century* (1936).

J. Pichon,   *The Life of Charles Henry Count Hoym, 1694-1736* (New York, 1889).

J. H. Plumb,   *Sir Robert Walpole* (2 vols., 1956, 1960).

G. Quazza,   *Il Problema Italiano e l' equilibrio europeo, 1720-1738* (Turin, 1965).

M. Ransome,   'The Reliability of Contemporary Reporting of the Debates of the House of Commons, 1727-1741', *Bulletin of the Institute of Historical Research,* 19 (1942-3), pp. 67-79.

C. B. Realey,   *The Early Opposition to Sir Robert Walpole, 1720-27* (Philadelphia, 1931).

O. Redlich,	*Österreich von 1700 bis 1740* (Vienna, 1938).
A. Rosenlehner,	*Kurfürst Karl Philipp von der Pfalz und die jülichsche Frage, 1725-1729* (Munich, 1906).
A. R. Saint-Leger,	*La Flandre Maritime et Dunkerque sous la domination Française, 1659-1789* (Paris, 1900).
J. C. Sainty,	*Officials of the Secretaries of State, 1660-1782* (1973).
H. Schilling,	*Der Zwist Preussens und Hannovers, 1729-1730* (Halle, 1912).
R. Sedgwick,	'Sir Robert Walpole', *Times Literary Supplement*, 2251 (1945), pp. 133-4.
R. Sedgwick (ed.),	*The History of Parliament: The House of Commons, 1715-1754* (2 vols., 1970).
H. Sée and H. Vignols,	'L' envers de la diplomatie officielle de 1715 à 1730: La rivalité commerciale des puissances maritimes et les doléances des négociants français', *Revue belge de philologie et d' histoire*, v (1926), pp. 471-91.
J. Shennan,	*Philippe, Duke of Orléans* (1979).
W. Sichel,	*Bolingbroke and his Times* (2 vols., 1902).
G. M. Slothouwer,	'Un effort pour la formation d'un Fürstenbund en 1728', *Revue d'histoire diplomatique* (1899), pp. 188-198.
A. M. W. Stirling,	*The Story of the Hothams* (2 vols., 1918).
G. Syveton,	*Une cour et un aventurier au XVIIIe siècle: le Baron de Ripperda* (Paris, 1896).
M. A. Thomson,	*The Secretaries of State, 1681-1782* (Oxford, 1932).
W. M. Torrens,	*History of Cabinets* I (1894).
P. Vaucher,	*Robert Walpole et la politique de Fleury (1731-1742)* (Paris, 1924).
L. Vignols,	'L'asiento français, 1701-1713, et anglais, 1713-1750, et le commerce franco-espagnol vers 1700 à 1730', *Revue d' histoire économique et sociale*, 17 (1929), pp. 403-436.
G. J. Walker,	*Spanish Politics and Imperial Trade, 1700-1789* (1979).
A. W. Ward,	*Great Britain and Hanover: Some Aspects of the Personal Union* (Oxford, 1899).
R. M. Wiles,	*Freshest Advices: Early Provincial Newspapers in England* (Columbus, Ohio, 1965).
B. Williams,	'The Foreign Policy of England under Walpole', *EHR* XV (1900), pp. 251-276, 479-494, 665-698; XVI (1901), pp. 67-83, 308-327, 439-451.
B. Williams,	'The Foreign Office of the first two Georges', *Blackwood's Magazine*, CLXXXI (Jan-June, 1907), pp. 92-105.
B. Williams,	*Stanhope. A study in eighteenth-century war and diplomacy* (Oxford, 1932).
B. Williams,	*Carteret and Newcastle* (Cambridge, 1943).
G. Williams,	'"The Inexhaustible Fountain of Gold": English Projects and Venture in the South Seas, 1670-1750', in J. E. Flint and G. Williams (eds.) *Perspectives of Empire* (1973).
A. M. Wilson,	*French Foreign Policy during the Administration of Cardinal Fleury, 1726-1743* (Cambridge, Mass., 1936).
T. Wright,	*Caricature History of the George* (1867).
M. Wyndham,	*Chronicles of the Eighteenth Century: Founded on the Correspondence of Sir Thomas Lyttelton and his family* (2 vols., London, 1924).

Index